WILL THE REAL CHRISTIANS PLEASE STAND UP!

BIBLICAL REFLECTIONS ON THE MEANING OF THE CHRISTIAN LIFE

By Robert J. Burton

Copyright © 2005 by Robert J. Burton

Will the Real Christians Please Stand Up!
by Robert J. Burton

Printed in the United States of America

ISBN 1-59781-486-5

All rights reserved solely by the author. The author guarantees all contents are original and do not infringe upon the legal rights of any other person or work. No part of this book may be reproduced in any form without the permission of the author. The views and opinions of the author do not necessarily reflect the views and opinions of Herschend Family Entertainment Corporation. The views expressed in this book are not necessarily those of the publisher.

Scripture quotations, unless otherwise noted, are from the HOLY BIBLE: NEW INTERNATIONAL VERSION®. NIV® Copyright © 1973, 1978, 1984, and are used by permission of The Zondervan Corporation.

The NIV and New International Version trademarks are registered in the United States Patent and Trademark Office by International Bible Society.

www.xulonpress.com

DEDICATION

First, I thank my Lord and Savior, and my best friend, Jesus Christ, who has been so patient with my imperfections, frailties and delays in the writing and completion of this book. The ultimate dedication is to Him so that people, including myself, may know, love and serve Him with ever increasing fervor.

I thank, too, the Holy Spirit, whose mission is to tell us about Jesus and to empower us to share the Good News of the Gospel. And it is all for the glory and honor of the Father, who sent us His Son and who invites us to share in His family life.

With regard to family and friends on this journey of life:

I dedicate the book first and foremost to my wife of 37 years, Barbara Marie, who knows my weaknesses better than anyone and who keeps on loving and supporting me even in the midst of her chronic pain and suffering. She is my inspiration, my friend and mate, and she is truly a great woman of God.

I dedicate the book to the owners and employees of Herschend Family Entertainment Corporation, with whom I have had the privilege of being associated since 1981.

I dedicate the book to the members of the Uninterrupted Prayer (UP) Team, who so faithfully pray for southwest Missouri, and, indeed, for all of Missouri, that God's perfect will be done and that this area be a catalyst for spiritual renewal in our nation.

I offer a special thanks to the people who have provided wise input and encouragement during the journey of the writing – and rewriting – of this book. Also, I thank Nancy, whose eagle eye and loving heart provided a proofing of the manuscript.

TABLE OF CONTENTS

INTRODUCTION xi

JOURNALING xvii

PART I:
    SALVATION HISTORY 19
        REFLECTION 1:   SACRIFICE 21
        REFLECTION 2:   SACRIFICE CONTINUED: BLOOD
                                COVENANT 35
        REFLECTION 3:   ENTER THE SANCTUARY 45
        REFLECTION 4:   LIVING TEMPLES 53
        REFLECTION 5:   A STORY OF FOUR
                                GARDENS 71
        REFLECTION 6:   THE REAL MEANING OF EASTER ... 85
        REFLECTION 7:   HEAVEN: OUR GOAL 95

PART II:
    THE SCRIPTURES SPEAK TO US 107
        REFLECTION 8:   PROVERBS 3: 5-7 109
        REFLECTION 9:   PSALM 3 119

REFLECTION 10: LIFESTYLE OF THE REAL
CHRISTIAN 127
REFLECTION 11: THE BURNING HEART 141
REFLECTION 12: SEEKING JESUS 149

PART III:
SPIRITUAL WARFARE IN SCRIPTURE AND THE
CHRISTIAN LIFE...157
REFLECTION 13: SPIRITUAL WARFARE 159
REFLECTION 14: SPIRITUAL WARFARE – APPLIED ..167
REFLECTION 15: THE EFFECTS OF SIN......................173
REFLECTION 16: WHY ME, LORD? 183
REFLECTION 17: THE DANGER OF THE NEW AGE
MOVEMENT 191

PART IV:
THE CALL TO SALVATION AND RELATIONSHIP 203
REFLECTION 18: MY LORD AND MY GOD 205
REFLECTION 19: NEW CREATION 211
REFLECTION 20: PERSONAL RELATIONSHIP............219
REFLECTION 21: WE WANT TO SEE JESUS 227
REFLECTION 22: WE WANT TO SEE JESUS,
CONTINUED 235

PART V:
LIVING THE CHRISTIAN LIFE 245
REFLECTION 23: HAVING A VISION 247
REFLECTION 24: RADICAL HOPE 255
REFLECTION 25: JUST HANGIN' IN THERE.................263
REFLECTION 26: A CALL TO INTERCESSORY
PRAYER 271
REFLECTION 27: THE SERVING LIFE 281
REFLECTION 28: LOVE FOR ONE ANOTHER 289
REFLECTION 29: BE CLOTHED WITH CHRIST 299

REFLECTION 30: A NEW HEAVEN AND A
NEW EARTH 305
REFLECTION 31: YOKE MINISTRY 313
REFLECTION 32: WHAT A CHRISTIAN IS NOT –
AND IS 323

CONCLUSION 337

INTRODUCTION

A subtitle for this book could well be:

IT IS TIME FOR CHRISTIANS TO STOP PLAYING CHURCH!

Over a period of time that covered about nine years, I had the privilege of doing something unusual for a Human Resources Manager. Every Sunday morning I conducted the employee church services in a log chapel on the grounds of Silver Dollar City, the theme park where I was employed. Through the picture window in the front of the church, the beauty of the Ozark Mountains and Table Rock Lake created an ideal setting for a worship service. The participants included both employees and customers (we call them guests), so I never knew from one Sunday to the next the background of my little congregation. I therefore had to turn to the Holy Spirit to guide me, in order to preach the truth and in a way that would touch the minds and hearts of folks from a wide variety of denominational walks. The result: I have without doubt learned and grown in my spiritual walk much more than my patient listeners.

Why the title? Why the subtitle? The world is searching desperately for meaning, hungering for true fulfillment, thirsting for something or someone lasting to place faith and hope in. Sadly, the one and only ultimate answer is repeatedly blocked by people who should be revealing the truth – the truth of Jesus Christ. Religious games and going through the motions of "faith" and a superficial and often hypocritical walk by "Christians" blind people to the immense and awesome beauty of the Church, the Body of Christ on earth, the vehicle the Father has chosen to bring light to a darkened world through the Love who is the Holy Spirit.

Now, those may appear to be harsh words, but they are accurate ones. I know, for I have been guilty of what I write about. So, this book of reflections addresses primarily those who call themselves Christians. I ask you to have open minds and open hearts, along with me, and to ask the Holy Spirit to show us what living the Christian life really means.

My hope and prayer is also that people who are not Christians, and those who have abandoned the Christian walk, will also pick up this book. If you have discounted Christianity as a way to true life and true peace, please look again. You may find in these pages a different and more vibrant version of Christianity – the real Christianity hidden from you by too many lives who talk it but do not walk it.

It is very fashionable these days to talk about "many paths to the same goal." Even many Christians, who should know better, espouse this deceiving and potentially damning belief. While we leave all judgment to God, and while I personally believe that God has His own ways to save those who really want the truth but have not found it, the Bible is very clear that Jesus is the Way, the Truth, the Life and the Light of the World; no one comes to the Father except through Him (even if we do not grasp the depth of what "through Him" means).

This book is based on God's Word. I firmly believe that the Bible is inspired and is true. The objective here is not to prove that; suffice it to say that the Bible has endured the test of time and criticism and stands tall and true as the living Word of God. That's right, the living Word. I believe that the Scriptures are unlike any other book ever written; when I read the Bible with faith, it is literally God speaking to me. That is a fundamental premise for these reflections.

There is another potential audience, in addition to the committed Christian, the "religious" Christian, the disillusioned Christian and the non-Christian. Perhaps the most difficult readers to reach are the people who are Christian in name only and who just are really not

Will the Real Christians Please Stand Up!

Christians at all – they are living a sham, even deceiving themselves.

To all, I say, "Wake up!" To myself also, I say, "Wake up!" Most important, to each and every one of us the Holy Spirit pleads, "Wake up!" It is time to let the Spirit show us Jesus as He really is and to teach us what it means to be His follower. It is time to let Jesus lead us to the Father so that we may worship and thank Him and live in the kind of intimate union with all three Persons of the Trinity that God has planned from all eternity.

"Wake up!" It is time to stop focusing on being "politically correct," on gathering the world's goods, on spending our lives on the worship of self. Time is short for each of us. Life on this earth is but a whisper in the wind compared to the eternity that is to come, with or without God.

Bearing the name "Christian" in no way necessarily means bearing Christ within. Am I a vibrant Christian, or a country club member of a religion? "Religious folk" have always been barriers to God's grace. The religion of Jesus' day killed Him, and the religion of today is stifling the saving work of Jesus. It is time to stand up and be counted. We are in a battle, and it has eternal consequences. There are real Christians, and there are artificial and superficial Christians. And there are people who do not understand Christianity because they have not seen Christ in Christians.

There are really two aspects of being a "real Christian." One is firmly holding to the essential doctrines of Christianity. The other is what we may call "lifestyle." Life is a process; we can always learn, grow and strive to be all of what God wants us to be. The real Christian is not perfect; no human being is. But the true Christian yearns with all of his and her mind, heart and spirit to be like Jesus Christ in every thought, word and action.

Now, I am sure that some "theologians," of either the trained or armchair variety, will immediately take issue with the phrase "real Christian." They may say that this is an oxymoron, that a person is either a Christian or is not. They may challenge me by saying that it is one thing to separate the wheat from the chaff when the chaff is the unbelieving world and the wheat is Christians, but it is quite another to attempt to identify the wheat and the chaff within the Church itself. They may say that if someone is a Christian, then the

xiii

word "real" is superfluous. **And right there is the whole point of this book.** The enemy (and we will explore in these reflections that belief in Satan and demons is one requirement for one to be a real Christian) tries to put blinders on people, or to influence minds and hearts toward a state of confusion and misdirection. I firmly believe that there are many people who use the title of Christian who have no true grasp of what it means to be one, to be a follower of Jesus Christ. As I have said, I have been there myself.

The Bible makes it clear that the true followers of Jesus will, by their lives and not just by their words, proclaim the love and sacrifice of the God-Man, Jesus Christ, and will point to Him as the Way to happiness, peace and eternal salvation.

So, this book is truly intended as a challenge. I bring no special credentials, save the fact that I spent many years as a nominal Christian as opposed to a real one, the less important fact that I have had the privilege of studying Christianity and theology for many years, and the fact that I have viewed the subject as a member of the clergy and as a member of the laity. For many years I mouthed "niceties;" I talked about the Savior; I was an active member of the Church; but it was like talking to God in a house by means of an intercom – I believed in Him, but it did not become real and personal for a long time, nor did I see the absolute necessity for a committed life as a Christian, day in and day out. As in marriage, there must be a deep, personal and total commitment to a person for the relationship to have any real and lasting meaning. For too many years I lacked a passion to become more and more like Him and to reveal His goodness and saving power to others. I did not listen to the quiet, insistent voice of the Holy Spirit; I did not grasp the immense and personal love of the Father. I was a living example of the Lord's hard words in Matthew 7: 21: *"Not everyone who says to me, 'Lord, Lord,' will enter the kingdom of heaven, but only he who does the will of my Father who is in heaven."* The will of the Father is expressed very succinctly in Mark 9: 7 when He spoke during the Transfiguration of Jesus: *"This is my Son, whom I love. Listen to Him!"* We can go to church, have daily devotionals, read the Bible, and not really know Him, much less listen to Him who talks to us daily, who knocks at our door and asks to come in and share our

xiv

life. (Revelation 3: 20)

For those of you who are still huffing and puffing over any challenge to the veracity of your Christianity, permit me to again use the marriage analogy. Two people who sign a marriage contract are legally married. But if there is no love, service or selflessness in the marriage – that is, no relationship – one could question whether they are really married in the full meaning of what marriage is all about. So, too, a person may have a baptismal certificate and an official church membership and still be a stranger, still not have a relationship of love with Jesus Christ. To be a Christian because "it is the thing to do" or because it is a family tradition is as empty and void of love and relationship as a "marriage of convenience." Worse, it is hypocritical because it portrays the trappings of love without any substance. Just as married couples sometimes find it helpful to have a third party be a mirror to them in order to help them recommit their lives to one another, so it is my hope that this book and, above all, the Word of God in this book and its Author, the Holy Spirit, will reintroduce some people to the God-Man knocking at the door of their hearts – and will also introduce some people for the first time to the real Jesus, to His Father and to the Holy Spirit, and to the gift of eternal life which They yearn to give us all.

Another difficulty some readers may have – the intensely social justice-minded among you – is that you would prefer to see more emphasis placed on social causes and service to the poor and underprivileged, as further indicators of "real Christianity." Well, this indeed is addressed; but to be frank, it does not receive nearly as much attention as developing a relationship with the Lord and having one's heart totally committed to Him. The reason is simple. The more we know Jesus, the more we follow Him, the more we will be sensitive to the needs of others and will reach out to help and serve others and defend the truth. Serving others as a result of following Jesus is a far cry from doing good works as a substitute for relationship, as a way to earn "eternal brownie points," or to have a "good name" to follow us after this life on earth. Relationship comes first – a free gift of love from God; works follow because of that relationship. Jesus came to serve, to give Himself, to die for us. He wants His followers to do the same, but as a result of the love relationship not instead of it.

This book is not about me. I seek only to be a vehicle, a vessel, through whom the Lord might touch hearts as He has touched mine. I am not going to theologize or be academic. My promise to you, the reader, is that everything I write will be based on the Bible, the Living Word of God, unbent and untainted by any denominational outlook. There are many, many Scripture quotations; they are far more important than any commentary I might have.

And this brings us to an important invitation and challenge to readers of this book:

Journaling.

JOURNALING

What is journaling? (According to the eminent Mr. Webster, the correct word is "journalizing", but "journaling" just sounds easier and is more commonly used.) A retired Senior Vice President of Herschend Family Entertainment introduced the President of the Silver Dollar City Foundation (a Christian ministry supported by the Company) and me to this marvelous way of studying the Word of God. John Baltes is the President of the Foundation, and my job has encompassed both working for this ministry and for Human Resources in Herschend Family Entertainment. For over two years, John and I did journaling together, using the One Year Bible. We privately read the same Scriptures for a two-week period – Old Testament, New Testament, Psalm, Proverb. We sought the guidance of the Holy Spirit and made notes, wrote prayers, and did whatever the Spirit brought to our minds and hearts. Then we came together and spent about two hours going over the Scriptures. It is amazing what revelations the Holy Spirit brings from the Living Word when two or more people share what the Lord has shown them. Later, a small group began meeting weekly in my office in Human Resources and doing basically the same thing, using the Psalms and John's Gospel. So, I challenge you to do journaling! Each chapter (I prefer to call them reflections) ends with some suggested Scriptures for journaling. For the most part they are Scriptures quoted and/or referred to in the reflection. Find another person, or more than one, spend time personally on them for an agreed-upon period and then share thoughts, prayers and insights. It may take some initial commitment and discipline, but the rewards will far outweigh the effort – I absolutely guarantee it.

PART 1:

SALVATION HISTORY

These seven initial reflections focus on the amazing reality that God did not leave us to our own devices when we sinned as a human race. He had a plan to redeem us – with the result that the latter state would actually be greater than the original one!

Following the expulsion from the Garden of Eden, as described in the early chapters of the Book of Genesis, God began fulfilling His promise to return us to right relationship with Him by entering human history in a dramatic way. After the great flood, by which God both punished a sinful world and spared a remnant through Noah and his family, God later entered human history by calling a man named Abram. Abram became Abraham, and eventually the people known as the Hebrews, the Jews, the People of Israel, became God's chosen vessel for the preparing of mankind for the coming of the Redeemer – a Redeemer beyond the wildest imaginings of any Jewish believer or any prophet.

In this section, we explore the central meaning of the Temple, of sacrifice and of covenant. We will compare the Temple of the Old Testament with the living "temples" of the New Covenant – each and every real Christian. We will look at the symbolic significance of "gardens" in the Bible. We will explore the meaning of the greatest event of all time, celebrated at Easter. And we will begin looking at our ultimate goal – a union with God in heaven.

So, let's join together on this exploration of God's Word and God's Love. Don't forget to do journaling. There will be suggested Scriptures at the end of each chapter, following a summary of the key points covered in the reflection.

REFLECTION 1:

SACRIFICE

Religion – mankind's acknowledgement and worship of divinity – pulsates through the arteries of human history. Giving homage to gods, to nature, to something or someone upon whom people recognize a dependence, or whom they fear, or before whom they stand in awe, is woven into every human culture, current and past.

Atheists are new in the grand scope of history, and the phenomenon is decidedly more western than eastern. Many wonder, myself included, if even atheists deep within themselves do not recognize a higher power or force of some kind, whether personal or impersonal. I have yet to find, for example, a "big bang" proponent of the formation of our universe who can logically explain or defend where the ingredients of that enormous explosion came from. Matter is, by its very nature, finite; it cannot have always existed by its own power. There is a story going around that makes the point: A scientist challenged God and claimed that he could now create life. God told him to go ahead, so the scientist picked up some dirt. God told him to stop, that he had to play by the rules – and told him to get his own dirt.

All people of all cultures since recorded human history began acknowledge a type of divinity – and worship it, pay homage to it, sacrifice to it. In fact, it is impossible to delve very deeply into a study of religions without finding right at the center of them some type of sacrifice. An integral element of religion is sacrifice. So, when God entered human history and formed a people who would follow Him, he included in His instructions to them: Offer sacrifices to Me.

Therefore, let's journey down the path of Salvation History, God's preparation for the coming of the Messiah. Let's travel to the ancient Middle East, the cradle of civilization. About 1,500 years before the birth of Jesus, the Middle East was home to a large variety of peoples and nations. They were all polytheists – worshiping many gods – and they all offered sacrifice, including human sacrifice. From the time right after Noah, mankind once again began a downward spiral into immorality, brutality and false worship. Right in the midst of this pagan soup, God established His own people. He revealed Himself as the One True God, something that seems obvious from our perspective, but something absolutely radical to the polytheistic societies of that age. In fact, over time, the Israelites became known to their pagan neighbors as the people who worshiped only one God and stood out as odd and out of step with the times. In point of fact, they were true revolutionaries, created and guided by the Divine Being who became the God of Abraham, Isaac and Jacob and later the "I Am Who Am" – Yahweh, the eternal and only God of the universe.

So, God called, made a promise to and entered into a covenant with Abraham, and asked him to follow and obey. The promise was that Abraham's descendents would become as numerous as the stars in the heavens, as grains of sand on the seashore. The covenant was an eternal one between God and Abraham and his descendents, a foreshadowing of the covenant forged between God and His Church, His people, through the death and Resurrection of His Son.

Following the age of the Patriarchs of the Jewish people, following the Exodus from Egypt by the guidance of Moses, through the wandering in the desert and the giving of the Commandments and laws for worship and sacrifice, through the entrance into the Promised Land as the people followed Joshua, through the establishment of the Kingdom and beyond, God's hand was with His people. He taught them about Himself, He showed them how to worship Him and serve and support one another – and

Will the Real Christians Please Stand Up!

He repeatedly told them to beware of the temptations all around them to follow false gods and worship idols. Indeed, the great temptation of God's people, and the sin into which they fell frequently, was idolatry. Living in the midst of nations and peoples who recognized many gods and who made sacrifice to those gods, the Israelites saw and often copied the religious practices of their neighbors. God instructed His people to offer sacrifice to Him, not to false gods made of clay and metal and wood, but time and again the people fell into grievous sin by recognizing as gods things other than the Living God. Jump ahead in history to our time. We think of idolatry as something ancient, or at best something in "uncivilized" parts of our world. But idolatry is, and always has been, putting anything, that's right, anything before us that takes the place of God as most important in our lives. Money? TV? Success? Sexual license? Comfort? The ultimate sin is always putting myself in the place of God. What is abortion if it is not placing comfort, convenience and personal "rights" ahead of the rights of innocent unborn babies? What is "same sex marriage" if not a way to put a human blessing on sexual immorality in defiance of God's divine law? What is the attempt to remove God from public life if not idolatry – worshiping human will and freedom over God's will? And these are just a few examples from modern life. The Jewish people in ancient times did the same – for when they sacrificed to idols they were taking the easy way out, avoiding persecution or mockery by their neighbors, in other words, looking out for #1, themselves. The choice of self – pride — has always been and always will be the basic sin and the root of all other sins. Look at what caused the downfall of Satan, and how Satan tempted our first parents: With idolatry – the choice of self-will over the One, True, Living, Eternal God, the Creator and Sustainer.

Let's explore sacrifice a little deeper. Even before the establishment of Israel, the Bible records sacrificial acts to the one God: The story of Cain and Abel, Noah after the flood. The descendents of Abraham, from Isaac to Jacob to the Patriarchs, to Moses and beyond, all followed God's instructions to offer sacrifice. The Covenant that God made with Abraham – the promise of a nation that would endure – includes as an integral aspect of man's

Will the Real Christians Please Stand Up!

response the offering of sacrifice. In the Pentateuch, the first five books of the Old Testament, there are many references to sacrifice. We find this prominent in the laws and instructions given by God through Moses regarding the fulfillment of religious responsibilities. The Mosaic Covenant included many practical regulations designed for the people's health and safety. But most prevalent in the Covenant was precise instruction regarding worship. This included sacrifice in a variety of forms – though never human sacrifice. Human sacrifice was an abomination to God.

The people understood sacrifice as primarily a form of substitution. This was especially true in blood sacrifice – the shedding of animal blood and the consuming of animals by fire to atone for sin. Many excellent and in-depth studies have been made of the nuances of sacrifice; these studies go beyond our purpose here. Hopefully readers will at least use such tools as a concordance and thematic studies of the Bible to increase knowledge of this important subject – especially in light of Old Testament sacrifice foreshadowing as a type the ultimate sacrifice of Jesus that would usher in the New Testament, the New Covenant. The relationship between Old Testament sacrifices by the Chosen People and the perfect and once-forever sacrifice of Jesus Christ is closely woven in God's design and is enlightening as to the overall beauty and goodness of God's salvific plan.

This awesome reality of God's plan bursts forth in its glory simply by a thoughtful study of the close-knit tie between the Old Testament and New Testament books of the Bible. The Old Testament was written over a period of about 1,500 years. In specific times and through specifically chosen individuals, the Holy Spirit inspired writers to record the oral tradition handed down over the centuries. The New Testament was written over a period of about 100 years. The early Christians had only the Old Testament writings and the oral tradition provided by the apostles and others who walked with Jesus. From that tradition, God guided the writing of the New Testament books through the inspiring of selected writers. Yet, regardless of this very long time period, a study of the relationships between the Old and New Testaments and the thread of thought within and between the Testaments reveals an awesome bond. The historical events and the messages all fit together, like a hand in a glove (admittedly, from a Christian perspective). One of the great miracles of human history is the interwoven perfection of the Bible, the greatest and most widely read book ever written. The promises and prophecies of the Old Testament find perfect fulfillment in the events of the New Testament. Why? Because the true Author of the Bible is the Holy Spirit. The Bible is a personal gift from God to mankind, really, God's autobiography. The infinite, perfect, all holy God has chosen to open Himself to His people and to invite us to enter into communion with Him. And, to be sure, one of the threads winding through the history of salvation and holding the tapestry together is the central place and meaning of sacrifice.

A pivotal historical event in Old Testament times became the greatest foreshadowing of a greater future fulfillment: The Exodus. Not only did God deliver His people from bondage, He instructed them to offer sacrifice both in preparation for leaving and as an annual remembrance. The people of Israel had migrated to Egypt to escape death by famine. God orchestrated this by permitting Joseph to be sold into slavery by his jealous brothers. Joseph found favor with Egyptian royalty but then suffered imprisonment through a false accusation of sexual harassment because of his commitment to purity. God delivered him from that as well and raised Joseph to a highly prominent place in the Pharaoh's court. Joseph recognized that God was using him to protect the people of Israel. He instructed the Israelites to protect his bones and carry them with them when they would in the future return to the Promised Land. Later Pharaohs forgot the great services that Joseph had performed for them – through a plan to preserve them from famine as well – and made the multitude of Israelites slaves. The early chapters of the Book of Exodus describe the familiar history of Moses' dealings with Pharaoh, based on the command to let God's people go. Time and again God punished the Egyptians for refusing, and time and again Pharaoh hardened his heart. With perfect hindsight as we study God's plan, this was all building up to the ultimate punishment, the one that would tip the scales in favor of the people of Israel – the destruction of the firstborn child of every Egyptian family, including Pharaoh's. This may seem harsh, but God permitted it because of Pharaoh's stubbornness of heart, that proud heart of a leader who put his authority ahead of the well-being of the Egyptian people he ruled over.

God gave the Israelites very specific instructions through Moses. Each family was to sacrifice a lamb, one without blemish. They were to put some of the lamb's blood on the doorway of their homes, so that the angel of death would "pass over" and thereby spare their own firstborn children. Then, each family cooked the lamb and prepared a special meal, to be eaten with unleavened bread (no time to wait for the bread to rise) and with staff in hand, as they were in haste preparing for a journey to freedom. Further, Moses gave instructions from God that the people of Israel were to have an annual Passover celebration, as a reminder of their miraculous deliverance from Egypt. Typology is the process of identifying signs and events in the Old Testament that point to the New, and of identifying signs and events in the New Testament that were initially seeds planted in the Old. The Word of God is so awesome! To use the tapestry analogy again, think of all human history as a large, beautiful and intricate tapestry, with one end at the beginning of creation and God's dealings with mankind and the other end at some time in the future – the tapestry is not yet complete. There are some threads that begin and end at a specific point in the tapestry; there are others that wind their way throughout the whole, holding everything in place by their constancy and strength. God's revelation and His guiding hand in human history are the primary thread. In fact, it is more a strong cluster of threads, around which are woven all the others. There are those who say that the universe and people are the result of chance, that human history is formed only by the actions of people throughout time. The Bible is powerful evidence that there is much more at work than chance. God exists, and, further, God is intimately involved in the affairs of mankind.

Returning to the Passover, we find in God's instructions and the response of the people of Israel an amazingly accurate foreshadowing of what was to come – of what the formation of the people of Israel was all about in God's plan of love. God required the slaying of a lamb without defect, pointing the way to the Lamb of God who as Deity Incarnate was the Sinless One. God instructed the people to put blood on their doorposts; it was the blood of the lamb that protected them from the angel of death, just as much later it would be the Blood of the Lamb slain on the Cross who would save us from our sins and give us the opportunity to avoid eternal death. God told the people to cook and eat the lamb; so, too, on the night before Jesus died, He told us to eat His Body and drink His Blood, not annually but frequently, as a way to remain in Him and renew our strength. God told the Israelites to eat with staff in hand, ready for a journey. So, too, Jesus our Lord asks His followers to take up the cross and follow Him. A sacrifice in Egypt led to the setting free of a nation of slaves, as God miraculously led them through the waters. A sacrifice on Golgotha led to the freeing of people from the slavery of sin and death, for all who would accept Jesus the Christ as Savior and Lord and who would follow Him through the waters of regeneration. This remembrance of the Passover by the people of Israel became a pivotal element of their worship, integrated later into the full body of worship and sacrifice as God instructed the people to build the Ark of the Covenant and later the Temple and bestowed on the sons of Levi the priestly office.

The reality and mystery of sacrifice permeate all of Salvation History. Further, the mystery of sacrifice is an eternal reality. The Book of Hebrews in the New Testament portrays Jesus as the Great High Priest, the Living Sacrifice who died once and for all on the Cross but whose offering of Himself to the Father for us goes on as He, the Resurrected Lord, is at the right hand of the Father. The love and obedience and offering of Jesus on the Cross constituted a spiritual giving that transcends the actual events at Golgotha. Even as the Risen Savior, He continues to give Himself for us while now in glory. He is the eternal High Priest offering the perfect sacrifice, His shed Blood is spiritually present to wash us clean, make us white as snow and make it possible for us to have eternal life as adopted sons and daughters in God's own Trinitarian Family. The writer of Hebrews pens the following in chapter 9, verses 19-26:

"When Moses had proclaimed every commandment of the law to all the people, he took the blood of calves together with water, scarlet wool, and branches of hyssop, and sprin-

kled the scroll and all the people. He said, 'This is the blood of the covenant, which God has commanded you to keep.' In the same way, he sprinkled with the blood both the tabernacle and everything used in its ceremonies. In fact, the law requires that nearly everything be cleansed with blood, and without the shedding of blood, there is no forgiveness. It was necessary, then, for the copies of the heavenly things to be purified with these sacrifices, but the heavenly things themselves with better sacrifices than these. For Christ did not enter a man-made sanctuary that was only a copy of the true one; he entered heaven itself, now to appear for us in God's presence. Nor did he enter heaven to offer himself again and again, the way the high priest enters the Most Holy Place every year with blood that is not his own. Then Christ would have had to suffer many times since the creation of the world. But now he has appeared once for all at the end of the ages to do away with sin by the sacrifice of himself."

Again, in Hebrews 9: 7-12 and Hebrews 10: 5-10:

"...Only the high priest entered the inner room, and that only once a year, and never without blood, which he offered for himself and for the sins the people had committed in ignorance. The Holy Spirit was showing by this that the way into the Most Holy Place had not yet been disclosed as long as the first tabernacle was still standing. This is an illustration for the present time, indicating that the gifts and sacrifices being offered were not able to clear the conscience of the worshiper. They are only a matter of food and drink and various ceremonial washings – external regulations applying until the time of the new order. When Christ came as High Priest of the good things that are already here, he went through the greater and more perfect tabernacle that is not man-made, that is to say, not a part of this creation. He did not enter by means of the blood of goats and calves; but he entered the Most Holy Place once for all by his own blood,

having obtained eternal redemption. The blood of goats and bulls and the ashes of a heifer sprinkled on those who are ceremonially unclean sanctify them so that they are outwardly clean. How much more, then, will the blood of Christ, who through the eternal Spirit offered himself unblemished to God, cleanse our consciences from acts that lead to death, so that we may serve the living God!...Therefore, when Christ came into the world, he said: 'Sacrifice and offering you did not desire, but a body you prepared for me; with burnt offerings and sin offerings you were not pleased. Then I said, 'Here I am – it is written about me in the scroll – I have come to do your will, O God.' First he said 'sacrifices and offerings, burnt offerings and sin offerings you did not desire, nor were you pleased with them" (although the law required them to be made). Then he said, 'Here I am. I have come to do your will.' He sets aside the first to establish the second. And by that will, we have been made holy through the sacrifice of the body of Jesus Christ once for all."

Delving more deeply into the meaning of sacrifice, we see a close bond between sacrifice and obedience. True obedience comes from the heart and does not focus simply on the letter of the law. True sacrifice comes from a person who passionately loves, worships, repents, thanks and intercedes. The Israelites were obedient to God's commands to perform sacrificial worship, following His instructions to the letter. That eventually became a problem, as some of the people and their leaders put more emphasis on form than worship from the heart (and that is a problem facing people of all religions and in all times). But in Jesus, we find the ultimate sacrifice, and one from the heart. It was Jesus' total obedience from His Heart to the will of His Father that made the sacrifice meaningful; and it was Jesus as the Second Person of the Blessed Trinity made flesh who made the sacrifice perfect. Looking back to the days of the early Kingdom of Israel, Saul disobeyed God and kept some of the fruits of spoil. So the prophet Samuel said to him, *"Does the Lord delight in burnt offerings and sacrifices as much as in obeying the voice of the Lord? To obey is better than sacrifice, and to heed is better than the fat of rams."* (I Samuel 15:22). What makes this all the more significant is that Saul's logic (and excuse) was that he had ordered keeping some of the enemy's livestock for the express purpose of making sacrifice to God. Nevertheless, God's anger burned and manifested itself through the holy man, Samuel. It is so easy to rationalize, so easy to go through religious rites and religious motions and, thereby, apply false salve to our consciences.

David understood this when he cried out in his great penitential Psalm 51: *"The sacrifices of God are a broken spirit; a broken and contrite heart, O God, you will not despise."* (51: 17) The prophet Hosea revealed God's heart when he wrote*: "For I desire mercy, not sacrifice, and acknowledgement of God rather than burnt offerings."* (Hosea 6:6) It is highly significant to recognize that Jesus quoted Hosea during His public ministry. After Jesus called the tax collector, Matthew, to follow Him and become a disciple, Matthew, in his joy and excitement, invited Jesus to dine with him. Jesus accepted the invitation and had supper with Matthew and some of the tax collector's friends. The friends probably had no more social standing with the religious leaders than Matthew did, and the Pharisees complained to Jesus' disciples about the company their Master was keeping. *"On hearing this, Jesus said, 'It is not the healthy who need a doctor, but the sick. But go and learn what this means, 'I desire mercy, not sacrifice.' For I have not come to call the righteous, but sinners.* (Matthew 9: 12-13). This is a clear indictment of those who think they are righteous because they look that way. "I go to church; I do not mingle with people from the gutter; I obey all the rules." Jesus cuts right through the pomp and circumstance and looks at the heart.

Gazing into your heart and mine, He says to us: "If you want to be my disciple, take up your cross and follow me." Sacrifice is truly an integral part of the Christian life. Far more important, and more costly, than the sacrifice of animals is the sacrifice of self. Jesus tells us plainly that the truly Christian life is a yielded life. It is asking God to break our will so that we will seek only to think, say and do what He wants in our lives. We, if we are born again, are members of the Body of Christ; but if we do not forsake all and follow Christ with our whole being (and keep on doing it, even when we fall and fail), we are not vital organs in that Body, enabling Christ to continue to walk in the world, to touch people, to save souls. We become simply "fatty deposits", still loved by the Lord but unusable by Him for the advancement of the Kingdom. We are all threads in the tapestry of God's plan, but without a surrender of self to the will of God, we are weak and even ineffectual. A European teacher of youth in the 19th century, a holy and committed man of God, had a dream. In that dream he went to heaven and found himself in the presence of the Triune God. God turned the man's attention to one direction where there were an uncountable number of souls praising God. God said to John Bosco, "These souls are here because you made your life a sacrifice of service much of the time and I was able to touch these people through you." John Bosco was about to praise and thank God, when God stopped him and turned his attention to another, even larger multitude of souls. "John Bosco, these are souls I wanted to touch and save through you, but I was unable to because of the times you did not yield and obey but served yourself. I had to find someone else to work through."

Peter wrote, *"As you come to him the Living Stone – rejected by men but chosen by God and precious to him – you also, like living stones, are being built into a spiritual house to be a holy priesthood, offering spiritual sacrifices acceptable to God through Jesus Christ."* (1 Peter 2: 4-5) Living temples of God, the Body of Christ – heady stuff, this, but it is the reality of the calling to the Christian life. Or, we can choose to be like Demas. Paul wrote, *"Do your best to come quickly, for Demas, because he loved this world, has deserted me and gone to Thessalonica."* (2 Timothy 4:10) Undoubtedly, Demas considered himself to be a Christian even after he left; but at a time of need he deserted Paul. He chose the world and its more comfortable ways. He did not heed the call of Jesus, the prompting of the Holy Spirit, and thereby he did not yield and obey. Thus, Demas did not offer "spiritual sacrifices", the spiritual sacrifice of his life – he did not take up his cross and follow Christ. What about us?

Paul wrote very clearly in his Letter to the Romans:

"Therefore, I urge you, brothers (and sisters), in view of God's mercy, to offer your bodies as living sacrifices, holy and pleasing to God – this is your spiritual act of worship. Do not conform any longer to the pattern of this world, but be transformed by the renewing of your mind." (Romans 12: 1-2)

As someone once said, humorously but with wisdom and insight, "The trouble with sacrifices is that they keep walking off the altar!" I confess that I have walked off the altar many times; but God, so rich in mercy, keeps gently calling me to climb back on. This I can do only by His grace. How do I know if I am a living sacrifice? Paul gives us the answer in that same twelfth chapter of Romans:

"Love must be sincere. Hate what is evil; cling to what is good. Be devoted to one another in brotherly love. Honor one another above yourselves. Never be lacking in zeal; but keep your spiritual fervor, serving the Lord. Be joyful in hope, patient in affliction, faithful in prayer. Share with God's people who are in need. Practice hospitality. Bless those who persecute you, bless and do not curse. Rejoice with those who rejoice, mourn with those who mourn. Live in harmony with one another. Do not be proud, but be willing to associate with people of low position. Do not be conceited. Do not repay anyone evil for evil. Be careful to do what is right in the eyes of everybody. If it is possible, as far as it depends on you, live at peace with everyone. Do not take revenge, my friends, but leave room for God's wrath, for it is written, 'It is mine to avenge; I will repay,' says the Lord. On the contrary: 'If your enemy is hungry, feed him; if he is thirsty, give him something to drink. In doing this, you will heap burning coals on his head.' Do not be overcome by evil, but overcome evil with good." (Romans 12: 9-21)

Christianity proudly bears the descriptive adjective "Judaeo-Christian." This means that the roots of the religion reach deeply into the soil of the Old Testament promises, of God's founding of and relationship with the Chosen People. Though Christians believe that the promise of the Messiah saw its fulfillment in Jesus of Nazareth, Jesus the Christ, the relationship between Jews and Christians is closely intertwined. Of all the failings of Christian peoples over the centuries – and make no mistake, Christians are guilty of many, many individual and corporate sins – one of the most heinous is the persecution and hatred of Jews by some Christians in the name of Christ. Anti-Semitism is a stench before God, because the Jews remain the Chosen People, because Jesus is Incarnate as a Jew, because Paul wrote eloquently in inspired Scripture about how much he and God love the Jews. Further, elements of worship as commanded by God of the people of Israel remain in Christian worship and are especially evident in the "liturgical" denominations (and in the worship in heaven as described in the Book of Revelation).

There are many beautiful ways in which Christians worship God. Some denominations focus more on preaching and singing, others incorporate those elements into formal patterns, called liturgy. All Christian churches focus on the once and forever sacrifice of Jesus on the Cross and His presence at the right hand of the Father as the Great High Priest. And Jewish faith and sacrifices were all pointing to the coming of the Messiah, whom Christians proclaim to be Jesus Christ. So, regardless of denomination, true Christians recognize the central importance of the Great High Priest in worship; when our praise and worship and intercession become joined with Jesus, our prayer takes on truly supernatural significance. He died once, never to die again; but the offering of Himself to the Father goes on, now from His position at the right hand of the Father as the Mediator, with the Holy Spirit as God's living Love bringing grace to those who worship in Spirit and in Truth.

I can think of no better way to end this reflection on sacrifice than to quote my wife, Barbara, who lives in almost constant physical pain but who is a deeply committed and loving Christian woman. She combines the thoughts of classical Christian writers with her own thoughts and experiences when she writes, "I find when I fight to love, to do, I see Jesus walk away. When I surrender and allow myself to give in – to pain and fatigue – Jesus comes in. I don't believe God is interested in how we struggle to live, but in how we die. I have spent much time trying to live and He only asks for death." The Word says it better, of course: "I no longer live, but Christ lives in me."

SUMMARY FOR REFLECTION AND DISCUSSION:

A real Christian:

1) Believes in the once only perfect sacrifice of Jesus Christ on the Cross, and sees and finds in that the way to salvation. Whether I look at a cross or a crucifix, do I recognize the immense and perfect love of God who became Man in order to offer a sacrifice far superior to any that others can offer? Do I recognize that He did it for me?
2) Places himself/herself on the altar of sacrifice by yielding body, mind and spirit to the will of God. What causes me to get back off the altar? What areas of my life am I unwilling to surrender?
3) Sees all of life as a glorious opportunity to be a living sacrifice, expressed above all by seeking to live each moment as an act of service and living prayer, under the Lordship of Jesus Christ. Do I listen to the Holy Spirit who whispers to me about how to serve? Am I interested, in final analysis, more about me and my agenda or more about God and His will?

SCRIPTURES FOR JOURNALING:

1) Exodus 12-13;
2) Romans 12;
3) Hebrews 9-10;
4) Ephesians 2 and 1 Peter 1-2.

REFLECTION 2:

SACRIFICE CONTINUED: THE BLOOD COVENANT

There is story that is very sad but worthy of repeating here. It is about a man and his son. The father as a young boy had read the books of Mark Twain, had lived for many of his growing-up years near the banks of the Mississippi river, and ever since he could remember had dreamed of being a riverboat captain. Most of his friends dreamed of escaping from the little town near the mighty river, talked about baseball and football and college and great financial success. But this boy wanted to draw ever closer to the river, to indeed live his life on the river – as the captain of a paddle wheeler or a tug or even a barge. Time passed; the boy grew up and moved away. He did, however, live close to a large river with some heavy boat and barge traffic. Though he was never able to captain a boat, he did have a job with some significant responsibility. He was in charge of raising a drawbridge. A railroad track passed through his town and a bridge carried both freight and passenger rail traffic over the river. As he attended to his job, he directed his attention as required to both lumbering and swiftly moving trains. But let a vessel churn through the waters below his post, and he would always smile. He was a husband and father now, and he had transferred his dream to his three-year-old son. If he could not be a riverboat captain, his son could! One day he brought his son to work with him. Letting him play on the floor in the small building where the controls were, Dad's mind drifted to the future. He could see his son, grown up, piloting a vessel down the mighty Mississippi. Then he was jolted back to reality by the sound of a train's long, loud whistle. The Limited, a normally packed passenger train, was approaching; his daydreaming had almost caused him to miss it. A large ship had passed through recently, and the bridge was still up! But he knew that he had ample time – nothing unusual here. As he started to activate the large gears and other machinery that would lower the bridge, he looked out the window with a sudden awareness of impending peril. His son had wandered away and was playing among the gears! If they began turning, they would crush him. The train's whistle echoed again, louder and closer now. The shock of the sound and the sight of his son caused him to tremble with fear. He thought, "I will run to my son, pick him up and return quickly." But he realized the futility of this. The train was just too close. If he did not engage the machinery immediately, it would be too late. He faced a seemingly impossible choice: Go get his son and cause hundreds of people to fall to their deaths; or lower the bridge and watch his son die. With tears streaming down his face and with his heart breaking, he lowered the bridge. And his son died. Could we do that? Put yourself in his place. Now put yourself in the place of the train passengers. What would you want him to do?

There are biblical parallels to this story; let's focus on Abraham and Isaac as a foreshadowing of Redemption. Genesis 22 tells us the story. This old man who was promised a son by God, who was promised that he would be the father of a mighty nation, rejoiced with his wife, Sarah, when Isaac was finally born. Then, some years later, God did the seemingly unthinkable. He asked Abraham to put his beloved son to death as a sacrifice to God. The very thought of this causes us to recoil in horror. Well, it did to Abraham as well; the difference was that pagan people surrounded him, people whose worship of the gods included human sacrifice. So Abraham at least understood the reality of such sacrifice; what he did not understand is why God would ask him to sacrifice his only son after giving Isaac to him long after his and Sarah's normal childbearing years.

But Abraham obeyed God, and, though the biblical account does not mention her, so did Sarah. Imagine the tears streaming down her face as she watched Abraham and their beloved son begin their journey to Mount Moriah. Imagine young Isaac asking his father where they were going, and why, and when he realized it was to offer sacrifice, asking Dad where the sacrifice was. With crushing sadness, Abraham told Isaac that God would provide the sacrifice. As they approached their destination, they gathered some wood, and Isaac carried it (very significant as typology, a foreshadowing of the future). It was only when Abraham made a crude altar and placed Isaac on it that his son realized with horror that he was the sacrifice and that his father was about to kill him. I am sure their eyes met, Isaac's with unbelief and fear, Abraham's with sadness and love; I am sure that Isaac watched Abraham raise the knife with trembling hands. It was at that wrenching moment that God stopped Abraham and told him that now He knew Abraham put obedience to his God over everything else. Abraham listened to God and followed him, even unto the impending death of his son.

Many centuries later, there was another impending sacrifice. It took place near the Jerusalem Temple, built on the very spot where Abraham took Isaac to sacrifice him. The hill was Golgotha, and there another only-begotten Son faced death. Nailed to a cross as if He were a criminal, He looked down upon His executioners and asked His Father to forgive them. The Father did not stay anyone's hand this time; He did not spare His Son. The Father from all eternity had willed that the Word made Flesh would shed His precious Blood and die for the sins of all mankind.

As we have seen, sacrifice is a key theme of the Old Testament, and of the New. God gave to the people of Israel a method of worship that included, in its very core, sacrificial offerings. Sacrifices were a way for the people to atone for their sins, to yield to God, to thank Him, to acknowledge His sovereign might. There were various types of sacrifice – such as wave offerings and grain offerings, but the most important of the sacrifices were those that involved the shedding of blood. To the Semitic mentality of ancient times, the life of people was in the blood; therefore, the shedding of blood was a symbolic way to move from death to life, from sin to right standing with God. Blood was the very seat and source of life. Different types of animals were sacrificed: The ox, representing the future patient endurance of Jesus, who would offer the only sacrifice that ever was, or ever will be, truly effective (and the only human sacrifice that God ever sanctioned); the sheep and the ram, representing yieldedness to God's will, even unto death; the turtle dove, representing the future purity, innocence and poverty of Jesus (the dove was the offering given by the poorest Israelite families; His parents provided doves at the time of His Presentation in the Temple); the goat, pointing to the Sinless One who would be numbered with transgressors and driven out of the city to die.

If we accept as a foundation of biblical interpretation that all of the Old Testament points to the New, it becomes challenging and exciting to find the relationship among events, writings and teachings. Applying this principle to sacrifice, accounts of sacrifices and sacrificial offerings have a rich and special meaning as we look backward in time from the perspective of Calvary. For example, read Leviticus 4: 3-12 and see therein a type of the sacrifice of Jesus:

"If the anointed priest sins, bringing guilt on the people, he must bring to the Lord a young bull without defect as a sin offering for the sin he has committed. He is to present the bull at the entrance to the Tent of Meeting before the Lord. He is to lay his hand on its head and slaughter it before the Lord. Then the anointed priest shall take some of the bull's blood and carry it into the Tent of Meeting. He is to dip his finger into the blood and sprinkle some of it seven times before the Lord in front of the curtain of the sanctuary. The priest shall then put some of the blood on the horns of the altar of fragrant incense that is before the Lord in the Tent of Meeting. The rest of the bull's blood he shall pour out at the base of the altar of burnt offering at the entrance to the Tent of Meeting. He shall remove all the fat from the bull of the sin offering – the fat that covers the inner parts or is connected to them, both kidneys with the fat on them near the loins, and the cover of the liver which he will remove with the kidneys – just as the fat is removed from the ox sacrificed

as a fellowship offering. Then the priest shall burn them on the altar of burnt offering. But the hide of the bull and all its flesh, as well as the head and legs, the inner parts and offal – that is, all the rest of the bull – he must take outside the camp to a place ceremonially clean, where the ashes are thrown, and burn it in a wood fire on the ash heap."

Young bull without defect (like the Lamb of God without defect)...sin offering...slaughter it before the Lord (the perfect sacrifice of the Incarnate Word for our Redemption)...sprinkle the blood seven times (seven meaning perfect/eternal)...blood on the altar (pointing to the altar of the Cross)...pour out the blood (blood and water gushed from the pierced side of Jesus)...burnt offering (signifying the totality of Jesus' offering)...outside the camp (Golgotha was outside the city walls of Jerusalem, where the Temple was). When Jesus died, the curtain of the Temple was torn asunder, signifying the end of the Old and the beginning of the New. The description of sacrifice in Leviticus predated the Temple, but also prepared the way for Temple worship and sacrifice. The divine tearing of the curtain, coinciding with the last breath of Jesus, and in anticipation of His Resurrection and Ascension, was and is a clear message that the Lamb who was slain and who now reigns as King of Kings, Lord of Lords, and the great High Priest, invites us into the very intimate presence of the Triune God. In fact, Paul writes twice that in the New Covenant we ourselves as believers are living temples, in which God dwells.

Let's explore now some New Testament scriptures emphasizing the significance of Jesus Christ's sacrifice for our sins:

"Then He took the cup, gave thanks and offered it to them, saying, 'Drink from it, all of you. This is the blood of the covenant, which is poured out for many for the forgiveness of sins.'" (Matthew 26: 27-28)..."This righteousness from God comes through faith in Jesus Christ to all who believe. There is no difference, for all have sinned and fall short of the glory of God, and are justified freely by his grace through the redemption that came by Christ Jesus. God presented him as

a sacrifice of atonement, through faith in his blood." (Romans 3: 22-25)...*"You see, at just the right time, when we were still powerless, Christ died for the ungodly. Very rarely will anyone die for a righteous man, though for a good man someone might possibly dare to die. But God demonstrates his own love for us in this: While we were still sinners, Christ died for us. Since we have now been justified by his blood, how much more shall we be saved from God's wrath through him! For if, when we were God's enemies, we were reconciled to him through the death of his Son, how much more, having been reconciled, shall we be saved through his life! Not only is this so, but we also rejoice in God through our Lord Jesus Christ, through whom we have now received reconciliation."* (Romans 5: 6-11)...*"In him we have redemption through his blood, the forgiveness of sins, in accordance with the riches of God's grace that he lavished on us with all wisdom and understanding."* (Ephesians 1: 7-8)...*"But now in Christ Jesus you who once were far away have been brought near through the blood of Christ."* (Ephesians 2: 13)...*"For God was pleased to have all his fullness dwell in him, and through him to reconcile to himself all things, whether things on earth or things in heaven, by making peace through his blood, shed on the cross."* (Colossians 1: 19-20)...*"When everything had been arranged like this, the priests entered regularly into the outer room to carry on their ministry. But only the high priest entered the inner room, and that only once a year, and never without blood, which he offered for himself and for the sins the people had committed in ignorance. The Holy Spirit was showing by this that the way into the Most Holy Place had not yet been disclosed as long as the first tabernacle was still standing. This is an illustration for the present time, indicating that the gifts and sacrifices being offered were not able to clear the conscience of the worshiper. They are only a matter of food and drink and various ceremonial washings – external regulations applying until the time of the new order. When Christ came as High Priest of the good things that are already here, he went through the greater and more perfect tabernacle that is not man-made, that is to say, not a part of this creation. He did not enter by means of the blood of goats and calves; but he entered the Most Holy Place once for all by his own blood, having obtained eternal redemption. The blood of goats and bulls and the ashes of a heifer sprinkled on those who are ceremonially unclean sanctify them so that they are outwardly clean. How much more, then, will the blood of Christ, who through the eternal Spirit offered himself unblemished to God, cleanse our consciences from acts that lead to death, so that we may serve the living God!"* (Hebrews 9: 6-14)...*"For you know that it was not with perishable things such as silver or gold that you were redeemed from the empty way of life handed down to you from your forefathers, but with the precious blood of Christ, a lamb without blemish or defect. He was chosen before the creation of the world, but was revealed in these last times for your sake. Through him you believe in God, who raised him from the dead and glorified him, and so your faith and hope are in God."* (1 Peter 1: 18-21)...*"But if we walk in the light, as he is in the light, we have fellowship with one another, and the blood of Jesus, his Son, purifies us from all sin."* (1 John 1: 7)...*"And they sang a new song: 'You are worthy to take the scroll and to open its seals, because you were slain, and with your blood you purchased men for God from every tribe and language and people and nation. You have made them to be a kingdom and priests to serve our God, and they will reign on the earth.'...And he said, 'These are they who have come out of the great tribulation; they have washed their robes and made them white in the blood of the Lamb'...'They overcame him by the blood of the Lamb and by the word of their testimony; they did not love their lives so much as to shrink from death'...He is dressed in a robe dipped in blood, and his name is the Word of God."* (Revelation 5: 9; 7: 14; 12: 11; 19: 13)

Wherever you are right now in your spiritual journey as you

read this, whatever your depth of faith, your Christian belief system, or any other belief system, you may and can have your own personal "altar call". You are invited, not by me but by God, to come to the altar of your heart, your inmost being, and bow down before the risen and glorified and living Jesus Christ, confess your sins, proclaim Him as your Savior and Lord. His precious blood will cleanse you from sin, no matter how heinous, as long as your heart is truly repentant because you have offended the God who created you and who died for you that you might have eternal life. He will dress you in the white robe of salvation, He will make you a member of His family through the waters of Baptism that both cleanse you and symbolize the inner cleansing of your spirit by the Holy Spirit. And God extends an invitation to partake of His family life, now and for all eternity. He asks that you accept His Son as Savior and choose to follow Him as the Lord of your life from this day forward. Or, if you are already a Christian, you may take this opportunity to renew your commitment to God, to ask for a new anointing by the Holy Spirit, to ask for the grace to ever better know and follow Jesus.

Real Christians believe in the power of the blood and understand its significance. If you are in a church or among Christians where the sacrifice of Jesus Christ is not emphasized – the bloody sacrifice of Jesus on Calvary and the eternal continuing sacrifice of Jesus as the great High Priest – then I say with utter conviction that you are among people who just do not get it, who do not understand what Christianity is all about. As the old hymn so powerfully proclaims, "There is power, power, wonder-working power, in the blood of the Lamb, in the precious blood of the Lamb."

It is very worthwhile for Christians to worship in a congregation of believers on a regular basis whenever possible – not because there is a rule requiring it, not because it is socially and politically correct, not because of a fear of consequences if they do not participate – but because they see uniting themselves with the High Priest, Jesus, by the power and presence of the Holy Spirit, for the glory and praise of the Father as the most absolutely sublime privilege they have on this earth, and because they know they will be doing it in an even more perfect and glorious way for all eternity in heaven.

SUMMARY FOR REFLECTION AND DISCUSSION:

A real Christian:

1) Grasps in the inner spirit the meaning and significance of blood sacrifices and blood covenant, foreshadowed in the Old Testament and fulfilled on Calvary by the death of Jesus, the Lamb of God;
2) Appreciates what has been handed down and preserved through the faith of our Jewish brethren;
3) Participates freely and joyfully in worship with other Christians (or in spirit when that is not possible), recognizing the reality of being united with our High Priest, Jesus, and of being loved by the Father with the very same Love (the Holy Spirit) with which He loves His Only-Begotten Son.

SCRIPTURES FOR JOURNALING:

1) Genesis 22;
2) Leviticus 4: 3-12;
3) Romans 3: 22-25; Romans 5: 6-11; Colossians 1: 19-20
4) Revelation 5: 9; 7: 14: 12: 11; 19: 13.

REFLECTION 3:

ENTER THE SANCTUARY

Some years ago there was a Reader's Digest article entitled "The Boy Who Dreamed of a Palace." It told the story of Bobby Atchison. As an elementary school student, Bobby came upon an old book, "I Am Anastasia." Anastasia had lived near St. Petersburg in the Alexander Palace with her parents, brother and three sisters. As a result of the 1917 revolution, the family was taken as prisoners to Siberia, where they were murdered – except, perhaps, for Anastasia. Bobby, a tall, thin second grader, studied the book with a growing fascination. He longed to learn more about the magnificent palace described in the book, so he read everything on Russian history that he could find. Bobby learned that the Alexander Palace, built by Catherine the Great in the 18th century, had more than 100 rooms, crystal chandeliers, parquet floors of rosewood and ebony, and much, much more. He even wrote a 100-page report on the Palace to fulfill a school history and writing assignment. Lying in bed at night, Bobby wondered if the Palace had been burned down during the revolution, as he had not been able to determine its fate. "Please let the palace be all right; if it has been ruined but is still standing, I'm going to fix it." So Bobby hoped as the passion within him built to a fever pitch. And so, a life's quest began. Having at last determined that the building was still in existence, as a sixth grader he told his teacher that his dream was to restore the Alexander Palace. She

Will the Real Christians Please Stand Up!

humored him, but many of his classmates ridiculed him for such an outlandish and impossible goal. In 1970 Bobby Atchison went to college, where he studied Russian culture. Following graduation he obtained a job as a travel agent. Finally, in 1977, at the age of 24, he had saved enough money to travel to the Soviet Union. He flew to Moscow and then rode a train to St. Petersburg, where he boarded a tour bus to the Alexander Palace. Heart pounding, Bobby saw the grand old palace of his dream – still standing tall and proud. But – guards denied Bobby access to the building! He discovered that since 1954 the army had been using it as an army installation for the Soviet Baltic Fleet. During the next decade Bobby traveled to St. Petersburg several times, trying to sneak in on each visit, but without success. Finally, in 1987 he used the strategy of taking with him a Russian friend, who explained to the guards that Bobby urgently wished to speak to the commandant. This time they granted him access, though only briefly. But at least he saw for his own eyes that some of the original treasures that he had read about were still present. As Bobby went on with his demanding business life, he never lost interest in the Alexander Palace. He went to libraries in the cities that his job required him to visit; there he made notes, copied and enlarged old photographs, and studied details of furniture and paintings, even window frames. He tried to enlist the support of museum directors in the St. Petersburg area, but no one wrote him back. He telephoned authors of books on Russia; most did not return his calls, but a few did and encouraged Bobby in his quest. At the same time they warned him that it was probably impossible for him as an American to become involved in any restoration work, and that even if he was successful, he was faced with a lifetime of work to achieve any lasting results. But, finally, success: He gained entrance again into the palace, he aroused the interest of people in Russia who shared his vision, and at long last Bobby became the leader of an organization with the mission of restoring the Alexander Palace. Bobby saw a dream fulfilled, one that began when he was a second grader, thousands of miles away from an all but forgotten palace in a vast nation politically unfriendly to the United States.

Now compare this story to the Books of Ezra and Nehemiah, which relate the account of the Jewish exiles returning to Jerusalem to rebuild the Temple and the walls of the city. The loss of Jerusalem and the Temple during the Babylonian exile is a tragedy that the non-Jewish mind cannot begin to fathom in terms of the emotion and pain and sorrow. Psalm 137 describes this raw emotion:

"By the rivers of Babylon we sat and wept when we remembered Zion. There on the poplars we hung our harps, for there our captors asked us for songs, our tormentors demanded songs of joy; they said, 'Sing us one of the songs of Zion!' How can we sing the songs of the Lord while in a foreign land? If I forget you, O Jerusalem, may my right hand forget its skill. May my tongue cling to the roof of my mouth if I do not remember you, if I do not consider Jerusalem my highest joy." A popular modern Irish tenor sings portions of this Psalm, and the rendition is truly rousing and enjoyable – but it does not in any way capture the deep sorrow poured out to God in that prayer. In contrast to this longing Psalm, the words of Psalm 126 describe the joy of the people of Israel in returning to Jerusalem and the Temple: *"When the Lord brought back the captives to Zion, we were like men who dreamed. Our mouths were filled with laughter, our tongues with songs of joy. Then it was said among the nations, 'The Lord has done great things for them.' The Lord has done great things for us, and we are filled with joy. Restore our fortunes, O Lord, like streams in the Negev. Those who sow in tears will reap with songs of joy. He who goes out weeping, carrying seed to sow, will return with songs of joy, carrying sheaves with him."*

The fervent quest of Bobby Atchison and the focus of the Israelites on Jerusalem and the Temple – they are similar in the account of zealous pursuit, to be sure. But what does that have to do with Christians? There is a very powerful phrase in Psalm 73, toward the conclusion of this beautiful Scriptural prayer. Let's reflect on the entire Psalm:

"Surely God is good to Israel, to those who are pure in

heart. But as for me, my feet had almost slipped, I had nearly lost my foothold. For I envied the arrogant when I saw the prosperity of the wicked. They have no struggles; their bodies are healthy and strong. They are free from the burdens common to man; they are not plagued by human ills. Therefore, pride is their necklace; they clothe themselves with violence. From their callous hearts comes iniquity; the evil conceits of their minds know no limits. They scoff, and speak with malice; in their arrogance they threaten oppression. Their mouths lay claim to heaven, and their tongues take possession of the earth. Therefore their people turn to them and drink up waters in abundance. They say, 'How can God know? Does the Most High have knowledge?' This is what the wicked are like – always carefree, they increase in wealth. Surely in vain have I kept my hands in innocence. All day long I have been plagued; I have been punished every morning. If I had said, 'I will speak thus,' I would have betrayed your children. When I tried to understand all this, it was oppressive to me TILL I ENTERED THE SANCTUARY OF GOD (emphasis mine); then I understood their final destiny."

Where is your sanctuary? Where do you go to discern the meaning of life, to determine the path you should choose, to find strength and light and wisdom and peace? You see, everyone has a sanctuary, a place they go to in their hearts, a source of meaning for life. When Jesus died, as we have seen, the curtain of the Jewish Temple was torn asunder. This was quite a feat when we consider the thickness and weight of the large cloth separating the people from the Most Holy Place. Thereby, through the redemptive death (and Resurrection) of the Son of God, the New Covenant began, with no need for anything separating God from the creatures made in His image and likeness. But, where is the Temple? Paul tells us in 1 Corinthians 3: 16-17:

"Don't you know that you yourselves are God's temple and that God's Spirit lives in you? If anyone destroys God's

temple, God will destroy him; for God's temple is sacred, and you are that temple." And again in 1 Corinthians 6: 19-20*: Do you not know that your body is a temple of the Holy Spirit, who is in you, whom you have received from God? You are not your own; you were bought at a price. Therefore, honor God with your body.*" Yet again in 2 Corinthians 6: 16-17*: "What agreement is there between the temple of God and idols? For we are the temple of the living God. As God has said, 'I will live with them and walk among them, and I will be their God, and they will be my people. Therefore come out from them and be separate,' says the Lord.*" Finally, the mysteriously beautiful promise given us by Jesus on the night before He died: *"On that day you will realize that I am in my Father, and you are in me, and I am in you.*" (John 14: 20)

The fully alive Christian walks in the awareness of being a living temple. The center of her/his heart is an intimate union with Jesus Christ, guided by and filled with the Holy Spirit, and all for the glory of the Father whom we can call "Abba," or "Dad," because of the personal and close relationship we are privileged to have with His only begotten Son, Jesus Christ. So, "entering the sanctuary" means entering into a conscious communion with the Trinity – with Father, Son and Holy Spirit. It is only in that encounter that life has ultimate meaning; it is only by the awareness of and living of this unspeakable gift we have that we can stay in balance as we are pushed and pulled by the forces of the world around us.

Let's conclude this reflection by focusing on some more Scriptures that encourage us to enter and live consciously within our sanctuary, to seek the Lord with all our hearts, and to really live the Christian life rather than simply give it lip service:

"Blessed are they who keep his statutes and seek him with all their heart...I have hidden your word in my heart that I might not sin against you. Praise be to you, O Lord; teach me your decrees...I meditate on your precepts and consider your ways. I delight in your decrees; I will not neglect your

word...My comfort in my suffering is this: Your promise preserves my life...Your decrees are the theme of my song wherever I lodge. In the night I remember your name, O Lord, and I will keep your law...My soul faints with longing for your salvation, but I have put my hope in your word...Oh, how I love your law! I meditate on it all day long...Your word is a lamp to my feet and a light for my path...I open my mouth and pant, longing for your commands...I rise before dawn and cry for help; I have put my hope in your word. My eyes stay open through the watches of the night, that I may meditate on your promises." (Psalm 119: 2, 11-2, 15-16, 50, 54-55, 81, 97, 105, 131, 147-148) (And the "word" is, for us, the living Word, Jesus Christ!) *"Be still before the Lord and wait patiently for him; do not fret when men succeed in their ways, when they carry out their wicked schemes."* (Psalm 37: 7) *"I love the house where you live, O Lord, the place where your glory dwells."* (Psalm 26: 8) *"One thing I ask of the Lord, this is what I seek: That I may dwell in the house of the Lord all the days of my life, to gaze upon the beauty of the Lord and to seek him in his temple."* (Psalm 27: 4) *"Better is one day in your courts than a thousand elsewhere; I would rather be a door-keeper in the house of my God than dwell in the tents of the wicked."* (Psalm 84: 10)

Finally, Jesus speaks to us*: I am the vine; you are the branches. If a man remains in me and I in him, he will bear much fruit; apart from me you can do nothing. If anyone does not remain in me, he is like a branch that is thrown away and withers; such branches are picked up, thrown into the fire and burned. As the Father has loved me, so have I loved you. Now remain in my love...I no longer call you servants, because a servant does not know his master's business. Instead, I have called you friends, for everything that I learned from my Father I have made known to you."* (John 15: 5-6, 9, 15)

SUMMARY FOR REFLECTION AND DISCUSSION:

A real Christian:

1) Recognizes that the Temple is a basic theme in the Old Testament and a foreshadowing of something much greater – that we have the invitation and privilege of not only passing through the curtain into the Most Holy Place but of actually being the place where God dwells;
2) Knows that when God created man and woman in His image and likeness and "walked with them in the cool of the garden", He wanted an intimacy of relationship, He invited His creatures to enter into His divine Family life of Father, Word and Holy Spirit;
3) Believes that when mankind sinned, God did not give up on us but promised Redemption – and in a way beyond our understanding and hope. The Word became Flesh and dwelled among us, and through Him we can enter once again into the family life of God;
4) Rejoices that God loves the followers of His Son with the very same love that He has for the Son – and that love is the Holy Spirit.

SCRIPTURES FOR JOURNALING:

1) Psalms 26, 37, 73;
2) 1 Corinthians 3: 16-17; 6: 19-20; 2 Corinthians 6: 16-17; John 14: 20

REFLECTION 4:

LIVING TEMPLES

Quick, answer this question: On what day should Christians wish a big "Happy Birthday!" to one another? What answer pops into your mind? Did you think maybe Christmas – because that is when God became a Man to redeem us? How about Easter – because that is when Jesus rose triumphantly from the dead, making possible the forgiveness of sin and our adoption into God's Family? Or is it our own personal day of accepting Christ as our Savior? Or is it our day of Baptism?

There are elements of beauty and truth in all of these events, to be sure. But the true birthday of the Church is the day of Pentecost.

Do you recall that Jesus, just before He ascended to His Father, told his apostles and disciples to go into Jerusalem? Do you remember why? He told them to pray and to wait to be clothed with power from on high. They needed to be equipped for the mission of going into the world and preaching the Good News, the Gospel. So, in obedience to Him, they – the eleven remaining apostles, some of the disciples, and Jesus' mother – went to the second floor of a building in Jerusalem. There, in that upper room, they prayed, reflected on the amazing events they had seen and been part of, comforted and encouraged one another, and sought whatever it was that God had for them. It must have been both a strange and an exhilarating time for them. There were surely conflicting emotions

Will the Real Christians Please Stand Up!

ging through them as they tarried in that upper room in Jerusalem. Their beloved Jesus was gone, after their hopes were first dashed by His horrible death and then rekindled by His glorious Resurrection from the dead. Most of them reflected with shame on their abandonment of Him, their doubts of His promises. He had spoken directly about His impending death, but they had not understood – perhaps they had chosen not to understand. They had believed He was the promised Messiah, they had come to begin to grasp that He was not simply a prophet, but the very Son of God. But then they saw their own religious leaders conspire against Him; they saw one of their own betray Him and their leader deny Him; they saw the cruelty of Roman might unleashed upon Him – and they saw Him die the death of a criminal, taunted by many, hung between two thieves. They had seen the people in Jerusalem first acclaim Him as He entered the city; then they had seen many of them turn on Him. They had seen people around the cross shaking their heads and shaking their fists at Him. They had experienced an earthquake and some startling events at the moment of His death – and they had heard about the great curtain separating the people from the Most Holy Place in the Temple tearing in two as He breathed His last. They had indeed wavered in their faith and hope, while still clinging to whatever threads of them they could. Then Mary Magdalene, about forty hours after some of them had laid Jesus in a borrowed tomb, announced with great excitement that she had seen Him! Surely Jesus also visited His mother, and He then appeared to the apostles. Even doubting Thomas eventually came to believe that what Jesus had promised had indeed happened. Jesus had been killed, but He had risen victorious over death and the grave. He appeared frequently to his apostles and disciples over the next forty days, and then He returned to His Father. An angel appeared to them and told them to quit staring into the heavens, for He would surely come again. The angel reminded them of their charge, to go to Jerusalem and wait – for something.

So this band of followers, for the most part simple, uneducated people, so unprepared in the world's eyes for being evangelists and spiritual leaders, waited obediently for their mission, their vision, for courage and strength. They knew now without any doubt or wavering that Jesus was the Messiah, and that His death and Resurrection were both foretold and the key reopening the door to eternal life. They believed He would be faithful to His promises. And, as they prayed and encouraged one another, they realized how deeply and intimately they loved Him.

We know what happened. On the Jewish Feast of Pentecost, something remarkable took place in that upper room. All of a sudden there was a sound like that of a rushing and mighty wind, and the Holy Spirit appeared and rested on each of them like a tongue of fire. Just as the Spirit had descended on Jesus in the River Jordan at the beginning of His public ministry, so the Spirit now descended on Jesus' followers. At that moment their lives changed forever. At that moment the history of the world altered its course forever.

In hindsight it is clear that Jesus all along was laying the foundation of what we call "the Church." That triumphant entry into Jerusalem prior to His arrest and execution immediately preceded, according to the Gospel accounts of Matthew, Mark and Luke, Jesus' angry cleansing of the Temple. As He threw out the money-changers, to the amazement and consternation of many, He said that His Father's house was a place for prayer, not a den of thieves. With this bold demonstration of authority, Jesus clearly and firmly laid claim to the Temple as His Father's domain, and therefore His. It is worthy of note that John, in his Gospel account, places the cleansing of the Temple at the beginning of Jesus' public ministry. Some believe that there must therefore have been two related incidents. However, most scholars agree that John's Gospel is much more theological than chronological. John had a spiritual reason for placing the Temple incident where he did, just as he had a specific reason for beginning his Gospel with a parallel to Genesis and the identification of the Word as God Incarnate in Jesus. So, why is the Temple cleansing near the beginning of John's account? When we study the Gospel and find the many narratives describing the conflicts between Jesus and the Jewish religious leaders, it appears clear that John, as inspired by the Holy Spirit, is teaching an important element of Jesus' life and ministry: Jesus was showing by word and action that He came not only to accomplish the plan of Redemption, but to lay the foundation for a Church that, under the

New Covenant, would replace the Church of the Old Covenant. Jesus confronted the Church of his day, the Church His Father had established as the people of Israel – the Chosen People – and in essence stated that the Church would consist of people of any land or nation who accepted Him as the Messiah, as the Savior of the World, as God Incarnate. Jesus did not confront for any reason other than to show the religious leaders that the promise of a Messiah was fulfilled in Him and that too many of them had changed God's guiding laws into rigid religious bondage. Jesus' cleansing of the Temple therefore symbolically pointed to the continuance of the Temple under the New Covenant – in two ways: First, the presence of God with His people is central to both Covenants. Under the Old Covenant, God was present in the Ark (as seen by the cloud) and later within the Temple, which housed the Ark in the Most Holy Place. When Jesus went through His mockery of a trial, one of the "witnesses" for the prosecution accused Jesus of being able to rebuild the Temple in three days if it was destroyed. The Lord was using symbolic language, referring to the Temple that was His Body, the Body that would be resurrected on the third day following His death. Applying that to us, we realize the import of Paul's words when He wrote that we who are united with Christ are living temples, because the Holy Spirit lives within us. Where the Holy Spirit is, there are the Father and the Son. Second, Jesus selected, taught and lived with the apostles clearly for more than to have them be witnesses to His life and death. He was preparing the Church of the New Covenant. Though there has been much confusion, especially over the last 500 years or so, as to what the "Church" is, the writings of the early Christian Church leaders – the Fathers of the first eight centuries, and especially the first four – make it clear that Christ established a very visible Church, with spiritual authority invested in its leadership (the apostles and their successors).

Whatever the points of dispute among Christians today, however, all true Christians agree that they are the Body of Christ and therefore temples of the Holy Spirit. This is the awesome truth that Jesus was preparing us for when He cleansed the Jerusalem Temple.

Will the Real Christians Please Stand Up!

Let's go on a Scriptural journey now, brief though it will be, exploring the Biblical meaning of "Temple." We begin in 1 Kings. There we read about the building of the Temple, promised to David but fulfilled during the reign of his son, Solomon. The Israelites ended their nomadic life, which including carrying the Ark of the Covenant with them, when they entered at last the Promised Land. After a period of rule by "judges," they clamored for a king; they wanted to be like their pagan neighbors, nations ruled by kings. God told them that He was their King, but they persisted in their request. The first king, Saul, began well and ended poorly. David, even though he sinned grievously, was the greatest of the kings, reigning for 40 years and writing a good portion of the Psalms. From the Davidic line would come the Messiah. David was a warrior king, establishing the Israelites as an entrenched nation in that part of the world. Because of his warrior ways, and even though God blessed him, God told David that a king with less blood on his hands would be given the responsibility for building the Temple as a permanent resting place for the Ark and thereby for God Himself. That king was David's son, Solomon. We read in 1 Kings 8: 6-11, 14, 23-24, 27-30:

"The priests then brought the ark of the Lord's covenant to its place in the inner sanctuary of the Temple, the Most Holy Place, and put it beneath the wings of the cherubim. The cherubim spread their wings over the place of the ark and overshadowed the ark and its carrying poles. These poles were so long that their ends could be seen from the Holy Place in front of the inner sanctuary, but not from outside the Holy Place...There was nothing in the ark except the two stone tablets Moses had placed in it at Horeb where the Lord made a covenant with the Israelites after they came out of Egypt. When the priests withdrew from the Holy Place, the cloud filled the temple of the Lord. The priests could not perform their service because of the cloud, for the glory of the Lord filled his temple. While the whole assembly of Israel was standing there the king turned around and blessed them. Then he said: ...'O Lord, God of Israel, there

is no god like you in heaven above or on earth below – you who keep your covenant of love with your servants who continue wholeheartedly in your way. You have kept your promise to your servant David my father; with your mouth you have promised and with your hand you have fulfilled it – as it is today...but will God really dwell on earth? The heavens, even the highest heaven, cannot contain you. How much less this temple I have built! Yet give attention to your servant's prayer and his plea for mercy, O Lord my God. Hear the cry and the prayer that your servant is praying in your presence this day. May your eyes be open toward this temple night and day, this place of which you said, 'My name shall be there,' so that you will hear the prayer your servant prays toward this place. Hear the supplication of your servant and of your people Israel when they pray toward this place. Hear from heaven, your dwelling place, and when you hear, forgive.'"

The Psalmist, echoing the faith and hope of the people of Israel, prayed: *"I will praise You, O Lord, with all my heart; before the 'gods' I will sing your praise. I will bow down toward your holy Temple and will praise your name for your love and your faithfulness, for you have exalted above all things your name and your word."* (Psalm 138: 1-2)

2 Chronicles records the lives and activities of Israel's kings, clearly indicating whether they were good, faithful kings or whether they did evil in the sight of the Lord and the people. The judgment on them had to do in great part with how they used and protected the Temple and the purity of worship of the one true God. Listen, for example, to 2 Chronicles 33: 1-7, telling us about King Manasseh:

"Manasseh was twelve years old when he became king, and he reigned in Jerusalem fifty-five years. He did evil in the eyes of the Lord, following the detestable practices of the nations the Lord had driven out before the Israelites. He rebuilt the high places his father Hezekiah had demolished. He also erected altars to Baal and made Asherah poles. He

bowed down to all the starry hosts and worshipped them. He built altars in the Temple of the Lord, of which the Lord had said, 'My name will remain in Jerusalem forever.' In both courts of the Temple of the Lord, he built altars to all the starry hosts. He sacrificed his sons in the fire of the valley of Ben Hinnom, practiced sorcery, divination, and witchcraft, and consulted mediums and spiritists. He did much evil in the eyes of the Lord, provoking him to anger. He took the carved image he had made and put it in God's Temple, of which God had said to David and to his son, Solomon: 'In this Temple and in Jerusalem, which I have chosen out of all the tribes of Israel, I will put my name forever.'"

As a brief but pertinent aside, this passage is a powerful denunciation of many of the cultic practices of today, for example, the New Age movement, witchcraft, Satanism, and related practices. Christians are never to engage in or even play around with such practices as astrology, séances and channeling. It is an abomination before God, who has ordained true and pure worship of Him. The more we become secularized, on the one hand, and the more we open ourselves to spiritual but ungodly practices such as those related to the New Age movement, on the other hand, the less sensitivity we will have to practices that are offensive to His holiness and to His Name.

Back to the Old Testament: Love of and reverence for the Temple was based specifically on love and reverence for God, for His name, for His holiness and purity. Ponder the following Scripture passages:

"When they see among them their children, the work of my hands, they will keep my name holy; they will acknowledge the holiness of the Holy One of Jacob, and will stand in awe of the God of Israel." (Isaiah 29: 23) "They were proud of their beautiful jewelry and used it to make their detestable idols and vile images." (Ezekiel 7: 20) "In the sixth year, in the sixth month on the fifth day, while I was sitting in my

house and the elders of Judah were sitting before me, the hand of the Sovereign Lord came upon me there. I looked, and I saw a figure like that of a man. From what appeared to be his waist down, he was like fire, and from there up his appearance was as bright as glowing metal. He stretched out what looked like a hand and took me by the hair of my head. The Spirit lifted me up between earth and heaven and in visions of God he took me to Jerusalem, to the entrance to the north gate of the inner court, where the idol that provokes to jealousy stood. And there before me was the glory of the God of Israel, as in the vision I had seen in the plain. Then he said to me, 'Son of man, look toward the north.' So I looked, and in the entrance north of the gate of the altar I saw this idol of jealousy. And he said to me, 'Son of man, do you see what they are doing – the utterly detestable things the house of Israel is doing here, things that will drive me far from my sanctuary? But you will see things that are even more detestable.'...And he said to me, 'Go in and see the wicked and detestable things they are doing here.' So I went in and looked, and I saw portrayed all over the walls all kinds of crawling things and detestable animals and all the idols of the house of Israel...He said to me, 'Son of man, have you seen what the elders of the house of Israel are doing in the darkness, each at the shrine of his own idol? They say, 'The Lord does not see us; the Lord has forsaken the land.' Again he said, 'You will see them doing things that are even more detestable.'...He then brought me into the inner court of the house of the Lord, and there at the entrance to his Temple, between the porch and the altar, were about twenty-five men. With their backs toward the Temple of the Lord and their faces toward the east, they were bowing down to the sun in the east." (Ezekiel 8: 1-6, 9-10, 12-13, 16-17)

Note: With regard to the quotation about backs toward the Temple and bowing down to the east: This may seem harsh to some, but it is entirely repugnant for a Christian to blend Eastern religious and

Will the Real Christians Please Stand Up!

healing practices with the Christian life. Anything – I repeat, any practice – that is not based on God's Word and Revelation is an abomination before God, regardless of any "benefits" gained.

Let's return to 2 Chronicles: We saw earlier how an evil king desecrated the Temple. Now let's study the opposite response to veneration of the sacred, that of the father of Manasseh, the great king Hezekiah:

"In the first month of the first year of his reign, he opened the doors of the Temple of the Lord and repaired them. He brought in priests and Levites, assembled them in the square on the east side and said: 'Listen to me, Levites! Consecrate yourselves now and consecrate the Temple of the Lord, the God of your fathers. Remove all defilement from the sanctuary. Our fathers were unfaithful; they did evil in the eyes of the Lord our God and forsook him. They turned their faces away from the Lord's dwelling place and turned their backs on him. They also shut the doors of the portico and put out the lamps. They did not burn incense or present any burnt offerings at the sanctuary to the God of Israel. Therefore, the anger of the Lord has fallen on Judah and Jerusalem; he has made them an object of dread and horror and scorn, as you can see with your own eyes. This is why our fathers have fallen by the sword, and why our sons and daughters and our wives are in captivity. Now I intend to make a covenant with the Lord, the God of Israel, so that his fierce anger will turn away from us. My sons, do not be negligent now, for the Lord has chosen you to stand before him and serve him, to minister before him and to burn incense.'...The priests went into the sanctuary of the Lord to purify it. They brought out to the courtyard of the Lord's temple everything unclean that they found in the Temple of the Lord...They slaughtered the bulls, and the priests took the blood and sprinkled it on the altar; next they slaughtered the rams and sprinkled their blood on the altar; then they slaughtered the lambs and sprinkled their blood on the

*altar. When the offerings were finished, the king and every-
one present with him bowed down and worshipped...Then
Hezekiah said, 'You have now dedicated yourselves to the
Lord. Come and bring sacrifices and thank offerings to the
Temple of the Lord.' So the assembly brought sacrifices and
thank offerings, and all whose hearts were willing brought
burnt offerings...So the service of the Temple of the Lord
was reestablished. Hezekiah and all the people rejoiced at
what God had brought about for his people, because it was
done so quickly." (2 Chronicles 29: 3-11, 16, 22, 29, 31, 35-
36)*

This was not the case of a king riding in on a white horse and
cleaning up the former ruler's mess. No, it is just the opposite, to
demonstrate the roller coaster of fidelity and infidelity the people of
Israel were riding during their history. Hezekiah was a truly
magnificent king, cleaning up Temple desecration before him; but
his son, Manasseh, turned the people back to idolatry and sacrilege.
And so it went. But key to this saga is the centrality of the Temple.
Faithfulness to God, primarily in His Temple, though also in avoiding idolatry anywhere, was the hallmark of Israel's times of
success. The temptations around them as manifested by the idola-
trous and shameful practices of their pagan neighbors were a
constant albatross around the corporate neck of the people of God.
Sometimes they threw it off; sometimes they succumbed.

This is all very powerful Scripture, readers! The historical
events are rich in meaning for us today. Remember, the Word of
God is alive, and what we read has eternal significance. The light in
the Temple had gone out: The typology is awesome, for the reference from our perspective is to the Holy Spirit. Where is the light in
the Church today? Why is the Church ridiculed, scorned, and –
worse – ignored so frequently? It is because too many of us for too
long have brought idols into the living temple – the temple that is
ourselves and that is the Church. Yes, idol worship is alive and well
today, for anything that takes the place of God in our lives is an
idol. Too many of us have chosen to mingle the Church with the
world. We have permitted Christianity to become all too often a

club, an organization, a way to grab respectability and salve consciences, a networking for financial gain, an empty social gathering that has little to do with the holiness of God and true worship of His Name. No, the Holy Spirit can never completely leave the Church; but we can in effect hide the light that is the living Love of God under a basket rather than show Him to the world. Hezekiah's first act was to repair the doors to the Temple; that is highly symbolic, for repentance requires first that we invite God back into our hearts and into the active life of His Church. When my treasure is elsewhere, the door to my heart becomes inoperable and grace cannot achieve what God wants it to – to mold me as a vessel through whom He can reveal His infinite love to mankind.

But let's delve even deeper into this subject. We move now from the Old Testament to the New. Throughout Scripture, and especially when we combine the words of the Old Testament with the New Testament, it is clear that the Temple of the people of Israel refers to the building in Jerusalem wherein the glory of God dwelt. Jesus began moving the meaning to new and wondrous depths when He referred to Himself as the Temple. Now follow along with Paul as he wrote to the New Testament Church:

> *"Don't you know that you yourselves are God's temple and that God's Spirit lives in you? If anyone destroys God's temple, God will destroy him, for God's temple is sacred, and you are that temple."* (1 Corinthians 3: 16-17) *"Do you not know that the wicked will not inherit the kingdom of God? Do not be deceived: Neither the sexually immoral nor idolaters nor adulterers nor male prostitutes nor homosexual offenders nor thieves nor the greedy nor drunkards nor slanderers nor swindlers will inherit the kingdom of God. And that is what some of you were. But you were washed; you were sanctified; you were justified in the name of the Lord Jesus Christ and by the Spirit of our God."* (1 Corinthians 6: 9-11) *"Do you not know that your body is a temple of the Holy Spirit, who is in you, whom you have received from God? You are not your own; you were bought at a price. Therefore, honor God with your body."* (1 Corinthians 6: 19-20)

"Do not be yoked together with unbelievers. For what do righteousness and wickedness have in common? Or what fellowship can light have with darkness? What harmony is there between Christ and Belial? What does a believer have in common with an unbeliever? What agreement is there between the temple of God and idols? For we are the temple of the living God. As God has said, 'I will live with them and walk among them, and I will be their God, and they will be my people. Therefore, come out from them and be separate, says the Lord. Touch no unclean thing, and I will receive you. I will be a Father to you, and you will be my sons and daughters, says the Lord Almighty.' Since we have these promises, dear friends, let us purify ourselves from everything that contaminates body and spirit, perfecting holiness out of reverence for God." (2 Corinthians 6: 14 – 7: 1)

The glorious, mighty truth is that in the New Covenant real Christians are living temples. The Almighty God who filled the Temple of the Old Covenant with His glory, who burned with anger when the Temple was sullied and turned into a place for idol worship, who gladly forgave when people repented and purified the Temple – that same God now makes His dwelling place with us and within us. On the day of Pentecost, the Holy Spirit came and not only founded a Church based on the cornerstone of Jesus Christ, He also made believers into living temples.

This gives deeper meaning to the horror of sin. Sin desecrates the temple. The Bible lists many such desecrating acts and life styles. We are all made in the image and likeness of God. This is what makes human beings distinct. More, we have seen that people have the potential to become living temples, in which the Trinity resides. And even for people who do not have that intimate relationship with God, they are still made up of body, mind and spirit. The mind and spirit have always been what is in the image and likeness of God, what have made it possible to live spiritually as members of God's family. And now, following the Resurrection and Ascension of Jesus Christ, the Second Person of the Blessed Trinity, at the right hand of the Father, has both a divine and a human nature. We

Will the Real Christians Please Stand Up!

have indeed been raised to an honor higher than angels! So, each person is special, with special privileges and responsibilities. Sin is an abomination before God, because every sin consists of the creature in effect "spitting in the face" of the Creator and saying, "I will choose myself, not You." Sin is such an offense that just one sin warrants annihilation of the person and of the entire human race. The angels in heaven recoil in horror before sin; the fallen angels in hell rejoice before it.

Each human being is unique, a jewel of creation. This is specifically true because of the spirit. People are spiritual in nature and they will live forever, with God or separated from Him. Regardless of what scientific wonders we have experienced and which may lie around the next bend, no scientist will ever create a human spirit, nor will any evolutionist prove the development of the spirit from other species. The spirit is spiritual and, as such, it cannot evolve from matter or be created in a test tube. It looks more and more as though human cloning will be possible, and if it becomes possible, someone at some time will do it. Should that indeed happen, one of two things will follow. Either we will be creating zombies or God will be creating human spirits to become part of that life. The answer to that question goes beyond the scope of this writing. I encourage you, however, to meditate on the infinite power and holiness of God, the treasure that every human being is, and the dark nature and terrifying reality of sin. If I could fully grasp the enormity of sin, I would flee for my very life from every temptation. The falling into idolatry and Temple desecrations of the people of Israel are actually models for every sin, including mine and the sins of secular society, which shakes its fist at any gods and chooses to chart its own course. Let's look again at abortion and homosexuality.

First, abortion: In modern life, there have been so many rationalizations, so many false justifications of things that go contrary to God's law and to God's very nature. The Scriptures make it abundantly clear (for example, Psalm 139) that life begins in the womb, at the moment of conception. Taking a "pro-choice" position in the name of protecting the rights of women really means taking a "pro-death" position in the name of denying the rights of new life in the womb. God creates the spirit, a unique never-before-seen-and-never-again-to- be-seen person at the moment of conception. It matters not that the new creation is unable to live outside the womb yet; that is another rationalization. Is an infant who is utterly dependent upon others for life sustenance therefore not fully a human being yet? (Actually, we are moving to that with the absolutely detestable practice of partial-birth abortion even being discussed as an option.) That newly created spirit, placed in a growing body that is initially only the result of a sperm and an egg, is more beautiful, more precious, more majestic than any Temple ever was. Christians must oppose laws protecting abortion because they are laws protecting the killing of human beings, totally innocent human beings. This has nothing to do with women's rights and has everything to do with the rights of vulnerable new people.

Second, homosexuality: I remember once as a boy reading a science fiction short story about a future society in which homosexual relationships were the norm and it was actually illegal for men and women to have sex together. I considered this one of those far-fetched science fiction imaginations at work. Well, we have not reached that point and probably won't. But who would have thought 25, 15, even 10 years ago that we would be at the point in our society in which people who oppose homosexual acts are branded as intolerant bigots and in which there are actual judicial and legal actions pushing our society to redefining marriage as the joining of two people, regardless of their gender? Modern skeptics, including many within the Church (in name, at least) discard the teachings of the Bible and the teachings of Church authority through the ages as old-fashioned and out of touch with societal changes. Nevertheless, both the Old Testament and the New Testament clearly describe homosexual acts as a grave sin. Paul even says that human beings know better based on the natural law engraved in their minds and spirits. Why did not God create just one gender – especially since God is genderless? Was it to add more variety to life? Was it a whim of an idea that came to Him? Was it really just because Adam complained that he was lonely? No, plain common sense tells us that we have two genders so that life can go on through reproduction. God commanded as well that a man and a woman not only reproduce, but that they leave their own families

Will the Real Christians Please Stand Up!

and create a new one, in a union of love. God never said that sex was bad; in fact, He made it very good. Anyone, and I literally mean anyone, in a good and lasting marriage will state that sexual relations are one important aspect of a union of love, though only one and not the most important. A man and a woman are called to a union of love. For a man and a man or a woman and a woman to claim this sacred right – sacred because it comes from God – is to again choose self instead of God, to disregard His wishes and His laws, to put self-pleasure and self-fulfillment ahead of selfless yieldedness and obedience to God. None of us has the right to judge the heart of a homosexual (just as we have no right to judge the heart of an abortionist). But we do have the right and the responsibility to stand up and proclaim what is right and wrong in the eyes of God and what is harmful to individuals and to society. Further, to leap right into the middle of a hotly debated issue: I have a friend whom I greatly respect. He is a husband and a father and has a ministry to gay people. Why? Because he was gay for many years, and even fell briefly into a homosexual relationship after he married. But he turned to God for help, and by God's grace he has not had a homosexual encounter for over 25 years. In fact, it is entirely accurate to say that he is no longer a homosexual. Listen to him – and he will speak at any opportunity given to him – and he will tell you that it is erroneous to call homosexuality genetic. We are not born gay; homosexuality is acquired. And while it is true that people with homosexual desires have a difficult journey, they simply do not have to yield to those desires and they can have lasting and fulfilling heterosexual relationships. Unfortunately, we live in a society which has as one of its slogans, "If it feels good, do it." Sexual union feels good, so, why fight or resist the desires, why channel them elsewhere? It does not matter what some old-fashioned Bible says, or what some old-fashioned idea of God might be, we are mature people, we live in an enlightened time, we can make our choices. And, readers, Satan is gleeful, for anytime he can turn us away from God and into ourselves, he is leading us into idolatry of self – the sin that led to his downfall and that of a third of the angels of heaven.

Abortion and homosexuality are just two examples of temple

desecration. They are prominent today, but there are many, many other types of sin. Again, the bottom line is that any time I choose myself over God, I sully the temple. I, the creature, dare the Creator to take action against me. And though He loves each of us deeply, He will indeed take action if we persist in sin. This is different than people who honestly believe that what they are doing is acceptable. God always looks at the heart. But we who have the blessing of God's grace and His very presence within us must speak the truth in love. Otherwise, we are closet Christians. It is time to come out of the closet!

It seems appropriate to end this Scripture-laden reflection with yet more Bible verses. First, I offer for prayerful reflection Romans 12: 1-2 and then Revelation 1: 12-18. They are fitting conclusions to a study of the Old Testament Temple, of the holiness of God, of the New Testament Church, and of the living temples that we are if we are real Christians.

> *"Therefore, I urge you, brothers, in view of God's mercy, to offer your bodies as living sacrifices, holy and pleasing to God – this is your spiritual act of worship. Do not conform any longer to the pattern of this world, but be transformed by the renewing of your mind. Then you will be able to test and approve what God's will is – his good, pleasing, and perfect will."* This is God's call to each of us.

> *"I turned around to see the voice that was speaking to me. And when I turned I saw seven golden lamp stands, and among the lamp stands was someone 'like a Son of Man,' dressed in a robe reaching down to his feet with a golden sash around his chest. His head and hair were white like wool, as white as snow, and his eyes were like blazing fire. His feet were like bronze glowing in a furnace, and his voice was like the sound of rushing waters. In his right hand he held seven stars, and out of his mouth came a sharp double-edged sword. His face was like the sun shining in all its brilliance. When I saw him, I fell at his feet as though dead. Then he placed his right hand on me and said: 'Do not be*

afraid. I am the First and the Last. I am the Living One; I was dead, and behold I am alive forever and ever! And I hold the keys of death and Hades.'" This is He Whom we will see face to face the moment we die. I pray that my temple be pleasing to Him.

SUMMARY FOR REFLECTION AND DISCUSSION:

A real Christian:

1) Sees everything in the Old Testament as having ultimate meaning and fulfillment in the New, and believes that the entire Bible is the inspired Word of God and the perfect guidebook for life, temporal and eternal;
2) Reads, studies and meditates on the Scriptures regularly, asking the Holy Spirit, the Author of the Bible, to bring meaning to this moment and hour of my life;
3) Knows that the essential Church is not a building, is not founded on any man's ministry, but is the Body of Christ and is the union of all true believers under the Lordship of Jesus Christ;
4) Believes that she/he is a true temple of the living God – that Father, Son and Holy Spirit dwell within the spirit;
5) Hates sin of any kind and avoids anything that would in any way contaminate the temple – anything seen, heard, read, watched, or participated in.

SCRIPTURES FOR JOURNALING:

1) 1 Kings 8;
2) Ezekiel 8;
3) 2 Chronicles 29, 33;
4) Revelation 1.

REFLECTION 5:

A STORY OF FOUR GARDENS

There is a children's movie, one that is equally valuable for and enjoyed by adults. It is a remake of the classic, "Secret Garden," based on a novel by the same name. An old garden (actually a small park) was unattended and locked behind high walls – and it lay in this state of disuse for many years. The garden was adjacent to a large house on the moors, a house of sadness and anger. The master of the estate was a recluse, embittered by the untimely death of his wife. The man's son, to make matters worse, was a terminally ill boy who rarely left his bed and room, and only then in a wheelchair. The nanny was a stern and rigid taskmaster. Then a visitor arrived: The master's young niece, a young and spoiled girl whose parents had been tragically killed in an earthquake in India. Filling out these characters was a mysterious neighbor boy, who appeared and disappeared just as unexpectedly on a beautiful horse. The boy always had a smile and was full of good cheer. To abbreviate the drama, the niece discovered the garden. Over time, she and the neighbor boy transformed it back to its original and wondrous beauty. Eventually, they coaxed the invalid lad to leave his room and enter the garden. There he took in the beauty and breathed in the smells of the lush foliage, and eventually he discovered that he was recovering, that he was not dying after all. The father found healing for his own internal misery through experiencing the new health and life of his son. The end result was joy and peace in lives where there had been misery and inner chaos. When I watched the movie, I found the garden to be an absolutely fascinating place; it was as though the allure of the park drew me through the movie screen into the beauty of the park. I had the same feeling that one has upon suddenly entering a forest glade, or discovering a breathtaking valley, or coming upon a mist-covered pond. Trees and flower gardens, even if man-made, and especially when they resemble the beauty of nature, are both mysterious and peaceful, reaching down somehow into the depths of our spirits and drawing out often forgotten feelings and memories.

It is not surprising, then, to discover that garden parks play important roles in the history of God's relationship with His people. Let's explore together four gardens, each rooted in Scripture and each of which was, or will be, the scene of a critically important event in God's plan of salvation.

Garden #1: Eden

In Genesis 2: 8-17 we read a description of the garden in which our first parents were permitted to live:

> *"Now the Lord God had planted a garden in the east, in Eden; and there he put the man he had formed. And the Lord God made all kinds of trees grow out of the ground —trees that were pleasing to the eye and good for food. In the middle of the garden were the tree of life and the tree of the knowledge of good and evil. A river watering the garden flowed from Eden; from there it was separated into four headwaters. The name of the first is the Pishon; it winds through the entire land of Havilah, where there is gold. (The gold of that land is good; aromatic resin and onyx are also there.) The name of the second river is the Gihon; it winds through the entire land of Cush. The name of the third river is the Tigris; it runs along the east side of Asshur. And the fourth river is the Euphrates. The Lord God took the man and put him in the Garden of Eden to work it and take care of it. And the Lord God commanded the man, 'You are free*

to eat from any tree in the garden; but you must not eat from the tree of the knowledge of good and evil, for when you eat of it you will surely die.'"

The prophet Ezekiel also wrote of the Garden of Eden, when, under the inspiration of the Holy Spirit, he recorded the words of the Lord directed against Satan in Chapter 28, verses 12-17:

This is what the Sovereign Lord says: 'You were the model of perfection, full of wisdom and perfect in beauty. You were in Eden, the garden of God; every precious stone adorned you: ruby, topaz and emerald, chrysolite, onyx and jasper, sapphire, turquoise and beryl. Your settings and mountings were made of gold; on the day you were created they were prepared. You were anointed as a guardian cherub, for so I ordained you. You were on the holy mount of God; you walked among the fiery stones. You were blameless in your ways from the day you were created till wickedness was found in you. Through your widespread trade you were filled with violence, and you sinned. So I drove you in disgrace from the mount of God, and I expelled you, O guardian cherub, from among the fiery stones. Your heart became proud on account of your beauty, and you corrupted your wisdom because of your splendor.'"

There are various interpretations of this passage. But if we just take it as written, there is a clear meaning: God is addressing an angel, one who existed at the time that Eden was created and prior to mankind's fall. The angel sinned and was cast down from his position of splendor and glory. It is no wonder, then, that that very angel appeared to Eve in the garden; he did so in the form of a serpent. We call him Satan, the father of lies. He who was thrown down because of his terrible pride tempted Adam and Eve with that very same sin. For, after all, pride is the root of all sin.

So, in the Garden of Eden we find a man and a woman created in God's image and likeness, existing in a state of total intimacy with God. God only asked one thing: They were not to eat of the tree of the knowledge of good and evil. He asked them for their faithfulness, their trust in Him, their willingness to yield to Him as their Creator who also wanted to share His eternal life with them. He asked that they depend on His guidance, not on their choices based on supposed self-interest. It was precisely here that Satan found their vulnerable spot. How well he knew it, for it was his as well. He lost everything except an eternity of separation from God. As a result, he hates God and everything about Him, and he hates mankind, created in God's likeness. So the great temptation, "to be like God," resulted in the horror and disruption of sin in the Garden of Eden, and God cast our first parents from the Garden.

Actually, God could have just annihilated creation, since He has no need of anyone or anything. But God is in His essence living Love. Therefore, God said that, though there were to be consequences to sin, He would redeem mankind and reestablish the possibility of intimate relationship with Him. Why did not God just forgive our first parents then and there? That very question arises from an ignorance of the enormity of sin. Saying "no!' to God and "yes!" to self creates a chasm of separation. Sin requires genuine repentance (not just regret) on the part of people and redemption by God (reestablishment of right relationship with Him, something only He can grant). From all eternity, God sees everything. Thus, even before He created us, He knew that we would rebel, and He had a plan that would actually make the redemptive state better than the original one! It is not for us to try to understand what God does, why He does it, when He does it; it is for us to yield to Him and accept His guidance with gratitude and humility – for our very existence totally depends on Him.

Garden #1 resulted in sin. What about Garden #2? This Garden was the result of sin; the horror is so terrible as to be almost unimaginable. Matthew writes in 26: 36-46:

"Then Jesus went with his disciples to a place called Gethsemane, and he said to them, 'Sit here while I go over there and pray.' He took Peter and the two sons of Zebedee along with him, and he began to be sorrowful and troubled. Then he said to them, 'My soul is overwhelmed with sorrow

*to the point of death. Stay here and keep watch with me.'
Going a little farther, he fell down with his face to the
ground and prayed, 'My Father, if it is possible, may this
cup be taken from me. Yet not as I will, but as you will.' Then
he returned to his disciples and found them sleeping. 'Could
you men not watch with me for one hour?', He asked Peter.
'Watch and pray so that you will not fall into temptation.
The spirit is willing, but the body is weak.' He went away a
second time and prayed, 'My Father, if it is not possible for
this cup to be taken away unless I drink it, may your will be
done.' When he came back, he again found them sleeping,
because their eyes were heavy. So he left them and went
away once again and prayed the third time, saying the same
thing. Then he returned to the disciples and said to them,
'Are you still sleeping and resting? Look, the hour is near,
and the Son of Man is betrayed into the hands of sinners.
Rise, let us go! Here comes my betrayer!'"*

Permit me to repeat one verse again, with different emphasis
this time: "My Father, if it is possible, may this cup be taken from
me. — — — — —-Yet,— — — — — —not as I will, but as you will." I
believe that heaven "held its breath" as Jesus prayed that He not
undergo the pain of rejection by the people He loved, that He not
suffer the physical and emotional pain of the crucifixion, the execution of the sinless One as He took upon Himself the total and awful
burden of every sin of every person who ever lived and who ever
would live. He began experiencing the weight of sin in the Garden;
the fear in His human nature from knowing what was to come and
the contact with the ugliness of sin on His holy Person caused Him
to sweat blood as His capillaries broke from maximum fear and
horror and blood mingled with His perspiration.

In that garden was the real battle, not on the cross. He went to
trial and execution with peace and conviction in His heart. He not
only took the cross, He embraced it and struggled on to Golgotha,
knowing that this was the final key to the divine plan of
Redemption. Satan, whom Scripture told us would return to tempt
Jesus following the encounter in the wilderness prior to His public

ministry, attacked with the full force of his evil intentions in Gethsemane. Jesus could have walked away; the Father would have granted His plea, had it not been accompanied by "Your will be done, not mine." If He had, there would have been no redemption, heaven's gates to eternal life with God would have remained closed and the sin of the first garden would never have been erased. But Jesus did submit to the will of the Father, just as He had during His entire life on earth. The Second Person of the Blessed Trinity was Man as well as God, because of the Incarnation. Jesus' human nature was just as much a part of this divine Person as was His divine nature. Jesus surrendered Himself totally – one Person with two natures, and because Jesus was a God-Man, His sacrifice was absolutely perfect, the one sacrifice that could get at the roots of sin in all people in the nature of all people since our first parents and destroy those roots.

So, all of heaven, and, too, all of the dead awaiting the redemptive love of the Messiah, breathed that sigh of relief. Jesus at that moment became the greatest hero of all time, the perfect example of love and service. It is truly admirable for a person to sacrifice his/her life for another; it is awesome to die that others might live. But it is beyond our wildest imagining that a sinless, pure, perfect, omnipotent God would take upon Himself every act of selfishness, pride, lust, rage, greed, and violence from the beginning of the world until its end. In a real and incredible way, He "became sin" so that we might be freed from Satan's grasp. Jesus really won the victory in that garden, because there He surrendered His will to the Father in love for all of us. Now all that remained was act of final immolation, the sacrifice that every Old Testament sacrifice was pointing to – the death and shedding of Blood of the good and perfect and once-for-all Sacrifice. Read how Paul describes this in Romans 5: 6-11 and 18-19:

"You see, at just the right time, when we were still powerless, Christ died for the ungodly. Very rarely will anyone die for a righteous man, though for a good man someone might possibly dare to die. But God demonstrates his own love for us in this: While we were still sinners, Christ died for us.

Since we have now been justified by his blood, how much more shall we be saved from God's wrath through him! For if, when we were God's enemies, we were reconciled to him through the death of his Son, how much more, having been reconciled, shall we be saved through his life! Not only is this so, but we also rejoice in God through our Lord Jesus Christ, through whom we have now received reconciliation. Consequently, just as the result of one trespass was condemnation for all men, so also the result of one act of righteousness was justification that brings life for all men. For just as through the disobedience of the one man the many were made sinners, so also through the obedience of the one man the many will be made righteous."

Thus the significance of all the blood sacrifices that the People of Israel had made, based on very specific instructions by God. They were important for their own spiritual growth, through acts of repentance, and thanksgiving, and worship, and intercession. The sanctuary and later the Temple, with the Most Holy Place in the center, defined the very essence of the corporate nature of the Israelites. God was at the center, and sacrifice to God – most importantly blood sacrifice – was the prescribed form of worship. But, these sacrifices were also types, pointing to a sacrifice in the future that would bring redemption to mankind. There is no better description and explanation of this than the beautiful one we have in the Book of Hebrews. We have already looked at it in an earlier chapter; let's revisit it:

"Therefore, since we have a great high priest who has gone through the heavens, Jesus the Son of God, let us hold firmly to the faith we profess. For we do not have a high priest who is unable to sympathize with our weaknesses, but we have one who has been tempted in every way, just as we are – yet was without sin. Let us then approach the throne of grace with confidence, so that we may receive mercy and find grace to help us in our time of need. Every high priest is selected from among men and is appointed to represent

them in matters related to God, to offer gifts and sacrifices for sins. He is able to deal gently with those who are ignorant and are going astray, since he himself is subject to weakness. This is why he has to offer sacrifices for his own sins, as well as for the sins of the people. No one takes this honor upon himself; he must be called by God, just as Aaron was. So Christ also did not take upon himself the glory of becoming a high priest. But God said to him...'You are a priest forever, according to the order of Melchizedek.' During the days of Jesus' life on earth, he offered up prayers and petitions with loud cries and tears to the one who could save him from death, and he was heard because of his reverent submission. Although he was a son, he learned obedience from what he suffered and, once made perfect (speaking of His human nature), *he became the source of eternal salvation for all who obey him and was designated by God to be high priest in the order of Melchizedek."* (Hebrews 4:14 – 5: 10) *"Now there were many of those priests, since death prevented them from continuing in office; but because Jesus lives forever, he has a permanent priesthood. Therefore he is able to save completely those who come to God through him, because he always lives to intercede for them. Such a high priest meets our need – one who is holy, blameless, pure, set apart from sinners, exalted above the heavens. Unlike the other high priests, he does not need to offer sacrifices day after day, first for his own sins, and then for the sins of the people. He sacrificed for their sins once for all when he offered himself. For the law appoints as high priests men who are weak; but the oath, which came after the law, appointed the Son, who has been made perfect forever."* (Hebrews 7: 23-28) *"It was necessary, then, for the copies of the heavenly things to be purified with these sacrifices, but the heavenly things themselves with better sacrifices than these. For Christ did not enter a man-made sanctuary that was only a copy of the true one; he entered heaven itself, now to appear for us in God's presence. Nor did he enter heaven to offer himself again and again, the way the high priest enters the Most Holy Place every year with blood that is not his own. Then Christ would have had to suffer many times since the creation of the world. But now he has appeared once for all at the end of the ages to do away with sin by the sacrifice of himself. Just as man is destined to die once, and after that to face judgment, so Christ was sacrificed once to take away the sins of many people; and he will appear a second time, not to bear sin, but to bring salvation to those who are waiting for him.*" (Hebrews 9: 23-28)

The third garden: "*...Joseph of Arimathea asked Pilate for the body of Jesus. Now Joseph was a disciple of Jesus, but secretly because he feared the Jews. With Pilate's permission, he came and took the body away. He was accompanied by Nicodemus, the man who earlier had visited Jesus at night. Nicodemus brought a mixture of myrrh and aloes, about seventy-five pounds. Taking Jesus' body, the two of them wrapped it, with the spices, in strips of linen. This was in accordance with Jewish burial customs. At the place where Jesus was crucified, there was a garden, and in the garden a new tomb in which no one had ever been laid. Because it was the Jewish day of Preparation, and since the tomb was nearby, they laid Jesus there. Early on the first day of the week, while it was still dark, Mary Magdalene went to the tomb and saw that the stone had been removed from the entrance. Mary stood outside the tomb crying. As she wept, she bent over to look into the tomb, and saw two angels in white seated where Jesus' body had been, one at the head and one at the foot. They asked her, 'Woman, why are you crying?' 'They have taken my Lord away,' she said, 'and I don't know where they have put him.' At this, she turned around and saw Jesus standing there, but she did not realize that it was Jesus. 'Woman,' he said, 'Why are you crying? Who is it you are looking for?' Thinking he was the gardener, she said, 'Sir, if you have carried him away, tell me where you have put him, and I will get him.' Jesus said to her, 'Mary.'*" (John 19: 38-42; 20: 1-2, 11-16)

In garden #3, the body of Jesus was laid to rest. But that is not what is most significant. No, in Garden #3, the greatest miracle of

Will the Real Christians Please Stand Up!

all time took place, the single event that has more eternal meaning than any other for every human being before, during or since. In that garden, Jesus Christ rose from the dead in glory. As important was His sacrificial death on the cross, far more important is His Resurrection. The Word of God states it very simply and eloquently in 1 Corinthians 15: 14: *"If Christ has not been raised, our preaching is useless and so is your faith."*

It is beyond our scope here to delve into the historical proofs of the Resurrection of Jesus Christ. From the accounts of eyewitnesses, to the size of the rock over the entrance to the tomb, to the presence of guards, to the explosion of Christianity based on the belief that He rose from the dead, it should be clear to people with truly open minds and hearts that a miracle took place in that garden. The eternal Father ordained that His only begotten Son should take on human flesh and a human nature and offer Himself as the perfect Sacrifice – the sacrifice of both Man and God – to take away sin and make it possible for mankind to once again have the possibility of an intimate union with God, both now and for all eternity. Just as that human body was immolated, so that human body rose triumphantly, transformed into a body both beautiful and glorious, as befitting the now eternal body of the Second Person of the Most Blessed Trinity. That glorious body was prefigured on the Mount of Transfiguration, witnessed by Peter, James and John, as Jesus spoke with Moses and Elijah.

Belief in the Resurrection is absolutely central to Christian faith. The real Christian lives daily in the joy and power of that great miracle, in the glorious though hidden presence of Jesus Christ, and the Holy Spirit, and the Father. The real Christian seeks to let the presence and love of the risen and glorified Christ shine through her/his life. And when trials and sorrows come – and, yes, stumblings and sins, as they do for all of us—it is faith in the Resurrected Jesus that gives renewed hope, renewed peace, renewed strength and courage. For the Resurrection means that Jesus is truly alive and well, that He is at the right hand of the Father as the great Mediator, the great High Priest, that He is living in the hearts of those who accept Him as their Lord and Savior, and that He will one day return. When Christians celebrate the memorial of the Lord's Supper, they are proclaiming both His death and

His Resurrection, as well as His presence among us. All Christians believe that Jesus is with His Church, the people who believe in Him – in our hearts, in His Word, where two or three are gathered together. All genuine Christians believe that the Second Person of the Trinity, the Word made flesh, is now forever both Man and God. This is how the sin of the first Garden resulted in a state of mankind even more wonderful than the first. The Godhead includes glorified flesh and a human nature!

Ponder again words from 1 Corinthians 15:

But Christ has indeed been raised from the dead, the first-fruits of those who have fallen asleep. For since death came through a man, the resurrection of the dead comes also through a man. For as in Adam all die, so in Christ all will be made alive. But each in his own turn: Christ, the first-fruits; then, when he comes, those who belong to him. Then the end will come, when he hands over the Kingdom to God the Father after he has destroyed all dominion, authority, and power. For he must reign until he has put all His enemies under his feet. The last enemy to be destroyed is death...I declare to you, brothers, that flesh and blood cannot inherit the Kingdom of God, nor does the perishable inherit the imperishable. Listen, I tell you a mystery: We will not all sleep, but we will all be changed – in a flash, in the twinkling of an eye, at the last trumpet. For the trumpet will sound, the dead will be raised imperishable, and we will be changed. For the perishable must clothe itself with the imperishable, and the mortal with immortality. When the perishable has been clothed with the imperishable, and the mortal with immortality, then the saying that is written will come true: 'Death has been swallowed up in victory.' Where, O death, is your victory? Where, O death, is your sting? The sting of death is sin, and the power of sin is the law. But thanks be to God! He gives us the victory through our Lord Jesus Christ." (1 Corinthians 15: 20-26, 51-57)

This brings us to the fourth and final garden. It is one yet to come,

Will the Real Christians Please Stand Up!

and the thought of it brings great hope and expectation. We find it described in the Book of Revelation, the Book that unfolds for us the panorama of heaven, based on the vision given John, and provides us with a description of the final triumph of God and His people.

> *"Then the angel showed me the river of the water of life, as clear as crystal, flowing from the throne of God and of the Lamb, down the middle of the great street of the city. On each side of the river stood the tree of life, bearing twelve crops of fruit, yielding its fruit every month. And the leaves of the tree are for the healing of the nations. No longer will there be any curse. The throne of God and of the Lamb will be in the city, and his servants will serve him. They will see his face, and his name will be on their foreheads. There will be no more night. They will not need the light of a lamp or the light of the sun, for the Lord God will give them light. And they will reign forever and ever. The angel said to me, 'These words are trustworthy and true. The Lord, the God of the spirits of the prophets, sent his angel to show his servants the things that must soon take place."* (Revelation 22: 1-6)

Thus, the tree of life found in the Garden of Eden reappears. Mankind could have eaten of that tree then and have lived forever in union with God. But mankind disobeyed, we sinned, and the tree of life disappeared along with the Garden of Eden. Yet, if I may dare to communicate this way, sin with its awful consequences resulted – as we have seen – in a reality far, far greater for us. And this is true because of the immense love and incredible forgiveness of our God. The Word became flesh! God became a Man! And, now, risen from dead in triumph after offering Himself upon the cross for our sins, Jesus Christ is back in heaven, the God-Man, making it possible for us to have an indescribably intimate union with God in His internal Family life of Father, Son and Holy Spirit. This goes beyond any human being's wildest imaginings! This is not fantasy; this is real. How do we find that life for ourselves? We find it through accepting Jesus Christ as our Savior, through being baptized in obedience to our Lord's command, through accepting

God's forgiveness and His invitation to enter into communion with Him.

The first garden was a beautiful gift from God, the place of dwelling for human beings, made in His image and likeness. The second garden became the place where Jesus began His Passion. The third garden contained the tomb wherein He was laid – and also the tomb from which He rose gloriously and triumphantly from the dead. The fourth garden is the recreation of the first, but it resides in the Kingdom of Heaven, the place where God dwells and to which we are invited to live forever.

SUMMARY FOR REFLECTION AND DISCUSSION:

A real Christian:

1) Praises God for "Salvation History" – the period of time in which God began direct involvement in the affairs of mankind, preparing us for the coming of the Redeemer. It began with the call of Abram and the establishment of a covenant with him, one that resulted in the formation of the People of Israel, from whom would come the Messiah, the Anointed One, the Redeemer. Salvation History continues now, in the final age, the age of the Church.

2) Firmly believes that the central and most important events in history revolve around the life, death, Resurrection and Ascension of Jesus Christ.

3) Knows that Jesus Christ came to establish a Kingdom – one that is not of this world.

4) Recognizes that the purpose and goal of life on earth is preparation for eternal life – for ourselves and for those whom God will touch through our obedient service during this life.

SCRIPTURES FOR JOURNALING:

1) Genesis 2; Ezekiel 28;
2) Matthew 26: 36-46; Romans 5;

Will the Real Christians Please Stand Up!

3) John 19: 38-42; 20: 1-2, 11-16;
4) 1 Corinthians 15;
5) Revelation 22: 1-6

REFLECTION 6:

THE REAL MEANING OF EASTER

Many of us look forward to Easter with high expectation. It is one of the truly exciting signs of spring; it signals the end of Lent; it invites us to break out the Easter bonnets and other finery (at least in much of the western world). Churches fill up with both lilies and people; none of the former have any awareness of why they are there, and, sadly, too many the latter do not have much conscious awareness either. We have permitted Easter to become too much like another secular celebration, Christmas. For Christians who do not recognize the importance of communal worship, Easter may be one of the few times they show up at the church doors. At another extreme on the spectrum, there are those who do not celebrate Easter because it has some similarities to pagan rites in its name and some of its traditions. Those same folks do not celebrate Christmas either, for the same reason. But, just as Christmas is the celebration of the Incarnation of the Divine Word, so Easter celebrates His glorious Resurrection from the dead. Easter is a time for real Christians to proclaim the glory of that Resurrection; but the celebration of this greatest event in the history of mankind is something that goes on daily – for we as Christians are privileged to live in intimate union with God even now, because of what our Lord Jesus did for us.

I heard a story once – whether a true one or not, it is still a great story – about a troupe of Shakespearian actors who traveled around England putting on performances of the writings of the Bard for any who would pay to attend. They were poor, they had little in the way of costumes, but they shared a passion for their craft. Nonetheless, the traveling from village to village was both hard and boring, the pay was small, and normally the audiences were both miniscule and unappreciative of the skills that the actors demonstrated. One cold, blustery, snowy night they were in a tiny hamlet miles from any significant population center. Their manager realized that few patrons would brave the elements; and all actors respond best to a large and lively audience. He knew that he needed a creative way to motivate his tired and somewhat depressed troupe of actors and actresses. So, quietly asking forgiveness from God for the "white lie," he invented a tale and called the group together just before curtain call. "I have an important and exciting announcement," he told them in his best breathless voice. "I have just received word that our beloved King is in the region tonight incognito, and he will be in the audience! Make it your best performance ever!" Filled with a new ambition to do their very best, they pulled off the performance of a lifetime. They outdid themselves, and they received a standing ovation at the conclusion of the play. The members of the troupe were flushed with pride and they were in the process of congratulating one another backstage, with the beaming manager right in the midst of them. All of a sudden, there was a commotion; and in walked the King of England! Unbeknownst to the manager or anyone else except a few trusted aides, the King was indeed present that evening for the performance!

For the real, the committed Christian, the King is always in the audience – always present, always watching, always loving and beckoning for us to give our very best, always leading and guiding and giving grace to open hearts. Easter is the celebration of the Kingdom of Heaven! The glorious fullness of it comes at death (unless we are still alive at the time the Lord returns); but in a real and awe-inspiring way we share in it even now, by faith. We are living temples, we are caught up in the heavenly mysteries. Jesus said that His Kingdom is not of this earth, and that is certainly true – the world cannot see or share in His Kingdom. But the King is here, spiritually, and where the King is, there is the Kingdom. When Jesus rose gloriously from the dead on that first Easter, the Kingdom of the New and Eternal Covenant was ushered in, with cries of acclamation by angels and those who had died days and centuries before and who had been waiting for that day with deep longing. When we celebrate Easter, we do not just memorialize a past event; no, the Resurrection is a living reality, the King lives and reigns each and every day. Our King is alive and well and asks us to serve Him with joy and gladness as He seeks to bring others into the Kingdom through our lives.

Psalm 24 is one of those mighty prophetic hymns, proclaiming a truth at the time of its writing and also pointing ahead mysteriously to an ever greater truth and reality. Let's meditate on the words of this majestic Psalm:

> *"The earth is the Lord's and everything in it, the world and all who live in it; for he founded it upon the seas and established it upon the waters. Who may ascend the hill of the Lord? Who may stand in his holy place? He who has clean hands and a pure heart, who does not lift up his soul to an idol or swear what is false. He will receive blessing from the Lord and vindication from God his Savior. Such is the generation of those who seek him, who seek your face, O God of Jacob. Lift up your heads, O you gates; be lifted up, you ancient doors, that the King of glory may come in. Who is this King of glory? The Lord strong and mighty, the Lord mighty in battle. Lift up your heads, O you gates; lift them up, you ancient doors. Who is he, this King of glory? The Lord Almighty – he is the King of glory."*

Jewish prophetic literature looked forward expectantly to the coming of a Messiah, a kingly figure who would vanquish their enemies and restore the throne of David. By the time of the birth of Jesus Christ, the poignant and powerful prophecies of the latter part of the Book of Isaiah were all but ignored and were for the most part seriously misinterpreted. (Even today, most of our Jewish brothers and sisters say that these prophecies pertain to the People of Israel, not to an individual Messiah.)

Why did Jesus say, *"Blessed are the poor in spirit, for theirs is the Kingdom of heaven"*? (Matthew 5:3) Because, according to Christian belief, He, the Servant and the Leader, came in fulfillment of this prophesy found in Isaiah 53: 1-3, 7, 9:

> *"Who has believed our message and to whom has the arm of the Lord been revealed? He grew up before him like a tender shoot, and like a root out of dry ground. He had no beauty or majesty to attract us to him, nothing in his appearance that we should desire him. He was despised and rejected by men, a man of sorrows, and familiar with suffering. Like one from whom men hide their faces he was despised, and we esteemed him not. He was oppressed and afflicted, yet he did not open his mouth; he was led like a lamb to the slaughter, and as a sheep before her shearers is silent, so he did not open his mouth. He was assigned a grave with the wicked."*

In spite of the references to sacrifice, the "suffering Messiah" was not a concept that the majority of the Jewish people embraced at the time Jesus began His public ministry. The people were subject to the dominion of the Roman Empire, and they yearned for deliverance, just as God had delivered them from enemies and captors in times past. Most of Jesus' contemporaries did not see Him as the true "Lamb of God who takes away the sins of the world" (though John the Baptist obviously did when he proclaimed this). Most did not understand that the Lamb had to be slain, to fulfill the meaning of all the sacrifices of centuries past. Also, when Jesus hung on the cross, most of the bystanders did not understand that when He cried out, "My God, my God, why have you forsaken me?", He was not only crying in anguish personally, He was praying Psalm 22. That great Messianic prayer, now prayed by the Messiah Himself, goes on as follows:

> *"Dogs have surrounded me; a band of evil men has encircled me, they have pierced my hands and feet. I can count*

Will the Real Christians Please Stand Up!

---

all my bones; people stare and gloat over me. They divide my garments among them and cast lots for my clothing." (Verses 16-18) But Jesus was not despairing. Listen to the end of this Psalm: *"All the ends of the earth will remember and turn to the Lord, and all the families of the nations will bow down before him, for dominion belongs to the Lord and he rules over the nations...Posterity will serve him, future generations will be told about the Lord. They will proclaim his righteousness to a people yet unborn – for he has done it.* (Verses 27-28, 30-31)

There is a sad irony recorded in John's Gospel. John 18: 28 recounts this:

"Then the Jews led Jesus from Caiaphas to the palace of the Roman governor. By now it was early morning, and to avoid cere-monial uncleanness the Jews did not enter the palace; they wanted to be able to eat the Passover." (By the way, "Jews" does not in any way indict the Jewish people. The reference is to a small group of Jewish leaders who wanted to eliminate whom they saw as a trou-blemaker.) The apostle John provides us with an account that is full of spiritual symbolism. These religious leaders, appointed to be spiritual guides to the people and prepare their hearts to receive God's word and the coming of the Messiah, missed it (which, by the way, the prophets had foretold). Not only did they not recognize Jesus as the long-awaited Redeemer, they followed their religious traditions and refused to enter pagan courts even at this most momentous of times. Why did they not enter? Here is the irony: They wanted to be sure they were ceremonially clean for the eating of the Passover meal. Passover! The great celebration of the libera-tion of the Israelites from Egyptian bondage was achieved, as we have seen, after God's angel struck down the first born of all Egyptian parents, including Pharaoh's, and spared the Jewish fami-lies who sacrificed a pure lamb and put its blood on their doorposts. The blood of the lamb was pointing to the coming of the pure Lamb of God, the One who would shed His blood and rise from the dead in order to reopen the gates to the Kingdom of Heaven. The Lamb was among the Jewish leaders, and that small band condemned Him

to death and found a way to ensure that their Roman conquerors would carry out the sentence. But it had all been planned and foreseen by the Father, as well as by the Son and the Holy Spirit. The leaders let religion blind them to reality; they complimented themselves on their adherence to ceremony, to ritual, to pomp and circumstance, and in so doing they failed to recognize the presence of the Messiah, who was also God Himself, in their midst.

And so it is in many churches and among so many Christians even today – when lip service is given to Christ but His dynamic, real, loving presence is either missed or ignored. Thus we become participants after the fact in the drama of those hours:

"Then Pilate took Jesus and had him flogged. The soldiers twisted together a crown of thorns and put it on his head. They clothed him in a purple robe and went up to him again and again, saying 'Hail, king of the Jews!' And they struck him in the face.'" (John 19: 1-3)

When we call Him King in worship but our hearts are elsewhere, we in effect treat Him with the same contempt that the leaders, that the soldiers displayed toward Him. That Jesus who suffered indignity quietly is the same Jesus, now glorified and seated at the right hand of the Father, who receives our worship and seeks to conform us to His image by the Holy Spirit. But even then God had His way! The very Pilate who condemned Jesus also ordered that a sign be attached to the cross: "*Jesus of Nazareth, King of the Jews.*" When the Jewish leaders objected, Pilate replied, "*What I have written, I have written.*" (See John 19: 19-22)

So, He died, He rose, and He is back with the Father and the Holy Spirit as the God-Man. He promised and sent the Holy Spirit to teach us about Him, to open our minds and our hearts to God's Word (another manifestation of the eternal Word Who became flesh), and to empower us as disciples hopefully following the Lord with every step and breath of our lives. That is what Easter means to a real Christian. That is how a real Christian lives – as a member of the Kingdom, proclaiming Jesus as Lord and following in His footsteps by taking up the cross with love and joy.

There are certain requirements to be a member of the Kingdom. A person has to be born again. (John 3:3) Born of water and the Spirit means being cleansed through Baptism, accepting Jesus as Savior, and committing oneself to be led by the Holy Spirit. It is meant to be a total conversion and commitment; it must be done consciously and freely; it is not just going through the motions of some religious rite or uttering some words, or running to an altar. In those denominations that perform infant baptism, while they see this as the way for the child to become a member of God's family (a practice that reliable historical sources confirm was implemented in the early Christian Church), they also recognize that at some point the choice to be a Christian must be deliberate and personal. Becoming a Christian is intended to be a life-altering decision. It means a life long personal walk with the Master. It means being able to recognize the sound of Jesus' voice as Mary Magdalene did at the tomb on that first Easter. (John 20: 16-17) It means crying out in our need for Him and giving our lives to Him as the thief on the cross did when he said, *"Lord, remember me when you come into Your Kingdom."* (Luke 23: 42) Lest we fall into any self-righteousness, remember, the first person to enter heaven under the New Covenant was a criminal.

Finally, being a member of the Kingdom means a commitment of service to others, with a true servant's heart, and being a servant leader in whatever situations the Holy Spirit prompts us to step up. Jesus, though He is God, demonstrated a perfect servant's heart when He walked among us. In Matthew 25, Jesus tells us for whom the Kingdom has been prepared: It is for those who serve. (25: 31-40) As the secular corporate world embraces the principles of servanthood and servant leadership in an ever-increasing number of companies, these leaders are learning that the greatest example of servant leadership in all of history is Jesus of Nazareth. Even when secular companies do not focus on Biblical teaching, the Person and presence of Jesus are at the heart of the principles taught by facilitators.

The Kingdom is here, the Kingdom is coming! The prophet Daniel proclaimed, *"The God of Heaven will set up a kingdom that will never be destroyed, nor will it be left to another people. It will crush all those kingdoms and bring them to an end, but it will itself endure forever...In my vision at night I looked, and there before me was one like a son of man, coming with the clouds of heaven. He approached the Ancient of Days and was led into his presence. He was given authority, glory and sovereign power; all peoples, nations and men of every language worshipped him. His dominion is an everlasting dominion that will not pass away, and his kingdom is one that will never be destroyed."* (Daniel 2:44 and 7: 13-14) Isaiah: *"And he will be called Wonderful Counselor, Mighty God, Everlasting Father, Prince of Peace. Of the increase of his government and peace there will be no end."* And the mighty words of the Book of Revelation: *"After this I looked and there before me was a great multitude that no one could count, from every nation, tribe, people and language, standing before the throne and in front of the Lamb. They were wearing white robes and were holding palm branches in their hands. And they cried out in a loud voice: 'Salvation belongs to our God, who sits on the throne, and to the Lamb.'...'The ten horns you see are ten kings who have not yet received a kingdom, but who for one hour will receive authority as kings along with the beast. They have one purpose and will give their power and authority to the beast. They will make war against the Lamb, but the Lamb will overcome them because he is Lord of Lords and King of Kings – and with him will be his called, chosen and faithful followers.'"* (Revelation 7: 9-10 and 17: 12-14)

Easter is the greatest of celebrations for the true Christian. It means the Lamb has overcome; it means the Kingdom of Heaven is real; it means that we live as members of the Kingdom now, and it means that we have the glorious privilege and awesome responsibility to take up the cross and follow our Lord and Savior, permitting Him by our lives to continue His work of redemption and salvation. Stand up and be counted, Christians! Put on the white robes, wave the palm branches of living love, worship and service, and follow the King!

Will the Real Christians Please Stand Up!

SUMMARY FOR REFLECTION AND DISCUSSION:

A real Christian:

1) Recognizes that Easter celebrates the consummate Christian event and, indeed, the single most important event in the history of the world;
2) Refuses to let the secular traditions, and even the religious ones, associated with the Easter season blind her/him to the joyous reality that every day is Easter, that Jesus is alive, that He has triumphed, that He lives with and within us;
3) Lets the glory of the risen Christ shine through daily life, bringing light to a darkened world.

SCRIPTURES FOR JOURNALING:

1) Psalm 22, Isaiah 53;
2) Psalm 24;
3) John 18-19
4) Revelation 7: 9-10; 17: 12-14

REFLECTION 7:

HEAVEN: OUR GOAL

I wrote the first draft of this reflection in preparation for a very special occasion in the Wilderness Church. This log cabin church dates back to the 19th century. In planning this service, which took place in the early 90's, I asked the Holy Spirit to guide my thoughts and words for a very personal reason: This message would be an emotional one and could either build up or tear down some people very important to me. You see, my wife, Barbara's, sister, Tami, was dying of rapidly spreading and inoperable cancer. She had been admitted into St. Joseph's Hospital in St. Charles, Missouri, with what she thought was pneumonia. Well, she had pneumonia, to be sure, but the physicians also discovered that she had cancerous growths in her chest, her lymph nodes, and her leg bones. Less than a year before that, Tami's husband, Danny, had died of a heart attack while he was watching television. There were two daughters: Amanda, 13, and Megan, 11. Tami was 34 years old. She had recently begun taking college courses, she bought a house and a car, and life was looking up for her. Tami had a difficult life, but she had been filled with new hope. Now things were still looking up, but in an entirely different way. Unless the Lord chose to heal her, she would be shortly be going home. Tami had recently recommitted herself to the Lord and her Christian faith, so she had an eternal home awaiting her. But it was difficult for her as a mother and it was difficult for Mandi and Megan.

Tami and the girls came to our home that weekend. So did Tami's dad; ill as he was with cancer himself, he drove up from Louisiana. They had not been close over the years, and a beautiful healing occurred that weekend. There had already been a healing in relationship with one of her brothers whom she had not seen for a long time. He drove to see her in the hospital, went home with her when she was discharged, and he took care of her for a few days. The other brother was also with us. He had been instrumental in the two girls establishing a personal relationship with the Lord. So, it was both a sad and joyful time in our household during those days together, as the work of the Lord was so obviously evident in people's lives.

They all came to the Wilderness Church on Sunday, along with Barb and one of our two sons. I told Tami that I would not embarrass her by referring specifically to her, but that the message would be for her, as would be the special music before and after the message. The Holy Spirit had prompted me to talk about heaven, and the nearness of the fall season (remarkably beautiful in the Ozarks) was a natural setting to remind ourselves of the death experience that we will all have – a doorway to eternal life or eternal death. For those who know and love the Lord, it will be a wonderful time as we enter the portals of heaven and achieve our intended destiny. The message was about what we would experience there. *"Though eye has not seen, nor ear heard, nor has it entered into our minds what things God has prepared for those who love him,"* we do have some clues that serve to give us a faint awareness of the glory of eternal life.

Over the years there have been recorded instances of "out of body experiences" of people who seem to have died but who quickly return to life. Most of these experiences relate to heaven. Without doubt, some of these are bogus, and some are frankly demonic in nature (especially references to an after life without any mention of God the Father, God the Son or God the Holy Spirit). But I am convinced that some are real, God-given testimonies to remind us why we are in this life. One of those experiences that appears to be genuine – based on the miraculous recovery, the

Will the Real Christians Please Stand Up!

description of heaven that is certainly in line with what we know from Scripture, and the commitment of the person to spread the word about our destiny from a Christian perspective—is that of Dr. Richard Eby.

In the prologue to his book, <u>Caught Up Into Paradise</u>, Dr. Eby writes: "Dick, you're dead! This seemed the most amazing and yet the most normal and sensible statement that I had ever uttered. I felt suddenly at home. I was instantly no longer in a strange world (as earth had seemed so often) but in Paradise personally prepared for my arrival. The peace was overwhelmingly ecstatic and instantly mine. Here I was, unaware of how I had died and that I had died and left the old body somewhere. I had no memory of earth. In a twinkling of an eye my memory had been erased, and my body replaced with the most exquisite mind and new body imaginable. I gasped with glee. God and His handiwork were everywhere. In that split second Jesus caught me up for a glimpse of His 'mansion' prepared for that moment alone. I find it difficult even now to phrase into English words the description of the total ecstasy and boundless love which pervade Paradise. The instant release from mortal shortcomings is really indescribable (St. Paul says 'unutterable')."

At the age of 60, Dr. Richard Eby fell from a balcony at the home of a relative and landed on his head on a concrete sidewalk. There was great loss of blood, the skull was exposed from ear to ear, the body was gray-white by the time his wife had rushed to him, and the blood had stopped flowing. There was neither pulse nor breath. (I had the misfortune once in Chicago of coming upon the body of a young man who had fallen from a window and landed on the sidewalk on his head. His skull was split open, and there was clearly no life and not even any remote possibility of recovery.) The paramedics took Dr. Eby to the nearest hospital, and they were convinced that he was dead. While all of this was going on, Dr. Eby was having quite a different type of experience! The following words are pulled from his book: "One moment in suburban Chicago, the next moment in the most exquisite place 'prepared for you, that where I am you may be also' – one moment with a flesh-restricted mind, the next moment with a heaven-released mind

Will the Real Christians Please Stand Up!

whose speed of function was that of light. I was enjoying a heavenly 'body' – aside from the complete absence of pain and the total presence of peace (neither of which I had ever known on earth). I looked like me, felt like me, reacted like me. I was me. I simply had suddenly shed the old body, and was now living anew in this fantastic cloud-like body! I was clothed in a translucent flowing gown, pure white, but transparent to my gaze…I could see through my body and noted the gorgeously white flowers behind and beneath me…I was instinctively aware that the Lord of Lords was everywhere about this place…The sense of timelessness made all hurry foolish…My eyes were unlimited in range of vision…There were no bones or vessels or organs. No blood…My mind which worked here in heaven with electric-like speed answered my unspoken query: They are not needed; Jesus is the Life here. He is the needed energy. There was no air to breathe, no blood to pump, no food to digest or eliminate…My gaze riveted upon the exquisite valley in which I found myself. Forests of symmetrical trees unlike anything on earth covered the foothills on each side. I could see each branch and leaf – not a brown spot or dead leaf in the forest…Each tree, tall and graceful, was a duplicate of the others – perfect, unblemished…The valley floor was gorgeous. Stately grasses, each blade perfect and erect, were interspersed with ultra-white, four petalled flowers on stems two feet tall, with a touch of gold at the centers…My thought to stoop and pick the flowers became the act! Here in Paradise I discovered that there is no time lag between thought and act…I found my hand containing a bouquet of identical blossoms. Their whiteness was exciting. I almost had time to ask myself 'why so white' when the answer was already given! 'On earth you saw only white light which combined the color spectrum of the sun. Here we have the light of the SON!' My excitement was too great to describe in words. 'Of course,' I thought, 'He is the light of the world.' I stood overwhelmed with the sights of Paradise…But He had more…It was music…I had been aware of the most beautiful, melodious, angelic background music that the ear of man can perceive. I was now ready to concentrate on it…It was truly a new song…Not instrumental, not vocal, not mathematical, not earthly. It originated from no one point – neither from the

Will the Real Christians Please Stand Up!

sky nor the ground. Just as was true of the light, the music emerged apparently from everything and every place. It had no beat – was neither major nor minor – and had no tempo…No earthly adjectives describe its angelic quality…Hallelujah! Music by Jesus. No wonder the cherubims and seraphims and multitudes sing around His throne!…I was not prepared for the sweetest revelation of all: the all-pervading aroma of heaven…Like the sights and the sounds, it was everywhere. I bent again and smelled the flowers – yes, it was there. The grasses also. The air was just the same. A perfume so exotic, so refreshing, so superior, that it was fit only for a King!…I simply stood quietly and let it bathe my being…I was allowed to share God's supreme perfume. Never can I be the same again…And it awaits whomsoever will come to Jesus! He said it; I believe it. He prepared it; I accept it. Fortunately for me, Jesus elected not to show me more of the heavenly wonders that day. I could not have coped with another revelation."

Dr. Eby returned to earth, in the body, in a hospital room, hooked up with tubes and monitors. He was given up for dead, but he did not die. God apparently performed a miracle. Dr. Eby walked out of that hospital to begin a ministry to tell all who would listen of what lies ahead for those who love the Lord.

By the way, the Lord later gave Dr. Eby another experience: For a few brief moments he descended into the pit of hell and experienced the horrors of silence, darkness, aloneness, despair, and agony that await those who die separated from Jesus Christ.

It is one thing to hear about an "out-of-body experience" that a contemporary Christian recounts. Praise God for such gifts to remind us of our destiny. But we do not really need these accounts, for we have beautiful descriptions right from the Word of God. The remainder of this reflection will be a journey to heaven via Scripture.

There is no question that we will, upon seeing God the Father, God the Son, and God the Holy Spirit, fall down in adoration of the supreme Godhead. We may cry out "Holy, Holy, Holy," or, as the song puts it, we may not be able to speak at first in the presence of God. But, wonder of wonders, we – puny creatures that we are – will actually be honored by God! Jesus gives us a hint in one of His parables: *"It will be good for those servants whose master finds them watching when he comes. I tell you the truth, he will dress himself to serve, will have them recline at the table, and will come and wait on them."* (Luke 12: 37) And focus also on the beautiful line in Psalm 23 (verse 5): *"You prepare a table for me in the presence of my enemies, you anoint my head with oil."*

Just as Dr. Eby experienced, the Word verifies the truth of transformed bodies. These weak, vulnerable, fleshly bodies will be replaced with glorified, strong, and beautiful ones.

Jesus gave us a foretaste of this at the time of the Transfiguration: *"Jesus took with him Peter, James and John, the brother of James, and led them up a high mountain by themselves. There he was transfigured before them. His face shone like the sun, and his clothes became as white as the light."* (Matthew 17: 1-2) After His Resurrection, Jesus showed how a glorified body operates: *"A week later his disciples were in the house again, and Thomas was with them. Though the doors were locked, Jesus came and stood among them.* (John 20: 26) Material things do not pose any barriers for glorified bodies! If you are thinking that perhaps these passages only describe the glorified Jesus and not His followers, Paul gives us the hope and the promise in Philippians 3: 20-21: *"But our citizenship is in heaven. And we eagerly await a Savior from there, the Lord Jesus Christ, who, by the power that enables him to bring everything under his control, will transform our lowly bodies so that they will be like his glorious body."* And, joyful reality that this is, we will see and be with our precious Lord in heaven for all eternity and with no fear of separation. *"Since, then, you have been raised with Christ, set your hearts on things above, where Christ is seated at the right hand of God. Set your minds on things above, not on earthly things. For you died, and your life is now hidden with Christ in God. When Christ, who is your life, appears, then you also will appear with him in glory."* (Colossians 3: 1-4) John tells us about this, too, in his first Letter: *"How great is the love the Father has lavished on us, that we should be called the children of God! And that is what we are! The reason the world does not know us is that it did not know him. Dear friends, now we are children of God, and what we will be has not yet been made known. But we know that when he appears, we shall be like him, for we shall see him as he is.* (1 John 3: 1-2) Stephen saw Jesus in glory, just before the deacon was stoned to death and joined his Lord: *"But Stephen, full of the Holy Spirit, looked to heaven and saw the glory of God, and Jesus standing at the right hand of God. 'Look,' he said, 'I see heaven open and the Son of Man standing at the right hand of God."* (Acts 7: 55-56)

We will be clothed with white robes – signifying the victory plus purity and holiness, which describe our existence in the Kingdom of Heaven where all sin is forever washed away. *"I delight greatly in the Lord; my soul rejoices in my God. For he has clothed me with garments of salvation and arrayed me in a robe of righteousness, as a bridegroom adorns his head like a priest and as a bride adorns herself with her jewels.* (Isaiah 61: 10)

"Now Joshua was dressed in filthy clothes as he stood before the angel. The angel said to those who were standing before him, 'Take off his filthy clothes.' Then he said to Joshua, 'See, I have taken away your sin, and I will put rich garments on you." (Zechariah 3: 3-4) *"He who overcomes will be dressed in white. I will never blot out his name from the book of life, but will acknowledge his name before my Father and his angels.* (Revelation 3: 5) *"There was a violent earthquake, for an angel of the Lord came down from heaven and, going to the tomb, rolled back the stone and sat on it. His appearance was like lightning, and his clothes were white as snow."* (Matthew 28: 2-3)

And keep in mind the beautiful symbolism in the parable of the prodigal son (Luke 15: 22). Just as the Father seeks now to forgive us when we turn to him, so one day, if we truly seek Him and are united with His Son, He will see us coming, He will run to us, and He will put on us the finest of robes and welcome us into His eternal kingdom.

We know also from Scripture that there is a mighty host of heaven, with whom we shall have fellowship for all eternity. Daniel had a vision: *"As I looked, thrones were set in place, and the Ancient of Days took his seat. His clothing was as white as snow; the hair of his head was white like wool. His throne was flaming with fire, and its wheels were all ablaze. A river of fire was flowing, coming out from before him. Thousands upon thousands attended him; ten thousand times ten thousand stood before him."* (Daniel 7: 9-10) Reflect, too, on Hebrews 12: 22-24: *"But you have come to Mount Zion, to the heavenly Jerusalem, the city of the living God. You have come to thousands upon thousands of angels in joyful assembly, to the church of the firstborn, whose names are written in heaven. You have come to God, the judge of all men, to the spirits of righteous men made perfect, to Jesus the mediator of a new covenant, and to the sprinkled blood that speaks a better word than the blood of Abel."*

In heaven, all time will cease. Our minds cannot grasp eternity, but the fact is that we will be in total joy and peace forever and ever – there will be no interruption and no ending to this marvelous life. *"On this mountain He will destroy the shroud that enfolds all peoples, the sheet that covers all nations; he will swallow up death forever. The Sovereign Lord will wipe away the tears from all faces; He will remove the disgrace of his people from all the earth. The Lord has spoken."* (Isaiah 25: 7-8) *"For the trumpet will sound, the dead will be raised imperishable, and we will be changed. For the perishable must clothe itself with the imperishable, and the mortal with immortality. When the perishable has been clothed with the imperishable, and the mortal with immortality, then the saying that is written will come true: 'Death has been swallowed up in victory.' 'Where, O death, is your victory? Where, O death, is your sting?"* (1 Corinthians 15: 52-55) And Jesus proclaimed, before He raised Lazarus from the dead: *"I am the resurrection and the life. He who believes in me will live, even though he dies; and whoever lives and believes in me will never die."* (John 11: 25) And Paul proclaimed: *"Now we know that if the earthly tent we live in is destroyed, we have a building from God, an eternal house in heaven, not built by human hands...Now it is God who has made us for this very purpose and has given us the Spirit as a deposit, guaranteeing what is to come."* (2 Corinthians 5: 1-5)

What better way to summarize God's revelation to us about heaven and eternal life than to turn to that greatest of all "out-of-body" experiences, John and the Book of Revelation? Read, prayerfully and joyfully: *"At once I was in the Spirit, and there before me was a throne in heaven with someone sitting on it. And the one who sat there had the appearance of jasper and carnelian. A rainbow, resembling an emerald, encircled the throne. Surrounding the throne were twenty-four elders. They were dressed in white and had crowns of gold on their heads. From the throne came flashes of lightning, rumbling and peals of thunder...Also before the throne was what looked like a sea of glass, clear as crystal...Then I looked and I heard the voice of many angels, numbering thousands upon thousands, and ten thousand times ten thousand. They encircled the throne and the living creatures and the elders. In a loud voice they sang: 'Worthy is the Lamb, who was slain, to receive power and wealth and wisdom and strength and honor and glory and praise.'...After this I looked and there before me was a great multitude that no one could count, from every nation, tribe, people and language, standing before the throne and in front of the Lamb. They were wearing white robes and were holding palm branches in their hands. And they cried out in a loud voice: 'Salvation belongs to our God, who sits on the throne, and to the Lamb.' All the angels were standing around the throne and around the elders and the four living creatures. They fell down on their faces before the throne and worshipped God, saying: 'Amen! Praise and glory and wisdom and thanks and honor and power and strength be to our God forever and ever. Amen!...Then I saw a new heaven and a new earth, for the first heaven and the first earth had passed away, and there was no longer any sea. I saw the Holy City, the new Jerusalem, coming down out of heaven from God, prepared as a bride beautifully dressed for her husband. And I heard a loud voice from the throne saying, 'Now the dwelling of God is with men, and he will live with them. They will be his people, and God himself will be with them and be their God. He will wipe away every tear from their eyes. There will be no more death or mourning or crying or pain, for the old order of things has passed away.'...The angel showed me the Holy City, Jerusalem, coming down out of heaven from God. It shone with the glory of God, and its brilliance was like that of a very precious jewel, like a jasper, clear as crystal. It had a great, high wall with twelve gates, and with twelve angels at the gates...The city was laid out like a square, as long as it was wide...The wall was made of jasper, and the city of pure gold, as pure as glass. The foundations of the city walls were decorated with every kind of precious stone...The twelve gates were twelve pearls, each gate made of a single pearl. The great street of the city was of pure gold, like transparent glass...The city does not need the sun or the moon to shine on it, for the glory of God gives it light, and the Lamb is its lamp...On no day will its gates ever be shut, for there will be no night there...Then the angel showed me the river of the water of life, as clear as crystal, flowing from the throne of God and of the Lamb down the middle of the great street of the city. On each side of the river stood the tree of life...No longer will there be any curse. The throne of God and of the Lamb will be in the city, and his servants will serve him. They will see his face, and his name will be on their foreheads. There will be no more night. They will not need the light of a lamp or the light of the sun, for the Lord God will give them light. And they will reign forever and ever...(And Jesus said, and says to us) 'Behold, I am coming soon...I am the Alpha and the Omega, the First and the Last, the Beginning and the End. Blessed are those who wash their robes, that they may have the right to the tree of life and may go through the gates of the city...The Spirit and the bride say, 'Come!' And let him who hears say, 'Come!' Whoever is thirsty, let him take the free gift of the water of life.'"* (Revelation 4: 2, 5-6; 5: 11-12; 7: 9-12; 21: 1-4, 10-12, 16, 18-19, 21, 23, 25; 22: 1-5, 12-15, 17)

We each have a choice. Our calling is to acknowledge Jesus as the Christ and as God, to confess our sins before Him, to examine our consciences daily and seek His forgiveness for what we have done or have failed to do contrary to His will, to not only accept Him as our Savior but to also make Him the Lord of our lives, and to serve Him the best we can with the help of the Holy Spirit and with every remaining breath that God gives us. And if we do, we shall one day hear Him say, *"Come, blessed of my Father, and receive the kingdom that has been prepared for you from the foundation of the world.* (Matthew 25: 34) The Lord Jesus who said that in His Father's house are many rooms, and who promised to come back for us, will welcome us, place a crown on our heads, and show us that beautiful Beulah land that Isaiah talked about (62:4).

Amen! So let it be! And, as the Book of Revelation ends,

indeed, as the very Bible itself ends: *"Amen. Come, Lord Jesus. The grace of the Lord Jesus be with God's people. Amen."*

Note: Tami Fleschert went home to be with the Lord on November 9, 1993.

Since this reflection began with a mention of the Wilderness Church, it seems appropriate to provide some additional information. The reflections in this book flow from messages I had the privilege of giving over a nine year period in this beautiful and historical log chapel, located in the heart of the Ozarks of southwest Missouri at Silver Dollar City, a Christian owned theme park near Branson. Silver Dollar City re-creates life as it was lived in the latter part of the 19th century, bringing to life the best of the fun and the heritage of that era. The picturesque log structure sits on the main Square of the Park and overlooks the Ozark hills and Table Rock Lake. On clear days the Boston Mountains of the Arkansas Ozarks can be seen. The Wilderness Church was one of the original buildings when the Park opened in 1960. However, the structure had been donated, dismantled and reconstructed there, after a colorful history as a church building, a schoolhouse and even a hay barn. The inscription over the large picture window behind the pulpit (fashioned from a tree stump and almost petrified by now) reads, *"I will lift up my eyes to the hills, from whence cometh my help."* There are worship services in the chapel every Sunday that the Park is open. The early service is the one I was privileged to be part of during those years just short of a decade, with a congregation composed of both employees before they began work ("Silver Dollar City citizens") and customers (guests). Though the entire Park did not open until later, the main Square was open at that time – with restaurants open for breakfast and music in the Gazebo – so every Sunday drew some "regulars" and some first-time or periodic visitors. The Holy Spirit used those years as highly formative for me, since there were people from many different denominations in attendance. This fluctuating mix of folks led me to focus on the themes of the Bible and to avoid any "theologizing." When I yielded to the Holy Spirit, it was amazing how clearly messages fell into place, with the ideas for the next service coming to mind and heart normally on my way home from the one just concluded. I remember one Sunday that I thought of a hymn during the service and asked if anyone knew it. A gentleman guest raised his hand, stood up and began singing. Well, the sweet spirit of that man was not matched by a sweet voice! Yet, everyone was deeply moved, and as I was reflecting on the experience during the drive home, the Holy Spirit gave me a continuation of the theme for the following Sunday – all because of a Christian who was unafraid to stand up and be heard.

My prayer has been – and is now, in the third drafting of this book – that the Holy Spirit will be totally in charge in the transferring of the messages to this collection of reflections. To make the words of John the Baptist my prayer with regard to the Lord Jesus: *"He must increase; I must decrease."*

SUMMARY FOR REFLECTION AND DISCUSSION:

A real Christian:

1) Has a vision of what is to come – eternal life;
2) Has a mission to be an eternal citizen of heaven and to be an instrument for God's grace to reach others and keep them from being eternal citizens of hell;
3) Lives this life to the fullest, but with an awareness that all is passing.

SCRIPTURES FOR JOURNALING:

1) Philippians 3: 20-21; Colossians 3: 1-4; 1 John 3: 1-2;
2) Daniel 7: 9-10; Hebrews 12: 22-24;
3) 2 Corinthians 5: 1-5;
4) Revelation 4, 5, 7, 21.

PART II:

THE SCRIPTURES SPEAK TO US

The five reflections in Part II focus on examples of how Scripture comes alive when we read it with faith in the presence and guidance of the Holy Spirit, the true author of the Bible.

In reality, this entire book is built on the living power of God's Word. "The Scriptures Speak to Us" is a prominent theme throughout all of the reflections. Nevertheless, this particular section seeks to be like a laser beam, highlighting the beauty of the Scriptures and their applicability for all people at all times.

In these reflections we explore the meaning of a Proverb for our Christian life, the power of a Psalm, and we focus in a special way on our Lord and Savior Jesus Christ from the perspectives of the Christian lifestyle He teaches us, the meaning today of Emmaus in Luke, and the challenge to seek Jesus daily

Each reflection ends with a summary and recommended Scriptures for journaling. Do not walk past the opportunity to meditate on and share insights with one person or several through mutual journaling.

REFLECTION 8:

PROVERBS 3: 5-7

I read a story in a newspaper about a man in a South American country. The account of his unusual life will serve as the introduction to this reflection. But, before we do that, that same paper had a joke at the bottom of the page; it is our "pre-introduction." Brace yourself; it is really a groaner. Why did the chicken walk to the middle of the road? So she could "lay it on the line." Well, Proverbs 3: 5-7, the heart of this reflection, really "lays it on the line" as a challenge for the real Christian, as we shall see.

But, first, the story: There was a man who was a husband and father, living in our time, who died not many years ago. He was also a miser. Having no faith in the financial institutions of that country or in paper currency, he developed a fetish for coin collecting – not as a hobby, but as his method for accumulating wealth. He would travel for miles to find old lost or carelessly discarded coins, and he stored them in a room of the house he and his family lived in. He kept the door locked, and he carried one key with him wherever he went, on a string around his neck. The other key he hid somewhere in the house, and only he knew where it was. Every evening after supper he retired to that room, locked himself in, and, ignoring his wife and children, spent his time counting and recounting his coins. The family lived in great poverty, just barely subsisting. But the head of the household continued to hoard coins, spending only what was absolutely necessary for survival. He looked forward to the day when he would have all the money he would ever need for the rest of his life. Then late one evening, his wife heard him choking and crying out from the other side of the locked door. She frantically searched the house and finally found the extra key. Upon entering the room, she found her husband dying of a heart attack. His final words as he died, surrounded by his coins, were, "Please lock the door." What his family and the authorities discovered in that mysterious room was astounding: Mounds and mounds of coins, worth one million dollars in face value! But in reality, they were worth nothing. That country's runaway inflation rate had reduced the value of the coins to the point that they were useless. In fact, the impoverished and embittered widow had to pay the equivalent of $250 to have the coins carted off!

Now compare this story with Luke 12: 16-21: *"And He told them this parable: 'The ground of a certain rich man produced a good crop. He thought to himself, 'What shall I do? I have no place to store my crops.' Then he said, 'This is what I'll do. I will tear down my barns and build bigger ones, and there I will store all my grain and goods. And I'll say to myself,' You have plenty of good things laid up for many years. Take life easy; eat, drink, and be merry." But God said to him, 'You fool! This very night your life will be demanded from you. Then who will get what you have prepared for yourself?' This is how it will be with anyone who stores up things for himself but is not rich toward God.'"* These are different circumstances, but they are based on exactly the same principle. As Jesus said elsewhere, *"Where your treasure is, there your heart will be also."* (Matthew 6: 21)

There is nothing soft or undemanding about Christianity. If you doubt that, reflect on what Jesus said as recorded later in that same chapter 12 of Luke, verses 49-53: *"I have come to bring fire on the earth, and how I wish it were already kindled! But I have a baptism to undergo, and how distressed I am until it is completed. Do you think I came to bring peace on earth? No, I tell you, but division. From now on there will be five in one family divided against each other, three against two and two against three. They will be divided, father against son and son against father, mother against daughter and daughter against mother, mother-in-law against daughter-in-law and daughter-in-law against mother-in-law."*

To choose Jesus above all, to seek first the Kingdom of God in all circumstances does not sit well with the spirit of the world; it is like oil and water trying to mix together. Well, sure, we can agree with that – in theory. But in practice surely we are not guilty of any of these things being talked about! Hopefully, that is true; but I strongly encourage you to have an open mind along with me. What this all really means is that if I place my trust in, if I am in any way obsessed with, if I have commitments to possessions, people or use of time that interfere with total commitment to God, then I have a problem. So, let's get to the Scripture that provides the challenge for this reflection: Proverbs 3: 5-7:

Trust in the Lord with all your heart and lean not on your own understanding; in all your ways acknowledge him, and he will make your paths straight. Do not be wise in your own eyes; fear the Lord and shun evil."

Analyze each phrase; take each word just as it is written; do not sugarcoat the passage or gloss over it. Do I trust in the Lord with ALL my heart? That means absolutely totally, in every situation, with every breath. Do I ever lean on my own understanding? In other words, have I fallen prey to the "American tradition" of "doing it my way," of "being all that I can be," of "picking myself up by my bootstraps," and all those other insidious clichés? – insidious because there is an element of truth in them, but in their essence they preach the philosophy of putting self first, taking care of #1, a way of life radically different than being a dependent, yielded servant of Jesus Christ who never makes a single decision without the Holy Spirit's guidance and who attributes any good accomplished to God's grace. Do I acknowledge God in ALL MY WAYS, meaning that when I awake He is first on my mind, and that at the end of each day I take time for a sincere examination of conscience by reflecting on how well I have listened to Him and followed His will – and seeking His forgiveness for putting myself and my own will and desires ahead of Him? Do I consciously consecrate every moment to

Will the Real Christians Please Stand Up!

Him and walk through my days conscious of His presence? Am I wise in my own eyes, or do I recognize that all I have comes from Him, and that the only wisdom worth having comes from the inspiration and guidance of the Holy Spirit?

You see, this is what it means to take the Word of God as truly inspired, with depths of revealed truth in every verse. If that kind of a totality of commitment is not present consistently – or at least a burning passion to live that commitment and a getting up with renewed determination every time I fall – then I am not a real Christian as Jesus sees His followers. I am playing games; I am building bigger barns; I am hoarding ultimately worthless coins; I am walking through life focusing on myself and my needs and my accomplishments rather than on Jesus Christ and His Father and the Holy Spirit.

In addition to falling into the trap of trusting self, we can also place inordinate trust in political leaders and/or in military might. Isaiah wrote it far better than I can:

"Woe to those who go down to Egypt for help, who rely on horses, who trust in the multitude of their chariots and in the great strength of their horsemen, but do not look to the Holy One of Israel, or seek help from the Lord. Yet he, too, is wise and can bring disaster; he does not take back his words. He will rise up against the house of the wicked, against those who help evildoers. But the Egyptians are men and not God; their horses are flesh and not spirit. When the Lord stretches out his hand, he who helps will stumble, he who is helped will fall; both will perish together. This is what the Lord says to me: 'As a lion growls, a great lion over his prey – and though a whole band of shepherds is called together against him, he is not frightened by their shouts or disturbed by their clamor – so the Lord Almighty will come down to do battle on Mount Zion and on its heights. Like birds hovering overhead, the Lord Almighty will shield Jerusalem; He will shield it and deliver it, he will 'pass over' it and will rescue it.' Return to him whom you have so greatly revolted against, O Israelites. For in that

day every one of you will reject the idols of silver and gold your sinful hands have made. (Isaiah 31: 1-7)

It troubles me when I witness super-patriotism in our nation, when people proclaim the USA not only to be a Christian nation, but to practically be a "messiah" for the rest of the world. There is no doubt that America has a Christian foundation; but that foundation is crumbling because of the passion of a few misguided people to remove God from our nation. I am grateful and proud to be a citizen of this country. But real Christians are repenting – for personal and national sins, present and past. The USA is becoming more and more hostile to religious expression, more and more mired in crime, violence, greed and immorality of all kinds, condoning the murder of millions of innocents in the name of "free choice", weakening the sanctity of marriage and family – more and more becoming akin to or even exceeding Sodom and Gomorrha in corruption and sin. I believe that there are several reasons why God has not yet rendered awful judgment on our nation.

First, there is a remnant of Christians who are passionately praying and working for revival in the land. (The Biblical theme of "remnant" is pervasive and fascinating, and it is found frequently in the Old Testament but also in the New. Regardless of how sinful we become, there will always be a small number – the remnant – who will hold to God's ways and through whom His grace will flow. The "remnant" is frankly another way to describe "real Christians" — people who not only believe in Jesus Christ, but who yield their very lives to following and obeying Him.)

A second reason why God is sparing this nation has to do with the fact that we send and support missionaries around the world, and we are a major supplier of Bibles and other Christian literature. What is sadly ironic about this is that we ourselves have become, without being generally aware of it, a country in need of missionaries. Any missionary will tell us that it is much harder to reach the indifferent than it is to reach any other people in need of the Gospel. There is a man whom I greatly value as a Christian brother. His name is Vassie Pillay. Vassie was born in India and grew up as a heathen. He moved to South Africa, where he ministered after he became a Christian.

Then the Holy Spirit called him to go and be a missionary to, yes, the United States of America. So now his missionary work includes the USA, South Africa, Australia, and, soon, India.

A third reason is one that is certainly controversial, because so many people have politicized it: America is an ally of Israel. Though there is not much religious or spiritual within the secular government of that nation, the land of Israel itself is very precious to God and should be to every Christian. The establishment of Israel as a nation in the 1940's was not a secular event; it was the fulfillment of a promise. If we falter in our support of that nation – which really means of God's Chosen People, for the Jews are just that, we are in trouble. If you have any doubts, read Romans. Does anyone doubt that a major reason why we are the "Great Satan" to the majority of the Muslim world (in addition to our examples of internal corruption) is that we are defenders of Israel? When the Lord returns – and none of us knows when that will be, in spite of all the proclamations and interpretations of Scripture that we hear and read – He will most certainly either appear at or go to the Jewish Temple, and there is not even a Temple there yet! But there will be, someday and somehow. Reflect with me. The place where Abraham almost sacrificed Isaac when God tested the obedience of the man who became the father of the Jewish nation, the place where Solomon built the Temple, the place where the other Temples have been built and destroyed, and the place where Jesus went as a young boy and as a man, the place where the Temple mount and the wailing wall are now – they are all exactly the same place! Woe to us if we let politics erode our support, not only of the Jewish people, but also of the nation of Israel to exist in freedom and security. In my mind there is no doubt that one of our major responsibilities is to help protect Israel. For a Christian to be anti-Semitic is not only an oxymoron; it is an abomination in the sight of God.

Now, back to trust. Instead of truly trusting the Lord, do I place my trust in other people? Oh, to be sure, we human beings are called to establish relationships of trust based on our being trustworthy; but what I am referring to is trust in people as a substitute to trusting the Father, Son and Holy Spirit.

"This is what the Lord says: 'Cursed is the one who trusts in man, who depends on flesh for his strength and whose heart turns away from the Lord. He will be like a bush in the wastelands; he will not see prosperity when it comes. He will dwell in the parched places of the desert, in a salt land where no one lives. But blessed is the man who trusts in the Lord, whose confidence is in him. He will be like a tree planted by the water that sends out its roots by the stream. It does not fear when heat comes; its leaves are always green. It has no worries in a year of drought and never fails to bear fruit.'" (Jeremiah 17: 5-8)

It is time for us to stop listening to people instead of listening to God. This does not mean that there are not godly people who give good counsel; it rather means that we offend God when we hang on every word of a man or a woman and do not put God first and test through the guidance of the Holy Spirit the words of people. We are foolish and we sin when we blindly follow anyone other than God. In these times it is becoming ever more difficult to truly discern good from evil, God's will from self-will and the will of other people who do not hear God. The Lord is calling us to places and times of quiet, to studying and praying God's Word, to listening to the Holy Spirit who yearns to tell us about Jesus, about the Father, and about God's love – for the Holy Spirit is indeed the living Love of God and God Himself. God actually seeks to communicate personally with each of us. We are also instructed to listen to the voice of His Church – though as denominations and "non-denominations" proliferate it is becoming more confusing to recognize that clear voice that communicates God's revelation and God's will.

We can fool ourselves about the strength of our spiritual life, but we cannot fool God. The section from Jeremiah quoted earlier has two verses following it that are timeless in their depth and importance: *"The heart is deceitful above all things and beyond cure. Who can understand it? I, the Lord, search the heart and examine the mind, to reward a man according to his conduct, according to what his deeds deserve."*

Finally, do I, contrary to the admonition of Proverbs 3: 5-7, forget God in my daily life of work and homemaking and fun and trials and triumphs and sorrows and joys?

> *"Can papyrus grow tall where there is no marsh? Can reeds thrive without water? While still growing and uncut, they wither more quickly than grass. Such is the destiny of all who forget God; so perishes the hope of the godless. What he trusts in is fragile; what he relies on is a spider's web. He leans on his web, but it gives way; he clings to it, but it does not hold. He is like a well-watered plant in the sunshine, spreading its shoots over the garden; it entwines its roots around a pile of rocks and looks for a place among the stones. But when it is torn from its spot, that place disowns it and says, 'I never saw you.' Surely its life withers away, and from the soil other plants grow."* (Job 8: 11-19)

Could it be that I am like that plant, seemingly well-grounded, living in sunshine, but really without any true foundation, no real roots? Will Jesus possibly say to me one day, *"Be gone, I never knew you."?* Not to the real Christian, He won't!

And, so, we conclude by focusing on the great need in each of our lives: To seek the Lord. Hosea expressed it this way: *Sow for yourselves, reap the fruit of unfailing love, and break up your unplowed ground; for it is time to seek the Lord, until he comes and showers righteousness on you."* (Hosea 10: 12) Paul wrote it this way in Romans: *"Therefore, brothers, we have an obligation – but it is not to the sinful nature, to live according to it. For if you live according to the sinful nature, you will die; but if by the Spirit you put to death the misdeeds of the body, you will live; because those who are led by the Spirit of God are the sons of God."* (Romans 8: 12-14) Moreover, this is how Paul puts it in Philippians: *"But whatever was to my profit I now consider loss for the sake of Christ. What is more, I consider everything a loss compared to the surpassing greatness of knowing Christ Jesus my Lord, for whose sake I have lost all things. I consider them rubbish, that I may gain Christ and be found in him, not having a righteousness of my own that comes from the law, but that which is through faith in Christ – the righteousness that comes from God and is by faith. I want to know Christ and the power of his resurrection and the fellowship of sharing in his sufferings, becoming like him in his death, and so, somehow, to attain to the resurrection from the dead.* (Philippians 3: 7-11)

Jesus said it simply and profoundly: *"Come, follow me."* (Matthew 4: 19)

SUMMARY FOR REFLECTION AND DISCUSSION:

A real Christian:

1) Seeks the Lord in all things, seeks the Holy Spirit's guidance in all decisions, seeks to follow Jesus every minute of every day;
2) Does not fall into the modern trap of taking pride in "doing things my way," but only wants to do things Jesus' way;
3) Recognizes that leaning on one's own understanding is the pathway to misery and ultimate failure.
4) Knows that the things of this world are passing and only the things of heaven are lasting.

SCRIPTURES FOR JOURNALING:

1) Proverbs 3: 5-7 (Delve deeply into the richness of meaning);
2) Isaiah 31: 1-7; Jeremiah 17: 5-8; Luke 12: 49-53;
3) Job 8: 11-19; Romans 8: 12-14; Philippians 3: 7-11.

REFLECTION 9:

PSALM 3

What does this Psalm, this prayer of the Old (and New) Testament Church, have to do with being a real Christian? Much! First, read it thoughtfully and prayerfully:

"O Lord, how many are my foes! How many rise up against me! Many are saying of me, 'God will not deliver him.' But you are a shield around me, O Lord; you bestow glory on me and lift up my head. To the Lord I cry aloud, and he answers me from his holy hill. I lie down and sleep. I wake again, because the Lord sustains me. I will not fear the tens of thousands drawn up against me on every side. Arise, O Lord! Deliver me, O my God! Strike all my enemies on the jaw; break the teeth of the wicked. From the Lord comes deliverance. May your blessing be on your people."

OK, now let's focus: Verse 3 is magnificent. Consider two translations: *"But you are a shield around me, O Lord; you bestow glory on me and lift up my head."* (NIV) *"But thou, O Lord, art a shield for me, my glory and the lifter up of mine head."* (KJV)

Both clearly point to three weapons in the arsenal of the Old Testament Israelite and the New Testament Christian – weapons made incredibly more powerful in the New because of the risen and glorious Messiah.

1) SHIELD: It is a word we certainly understand today but one we perhaps do not appreciate as much as did the soldiers of ancient times. In the days of the Old Testament, the shield was in important and generally effective – thought at times crude – defensive weapon. God spoke of the shield in spiritual terms, when He said to the father of the Jewish people, *"Do not be afraid, Abram, I am your shield, your very great reward."* (Genesis 15: 1) In 2 Samuel 22: 1-3, we read: *"David sang to the Lord the words of this song when the Lord delivered him from the hand of all his enemies and from the hand of Saul. He said: 'The Lord is my rock, my fortress and my deliverer; my God is my rock, in whom I take refuge, my shield and the horn of my salvation."* And we discover the shield again in Psalm 28: 6-7: *"Praise be to the Lord, for he has heard my cry for mercy. The Lord is my strength and my shield; my heart trusts in him, and I am helped. My heart leaps for joy and I will give thanks to him in song."*

It is clear from these verses that the inspired writers used the word "shield" to describe the protective love of God toward those who trusted in Him and were faithful to Him. The word was highly descriptive to people in those often battle-weary times, and it brought to mind images of soldiers on the battlefield carrying shields of various sizes based on need – from quite large ones for protecting the entire body, to small ones for use in hand-to-hand combat. King Solomon, who received a "salary" of 25 tons of gold annually (1 Kings 10: 14), once ordered to be constructed two hundred large shields (each of 7+ pounds of hammered gold) and three hundred small shields (each just under 4 pounds of the same precious material). These were placed in his palace and were probably used for decoration and for gifts. On the battlefield shields were normally wooden frames covered with leather, brass or copper. In battle, soldiers needed two types of weapons – offensive and defensive ones – and the shield served as the primary defensive weapon.

A good example of this can be found in the familiar story of David and Goliath (1 Samuel 17). Twice, as the description of the Philistine warriors is provided in the account, there is reference to a shield bearer. The large shields were normally carried by people

Will the Real Christians Please Stand Up!

who had been given this task; they handed them over to the soldiers at time of battle. Scripture tells us that Goliath's armor weighed 125 pounds, and that just the iron point of his spear weighed 15 pounds. Imagine what a job his shield bearer had carrying around a shield to protect this man who stood over 9 feet tall! As David challenged the warrior and approached him, verses 41-42 tell us, *"Meanwhile, the Philistine, with his shield bearer in front of him, kept coming closer to David. He looked David over and saw that he was only a boy, ruddy and handsome, and he despised him."* It is not stated, and it is a fact usually overlooked, that Goliath was apparently so confident of his prowess and so disdainful of this stripling of an Israelite that he did not bother to take the shield from his shield bearer! It was a fatal mistake. David, on the other hand, who had refused to wear the armor of an Israeli soldier, because it weighted him down too much, trusted in God, found the shield of the Almighty walking with him, and prevailed in the name of the Lord and for the glory of God.

In the New Testament, there is a significant reference to the armor of that day in Ephesians 6: 10-18. Paul writes of spiritual warfare, stating emphatically that for the Christian *"our struggle is not against flesh and blood, but against the rulers, against the authorities, against the powers of this dark world, and against the spiritual forces of evil in the heavenly realm."* He then urges us to put on God's armor; and that armor includes a shield – *"the shield of faith,"* he writes, *"with which you can extinguish all the flaming arrows of the evil one."* The enemy is Satan and his demonic hordes. The shield with which to ward of their attacks is faith – faith in the love, power and presence of the Lord. It should be clear here that the life of every Christian includes spiritual attacks. We are at war. The fact that so many people of our time, including some Christians, laugh at the idea of Satan and spiritual warfare is actually verification of the wiles and deceit of our archenemy. The truth is that without spiritual awareness of what is really going on around and without a response with the help of grace we will fall victim to Satan's devices. We will lose effectiveness as Christians; we will, frankly, not be "real Christians," for every committed Christian puts on and uses the armor, both the defensive and offensive weapons that we are called to bear against the enemy – in order that the Church may triumph, that souls be saved, and that God may be glorified.

2) GLORY: One rather formal but accurate definition of glory is that it is "the exercise and display of what constitutes the distinctive excellence of the subject about which it is spoken." ("The New Ungers Bible Dictionary," Moody Press) (Whew!) What is God's glory? It is the manifestation of His attributes, His presence, His very being.

Some Scriptures: *"Arise, shine, for your light has come; and the glory of the Lord rises upon you. See, darkness covers the earth and thick darkness is over the peoples, but the Lord rises upon you and his glory appears over you."* (Isaiah 60: 1-2) This messianic prophecy was fulfilled when the Light of the World, Jesus Christ, appeared. When Jesus was born, an angel appeared to nearby shepherds. After his announcement that the Messiah had come, the heavenly host joined the angel and said, *"Glory to God in the highest, and on earth peace to men on whom his favor rests."* (Luke 2: 14) In the early days of the Hebrews, after their deliverance from Egypt, Moses went up the mountain to receive the Ten Commandments. (One of my favorite cartoons shows Moses coming down with three tablets, dropping one and saying "Here are God's Fifteen – Whoops, Ten – Commandments. I confess: It is my sick humor coming out!)

Exodus 24: 15 states that when Moses went up that mountain, the glory of God covered it in the form of a cloud. Then Exodus 34: 29-33 describes Moses coming down (after he ascended it a second time to receive the tablets again following the punishment of those who had been worshiping a golden calf instead of the Lord): We read that his face was shining because he had been in the presence of God, and he had to wear a veil. This is not some fairy tale in a far distant time and land; this is a description of God and a man in His presence – the God who is the same yesterday, today, and forever. Think about this: Christians today have more intimate contact with God than Moses did; for we have the awesome gift of God dwelling within us! Why does not my face shine with His glory? Why do I seem so often to take His presence and His holiness for granted?

2 Chronicles 5: 13-14 describes what happened when the Ark of the Covenant was brought to the newly constructed Temple for the

dedication. *"Then the Temple of the Lord was filled with a cloud, and the priests could not perform their service because of the cloud, for the glory of the Lord filled the Temple of God."* Again, how about us? We are living temples of God! John, in the magnificent prologue to his Gospel, writes: *"The Word became flesh and made his dwelling among us. We have seen his glory, the glory of the One and Only, who came from the Father, full of grace and truth."* (John 1: 14) John also records some of the final words of Jesus before His Passion: *"And now, Father, glorify me in your presence with the glory I had with you before the world began."* (John 17: 5) And, of course, John could write with confidence of Jesus' glory because he was one of the witnesses to the Lord's Transfiguration, when Moses and Elijah appeared to Him, and His clothes and countenance became dazzling white. John surely began to understand that Jesus, a Man in the flesh, was also God, full of eternal glory. It was again perhaps John who, as an elderly and persecuted Christian, was privileged to see heaven open and to write about it in the Book of Revelation.

Chapter 5: 11-14 preserves for us a beautiful portion of that vision: *"Then I looked and heard the voice of many angels, numbering thousands upon thousands, and ten thousand times ten thousand. They encircled the throne and the living creatures and the elders. In a loud voice they sang: 'Worthy is the Lamb, who was slain, to receive power and wealth and wisdom and strength and honor and glory and praise!' Then I heard every creature in heaven and on earth and under the earth and on the sea, and all that is in them, singing: 'To him who sits on the throne and to the Lamb be praise and honor and glory and power, forever and ever!' The four living creatures said, 'Amen,' and the elders fell down and worshiped."* And, more good news: Paul, in Colossians 3: 3 writes that *"When Christ, who is your life, appears, then you will also appear with him in glory."* Paul again in Romans 8: 18: *I consider that our present sufferings are not worth comparing with the glory that will be revealed in us."* Finally, in 2 Corinthians 4: 17: *"...our light and momentary troubles are achieving for us an eternal glory that outweighs them all.*

Thus, God's revealed Word tells us that 1) His essence is glory (light, holiness, awesome splendor, 2) Jesus is the supreme manifestation of God's glory on this earth, 3) there is an overwhelming celebration of glory in heaven going on right now, 4) it is our promised home if we remain faithful to Jesus, and 5) the glory of God is with and within us right now and we are called to manifest it through our lives in order to bring light to a dark and lost world.

In other words, just as the shield is our primary defensive weapon, the glory of God living in His Word and living within us who are living temples constitutes our primary offensive weapon. Both are important.

3) LIFTER OF MY HEAD: More marvelous news: God Himself is the lifter of my head if I place my trust in Him. That means He gives me hope, and He gives me comfort. It means that we can take to ourselves the words of the prophet Elisha: *"Don't be afraid. Those who are with us are more than those who are with them."* (2 Kings 6: 16) The Bible is replete with examples of God loving, guiding, forgiving, protecting, promising, delivering – and then finally God became Man, the Word became flesh and dwelt among us to show us the infinitely amazing love of God in action. He walked in ministry without a place to lay His head so that He could lift ours to new life; and He finally laid His thorn-ravaged head on the hard wood of a cross so that we could find ultimate hope and peace and, finally, eternal salvation.

We have the shield; we have the glory; we have One to lift our heads. So it is that Paul prays for us – for you and for me: *"...we have not stopped praying for you asking God to fill you with the knowledge of his will through all spiritual wisdom and understanding. And we pray this in order that you may live a life worthy of the Lord and may please him in every way: bearing fruit in every good work, growing in the knowledge of God, being strengthened with all power according to his glorious might so that you may have great endurance and patience, and joyfully giving thanks to the Father, who has qualified you to share in the inheritance of the saints in the kingdom of light. For he has rescued us from the dominion of darkness and brought us into the kingdom of the Son he loves, in whom we have redemption, the forgiveness of sins.* (Colossians 1: 9-14)

As we look around us in this modern world we live in, we see

Will the Real Christians Please Stand Up!

so many brightly shining and appealing baubles of the material world; yet, they cannot be compared with the glory of the Kingdom of Heaven. It seems fitting to close this joyful and hopeful and triumphant reflection with the words of an unknown author:

"God is like the Ford...He has a better idea.
God is like Coke...He's the real thing.
God is like Pan Am (remember them?)...He makes the going great.
God is like Pepsi...He has a lot to give.
God is like Standard Oil...You expect more from Him and you get it.
God is like Dial Soap...Aren't you glad you know Him? Don't you wish everybody did?
God is like Alka Seltzer...Try Him, you'll like Him.
God is like Bayer Aspirin...He takes the pain away.
God is like Hallmark Cards...He cared enough to send the very best.
God is like Tide...He gets the stains that others leave behind.
God is like VO-5 Hair Spray...He holds through all kinds of weather.
God is like a Mattel toy...You can tell He's swell.
God is like Frosted Flakes...He's GRRRRRRRREAT!!"

SUMMARY FOR REFLECTION AND DISCUSSION:

A real Christian:

1) Sees with spiritual eyes the spiritual warfare that is part of the Christian life;
2) Also sees the spiritual weapons available, which include a shield and the glory of God;
3) Travels through life with hope and joy and peace, knowing that the Father, Son and Holy Spirit are present as the lifter of one's head;
4) Recognizes the power of Scripture and incorporates it into daily life;

Will the Real Christians Please Stand Up!

SCRIPTURES FOR JOURNALING:

1) Psalm 3 (again, explore deeply);
2) 1 Samuel 17; Ephesians 6: 10-18 (examples of "shield");
3) 2 Chronicles 5: 13-14; Revelation 5: 11-14 (examples of "glory");
4) 2 Kings 6: 16 (example of "lifter");
5) Colossians 1: 9-14.

REFLECTION 10:

LIFESTYLE OF THE "REAL CHRISTIAN"

We have been looking at "real Christianity" from a variety of perspectives. Let's now hit it head on.

The Bible never ceases to amaze. Just when we think that we might have at least a basic grasp of content and meaning, new revelations burst forth like a meteor flashing through the night sky. I can absolutely guarantee that you and I can never plumb the depths of the Word, can never exhaust the riches of the Scriptures – for the Bible is the Living Word of God, authored by the Holy Spirit, an expression of the mind of God, and God is infinite. For all eternity, if we are with Him, we will continue to explore and find awesome treasure. What an absolutely marvelous gift! All we must do is approach the Bible with humility, with a belief that it is God's Revelation, with a desire to learn from the Holy Spirit, with a firm conviction that God speaks to us through the Bible – that this Book is totally unique in that it is a living Word speaking every time we read it – and that the Spirit will give us insights, wisdom, direction and strength.

I share two examples in this reflection (please take time to come up with your own by seeking insights from the Holy Spirit). First, a recent one: I was in a time of prayer and had been reflecting on the Garden of Gethsemane – not long after going to see "The Passion of

Will the Real Christians Please Stand Up!

the Christ." The Holy Spirit nudged me and told me to just be quiet and listen (not an easy thing for me in prayer). So I tried to be obedient, and after about five minutes I saw something in the Garden account that I had never grasped before. This was the only time in the history of mankind in which God asked humans to pray for Him! Think about it: Jesus was wrestling, in His human nature, with fear and above all with the loathing of taking on the sins of every person – past, present, future – and He turned to the three friends He had asked to accompany Him into the Garden. But they were asleep. They blew it. But, the Holy Spirit was not finished. He then reminded me that Jesus lives on in the Body of Christ, and every day I have the opportunity to serve Him by serving others. But, how often am I asleep, wrapped up in myself, in moments of need? Wow! I am not deep enough to come up with that on my own; the Holy Spirit used the Word, His presence, and a mind and heart trying to be open to give a new revelation to a familiar Biblical account.

The second example is actually two chapters of Luke's Gospel account – 18 and 19. They are a slice of Jesus' life and ministry as recorded by Doctor Luke, under the inspiration of the Holy Spirit. The passage relates certain events and teachings of Jesus, some common to other Gospels and some peculiar to Luke's account. While I was reading those chapters one day, knowing that I had read them many times before, the Holy Spirit showed me something very special. Instead of seeing separate events, I saw a composite of a teaching – even though it was obviously not the original or primary intent of these Scriptures. I realized that the chapters describe, in a very vivid and beautiful way, what the life of a real Christian is all about. So, let's become explorers of the Word and discover some new and uncharted depths.

Luke 18 and 19 record events toward the end of Jesus' public ministry, as He was making a resolute journey to the cross. There is an increased sense of urgency in His teaching, in His contacts, in His exhortations, for He knew that His time was short. I encourage you to stop here, take your Bible, and read – carefully and prayerfully – the 18th and 19th chapters of the Gospel according to Luke. In these chapters we can find some key attributes of a true Christian's life.

Will the Real Christians Please Stand Up!

1) <u>Continuous prayer</u> (Luke 18: 1-8): Jesus told His disciples the parable of the persistent widow. As the Word states, He did this *"to show them that they* (we) *should always pray and not give up."* Jesus ends this story – about the lady who kept after the judge until he granted her justice against her adversary – by saying, *"And will not God bring about justice for his chosen ones, who cry to him day and night? Will he keep putting them off? I tell you he will see that they get justice, and quickly. However, when the Son of Man comes, will he find justice on the earth?"*

This is powerful teaching! Guess who the "chosen ones" are? Real Christians, ones not in name only – whether Protestants or Catholics or Orthodox, people who are washed in the Blood, who have accepted Jesus as their Savior and Lord and have become members of the Church, the Body of Christ, and who have set the course of their lives in a determination to be yielded and obedient to Him. So, one description of the "real Christian" is that she and he are people who cry out to God day and night, who heed Jesus and also Paul who wrote that we are to pray without ceasing. This means journeying through life in awareness of our relationship with God (Father, Son and Holy Spirit) and of our calling to be people of prayer (worship, thanksgiving, repentance and intercession) as the Body of Christ on earth. It means that we seek to have daily times of prayer, not as a duty but a joy, because we are communicating with the Beloved. Yet, it means more than that. It means we are called to be people of prayer throughout the day, every day – and that is truly possible. Obviously, we live in a busy world, most of us, and there are many duties and responsibilities at home and at work. But we can, with the help of the Holy Spirit, develop an "attitude of prayer," based on an awareness that we are always in the presence of God as living temples. Thus, we can be sensitive to calls to prayer – communication with God – even in the midst of other activities. The sight of a beautiful tree, of a baby, or of a sunset brings internal exclamations of praise and thanksgiving. Hearing about or reading the news about famine or war, about a person on death row, about people suffering or inflicting suffering prompts immediate intercession. Seeing a friend, work associate, or family member hurting or without a relationship with God causes

Will the Real Christians Please Stand Up!

quiet prayer at that very moment. Experience of pain, sickness, disappointment, or a sharp word or snub from someone brings forth a prayer for others who are similarly hurting somewhere in the world – and immediate forgiveness of and prayer for the person who hurt us. Thus it is that every day is an exciting adventure and opportunity to make an impact in the world. God has made it clear that He has chosen to touch people's lives through the faithful and loving prayers of His followers. Our prayers are mighty, not because we in ourselves are special, but because God has given us both a commission and the grace to fulfill it. When we pray, as guided by the Holy Spirit (and I have come to learn that random, distracting thoughts are a call to pray) our prayer as members of the Church in some mysterious and actual way becomes the prayer of the Mediator, the great High Priest, Jesus Christ – and the Father always listens to His Son!

Another note: Obviously, not all of our prayers appear to be answered. If a loved one is ill, or if we are having a problem of some kind, and prayer does not seem to be having results, does that mean that the Word is wrong, that I do not have enough faith, that I am in some kind of sin and therefore ineffective in prayer? Well, to be sure, we need to explore the latter two possibilities with the Lord. But – and I state this with all possible conviction – do not listen to those who may tell you that if there is an illness or some other problem and prayer is not working it automatically means there is something wrong in your relationship with God. I repeat: Prayer from the heart, under the guidance of the Holy Spirit and therefore in keeping with God's will, is always heard and always bears fruit. But that fruit may not be what we expect or when we hope to receive it. Christians who, regardless of good intentions, put guilt trips on people by proclaiming that they have already received what they obviously do not have, or by telling or intimating to them that there must be a faith or sin problem blocking God's grace, are not speaking for God. I have seen many people hurt because of this misapplication of the Word of God. God is sovereign and infinitely wise; He knows what is best, and when. A prayer for healing, for example, while it may not result in a healing now or ever in this life, will certainly result in renewed strength and hope and purpose when it is received with a yielded spirit. Internal healing – the interior fruit of the Holy Spirit – is far more important than physical healing. And, of course, the good news is that the prayer for healing (or release from some other difficulty) will ultimately be answered for the true Christian – if not on this earth, then in the eternal home of heaven. We see things from the perspective of time; God sees them from that of eternity.

2) <u>A state of repentance and awareness of my sinfulness:</u> (Luke 18: 9-14) Jesus then told the parable of the Pharisee and the tax collector. The proud, sophisticated, urbane "man of God" loudly proclaimed a prayer of thanksgiving that he was not like the scum of the earth, including the tax collector who was invading his space. The tax collector, a member of a despised group of Jews hired by the Romans, just beat his breast and begged God to be merciful to him, a sinner. Now let's not lose sight of something: The tax collector <u>was</u> a sinner; he was not displaying a false humility. The real difference between the two was that one recognized his sinfulness and the other one did not.

Do I recognize the horror of sin? Do I recognize that I am a sinner? John wrote that the person who says he or she is without sin is a liar. (I John 1: 8) The whole point of the masterful movie, "The Passion of the Christ" was what Jesus endured for our sins, and because of them. John the Baptist prepared the way for the public ministry of Jesus by crying out to the people to repent – so that they would recognize the coming of the Messiah. Every prophet in the Old Testament had the mission to call people to repentance. The first "sermon" of Jesus was to repent because the Kingdom of God was (is) at hand. The call to repent is not just for unbelievers; it is the cry to and within the heart of every believer as well. John writes in his first Letter that if we say we sin not, we are liars. But he also writes that we have Jesus as our Mediator. I listened to a message some years ago; it was a teaching by an evangelist. In the tape he proclaimed, even bragged, that since he had a relationship with Jesus Christ he had no need to ever repent again, no need to ask forgiveness for sins. Some of this man's teachings were excellent; but this one veered far off the path of true Christian doctrine. If I do not see a need to regularly repent, I have become like the Pharisee in Jesus' parable.

Every true Christian proclaims as absolutely true that sin is the greatest of horrors. It is the creature saying 'No!" to the Creator and "Yes!" to oneself. It is the ultimate idolatry, setting oneself up as an object of worship rather than God. John ends his first Letter with the short, abrupt plea, "Little children, stay away from idols." Idolatry is unfortunately alive and well today. Idols do not have to be images of stone or wood or precious metals; the worst and most destructive idolatry is the elevation of the self above God.

So, it is indeed true, as Paul writes forcefully, that only when I bow before the Lord, admit my sinfulness and need for redemption, and accept Him as my Savior that I begin walking on the fork of the path leading to eternal salvation. Even though I stumble and fall, I believe that as long as I am aware of helplessness without God, as long as I keep returning to Him, as long as I genuinely seek His guidance and inspiration and to do His will, I will be clay in the Master Potter's hands, and His plan for my life will be accomplished.

If a critical step is choosing to become a Christian – accepting Jesus Christ as Savior – then an important next step is to make a commitment to make Him Lord of my life, day in and day out. Paul's writings were the instrument used by the Holy Spirit to teach us God's truths about faith. On the other hand, when we focus on the teachings of Jesus, we find a very strong emphasis on the importance of His followers bearing fruit, as well as, of course, an emphasis on faith. Think, for example, of the fig tree He cursed because it did not bear fruit and of His proclamation on the night before He died that we must abide in Him, remain in Him, if we are to bear fruit. Think about the parable of the sower and the seed, of the fields ripe for harvest, of the parable of the sheep and the goats and the emphasis on serving our fellow men and women. Think of His challenge to us to be willing to give up all and follow Him.

The Christian life begins with an awareness of sin and our separation from God, with Jesus as the bridge to life with God. The Christian journey continues with us seeking to follow and serve, asking the Holy Spirit to tell us about Jesus and His will. When we fall, God's grace is there to help us rise. It is a glorious, challenging journey for the real Christian – who recognizes that she and he can only bear fruit by yielding to the guidance and grace of God. God does not forsake us, He does not abandon us; He is always right here to strengthen hearts open to His love and forgiveness and His will.

The closer we come to God, the more we recognize God's utter holiness and our sinfulness and unworthiness in and of ourselves to be in His presence. It is not at all a contradiction to be a member of God's family, to be a temple in which the Holy Spirit (and thus also the Father and Son) lives, to have the righteousness from grace that Paul writes about, and at the same time to be weak and sinful vessels. Therein lie the great love and power and majesty of God!

3) <u>The heart of a child</u> (Luke 18: 15-17): The apostles were rebuking people for letting their children bother Jesus (reminiscent of bodyguards protecting some TV evangelists!). But Jesus in turn rebuked the apostles and took the children in His arms. This was Jesus' love in action; He also seized the opportunity to teach a lesson. Jesus said very plainly that the only people who will be part of the Kingdom of God are those who accept it with a child's heart. Note the word "only." That is quite a dogmatic statement, and it is from the mouth of the Incarnate Son of God, God Himself. Now, we know that children can be selfish, demanding, short sighted, and even cruel (as can adults). Jesus was not talking about those qualities that are part and parcel of a fallen human nature. Rather, He was talking about trust and an awareness of need and dependency. Jesus, and His Father and the Holy Spirit, seek people who recognize that we are totally dependent upon God for life itself, for redemption, for any good that we do or receive. The Persons of the Trinity seek people who believe in God's goodness and sovereign power and trust that His love will prevail. Our challenge is to have the loving, trusting heart of a child every minute of every day, with the help of God's grace. It is not "I did it my way," but "I did it His way."

4) <u>Walking the talk</u> (Luke 18: 18-30): In these verses we read the account of the rich man who asked how to inherit eternal life. Jesus referred him to the Commandments. The man replied that he had kept them from his youth. So, Jesus looked at him (Mark's account of this event states that Jesus, looking at him, loved him) and challenged him. He said: *"You still lack one thing. Sell everything you have and give to the poor, and you will have treasure in heaven.*

Then come, follow me." The man went away sad, for he had many possessions. Jesus then went on to shock His apostles by telling them that it was hard for a rich person to enter heaven. Now, don't indulge in a big sigh of relief if you are not wealthy! And, do not despair if you have a yacht or two! Jesus is saying something critically important, applicable to each and every one of us. He is not talking about the amount of money and goods that we possess; He is talking about our attitude toward whatever those possessions might be. The poor person who grasps and clings fiercely to whatever he or she has or dreams of having is in no less difficulty than the rich person who does the same. For the true Christian, the perspective is, I may or may not be wealthy; but my riches in Christ are far superior to and more important than any worldly wealth or lack thereof. This passage does not mean that you and I must immediately sell everything we have in order to be citizens of heaven. It could mean that for some, when God calls for it specifically; it certainly meant that for the man in the Gospel account. But what it does mean for each of us is a willingness to give all up – possessions, dreams, everything. It is based on the realization, by grace, that everything we have is given by God, no matter how hard we worked for it. It means we recognize that all material possessions are temporary and fleeting; it means that we want with all our hearts all and only what God wants for us. If there is anything in my life that is so important to me that it interferes with my relationship to or service of the Lord, then it must go. If I recognize the problem and choose to do nothing about it, then I have in effect proclaimed that I choose myself and my desires rather than God and His – and that makes me something other than a "real Christian." So, it is something to seriously pray about. I urge each of us to find some quiet time and to lay everything we have, and are, before the throne of God and say, in effect, "Lord, everything is from You, and I give it back. I only want what You want; please give me guidance and the strength to serve You by doing Your perfect will." In that submission comes the greatest of all possessions and the greatest of all joys.

5) <u>Spiritual vision</u> (Luke 18: 35-43): Chapter 18 ends with the account of the blind man at Jericho. Hearing that Jesus was passing by where he was seated as a beggar at the roadside, he cried out,

"Jesus, Son of David, have mercy on me!" People standing nearby told him to be quiet, but, undaunted, he cried out again and more loudly. Jesus heard him, stopped, and asked the sightless man who had been given the grace to see the love and power of Jesus in his heart what he wanted. The reply was simple, yet a profound exclamation of courage, faith and hope: *"Lord, I want to see."* Jesus' reply was instantaneous and commanding: *"Receive your sight; your faith has healed you."* And notice what the man, now seeing physically as well as spiritually, did: He praised God, and he followed Jesus. All of the people who witnessed the miracle also praised God. That blind man is I, and that blind man is you. I am sitting by the roadside, and I know that Jesus is nearby. I might say nothing, depressed over my situation, believing that no one can help me. I might cry out once but then lapse back into silence because people will find me annoying or even think I am crazy. I might stop hoping, because deep down I believe that God could not possibly be interested in someone as insignificant as I. Or, I might recognize that Jesus is looking at me with love, asking me to trust Him and to reach out to Him. You see, wherever we are in our spiritual walk, there are elements of blindness that the Light of the world wants to remove. I can always learn more, especially in my heart, about God and His love. There are always new depths of relationship and service possible in my life – and new depths of peace and joy and spiritual fulfillment. As I realize this, my prayer becomes: "Lord, help me to see – You, and life, and what You want me to do in service to You and other people." And when new sight comes, it results in praise and following Jesus ever more closely and consistently. Is that my heart's desire? It is if I am a real Christian!

6) <u>A sense of urgency</u> (Luke 19: 1-10): The account of Zacchaeus, a chief tax collector (and therefore, a Jew despised by other Jews) really deserves an entire reflection on its own. But for our purposes here, let's focus on a few critical points regarding the Christian walk: Zacchaeus was determined to see Jesus. In fact, he was so determined that he made a fool of himself by climbing a sycamore tree in order to see Jesus passing by. Zacchaeus was a short man, as well as a sinner (I can identify with both qualities!)

and he climbed the tree in order to be able to see over the crowd. Jesus stopped, looked up (and probably smiled) and told Zacchaeus to come down because He wanted to dine in his house. Zacchaeus responded immediately with joy, followed by repentance. Many of the bystanders grumbled because Jesus was going to the home of a sinner – a strong reminder of how easy it is to fall into judgmentalism. Zacchaeus promised restitution of his gains obtained by greed; and Jesus rejoiced and said that salvation had come to this household. This is the only time we meet Zacchaeus; but there can be little doubt that another tax collector became a committed disciple of Jesus. The key for Christians here is the clear message that we are called at times to be fools for Christ! If Zacchaeus had not climbed that tree, nothing would have happened. If I really love Jesus, I will do anything and everything I can to grow closer to Him; it will be a consuming passion. Further, I will immediately follow His guiding when He asks me to share the Good News or reach out to people in need. The true Christian has a sense of urgency. Also, the theme of repentance repeats here. Woe to me if I become puffed up and feel that I have it made and am one of the elite. There will always be a need in my life to make restitution. But the glorious news is that when I do indeed have a sense of urgency, when I reach out, when I seek God, when I do what is right even though some people will grumble (the religious ones and the worldly ones), salvation will come to people around me because God can use me as He wants to – and that is what the Christian life is all about.

7) Use my gifts (Luke 19: 11-27): Here we find the parable of the three servants and their use of the money given them by their master as he was leaving for a journey. Two invested the money, but the third buried his in the ground because he was afraid. The lesson is *"I tell you that to everyone who has, more will be given, but as for the one who has nothing, even what he has will be taken away."* Again, there is much meat here. The overriding message for the Christian is this: We are called to use the gifts that God has given us, to the very best of our ability, for the sake of the Master. We all have gifts – every one of us. God does not want us to compare our gifts with others, for that is foolish and useless. He has given to

each person according to His divine plan, and it does not matter in God's sight whether the glass is small or large, only that it is full. When I enter into a personal relationship with Jesus Christ and the Holy Spirit begins working in my life, I receive spiritual gifts and the natural ones I already have become refined for spiritual purposes. From that moment on, every gift, talent, action, word, breath is to be used for the glory of God and the spreading of the Kingdom. Period!

8) <u>Follow Jesus all the way</u> (Luke 19-28-40): The account of the entry of Jesus into Jerusalem, for the last time before His death, has been memorialized in many churches by the celebration of Palm Sunday, the Sunday before Easter. Jesus rode a donkey into town, to fulfill the prophecy of Zechariah (and this was the King of Kings, riding into His city on a humble beast of burden). The crowds, caught up in the emotion of the moment, hailed Him, waved palm branches, and proclaimed Him as the Messiah. Five days later, many were caught up in another emotional moment and were calling for the release of Barabbas and the death of Jesus. Then, on the hill of Golgotha, most of that crowd was nowhere to be seen. It is one thing to say that I am a Christian. It is quite another to follow Him with all my heart and mind and life. To truly follow Jesus the way He expects is radically different than what most people think and do. Follow Jesus totally, and there will be grumbling by others, there will be laughter at times, there will be discomfort, there will be criticism and even persecution – both by the world and, sadly, some members of the Church. It is one thing to follow Him when it is easy, to wave and sing when everyone else is doing it. It is quite another thing to follow Jesus when He is branded a criminal, or insane, or irrelevant and out of touch with "modern" times. Would I have been among the throng on Palm Sunday and would I have remained faithful on Good Friday? I do not have to know the answer to that; I just have to know how I will stand up for Him in the here and now, in church and at home and in the marketplace. Do I really follow Jesus, day in and day out, regardless of the consequences? I am echoing Billy Graham here, who once proclaimed during one of his crusades: "To take up the cross is to stand up for Jesus – at home, in the marketplace, every-

where, regardless of the consequences."

9) <u>Love the Church</u> (Luke 19: 41-44): Jesus wept over Jerusalem, the symbol and central focus of the Old Testament Church, for He was the long-awaited Messiah, the very reason that the Jewish people and the Temple in Jerusalem existed. Here He was, among His people, and He was being rejected by many as a charlatan or a rabble-rouser. But Jesus deeply loved the Church. Do I? Do I love the Church as the Living Body of Christ on this earth? Am I able as a Christian to look beyond my denomination or local church, even if I believe that it possesses the fullness of truth, and recognize that all believers are together the great Body of Christ and that we all have much more in common that we have differences? The real Christian is one who is able, by grace, to see the vision of the Church, composed of all believers who have accepted Jesus as Savior and who have made Him Lord of their lives. The real Christian weeps for the Church of our day while he and she also praise God for it. We weep because we see how religion has once again prevented the full glory of God from shining through; we rejoice, because we know that the Church will prevail, even if as the remnant of true believers. The real Christian recognizes the privilege and responsibility of being a member of the Church and walks through life with a sense of mission and purpose. This Christian prays daily for the Church, that Jesus Christ be glorified and revealed to the people in this world, hungering as they are for light and truth, that they find the Messiah, the living Lord, through His Church -- which means through the Holy Spirit anointing the members of the Body, teaching them about Jesus and conforming them ever more completely to His mind and heart.

10) <u>Thirst for holiness</u> (Luke 19: 45-46): Chapter 19 ends with Jesus cleaning out the Temple. Jesus had such a love for His Father, such an awareness of His holiness, that He could not tolerate turning the Temple – the Old Testament presence of God – into a marketplace, with buying and selling going on and little thought given to the presence, holiness and glory of God. I find it highly significant that John, in his Gospel account, puts this event at the beginning of Jesus' public ministry. John was much more interested in symbolism than in chronological detail. By telling the account of

the cleansing at the beginning, he was teaching, in effect, that Jesus was consumed by a passion for His Father and His will and that Jesus knew the Old Testament Temple would be replaced by the presence of God living within the hearts of His followers.

I am indeed a temple of God, if I am a true Christian, for God literally dwells within me. Do I thirst for holiness, to be as pure a dwelling place for the All-Holy God as possible? Do I permit anything unclean and unworthy of God into my temple – by what I choose to watch, where I go, what I think, what I do? A real Christian has a horror of sin, has an ever-growing awareness of just how holy God is, has a burning desire to glorify Him and serve Him, to the point that it is the number one goal in life. I confess that it is my daily prayer to grow in this awareness and passion and to overcome my tendencies to let my spiritual senses become dulled by the attractions and distractions of the world.

Thank you, Doctor Luke; thank you, Holy Spirit. Thank you for this description of true Christianity. Will we accept the challenge?

SUMMARY FOR REFLECTION AND DISCUSSION:

A real Christian:

1) Makes all of life a prayer;
2) Is acutely aware of sin and is repentant;
3) Has the trusting heart of a child;
4) Does not just talk about Christianity, but lives it heart and soul;
5) Has a clear vision of life and heaven, and has a mission and a passion to fulfill it;
6) Uses gifts from God fully and wisely;
7) Has a sense of urgency because of the fleeting nature of life and the many who are lost;
8) Understands and loves the Church, the Body of Christ;
9) Follows Jesus closely and totally, as the #1 priority;
10) Has a thirst for holiness, for an ever deepening relationship with Jesus Christ through the guiding of the Holy Spirit, for the glory of the Father.

SCRIPTURES FOR JOURNALING:

1) Prayerfully study Luke 18-19 and look for additional pearls of truth and wisdom. Also, check the related Scriptures in the margins.

REFLECTION 11:

THE BURNING HEART

In Luke 24, the two disciples who met the risen Jesus on the road to Emmaus said to one another after they recognized Him in the breaking of the bread, *"Were not our hearts burning within us while he talked with us on the road and opened the Scriptures to us?"* (Luke 24: 32) When we read the Word of God prayerfully and thoughtfully, in the belief that the Living Word is speaking to us, that the Holy Spirit is guiding us, we must logically ask ourselves an intimate and important question: Does my heart burn in and for the presence of Jesus? It may make us squirm a bit, but the fact is that only the real Christian can answer in the affirmative to that question. In fact, it is one of the most distinguishing characteristics of the true Christian.

We find the word "heart" used over 800 times in the Bible. Its meanings include: Center of one's natural condition; center of the spiritual nature; center of the moral life; a field for the seed of the divine Word; the center of feelings and affections; the dwelling place of Christ; the dwelling place of the Holy Spirit; the source of good and evil in one's thoughts, words and actions; a receptacle of the love of God; a closet for secret communion with God; the center of the entire person. (See The New Ungers Bible Dictionary, Moody Press)

No human heart ever burned with more love than the heart of Jesus; but no human heart was also united with a divine nature in a divine Person either. When Jesus cried out from the cross, *"I thirst,"* He was almost certainly speaking of a spiritual thirst for the salvation of mankind. To honor the heart of Jesus is to honor the Person; it is an expression of faith in His love and an expression of love in His faithfulness. It is not focusing on a heart; it is focusing on the immensity of divine love symbolized by the beating and pierced heart – which by the way is still beating in the Resurrected Jesus as the great High Priest at the right hand of the Father.

Let's do a brief word search of "heart" as it occurs in the Bible:

God spoke through Jeremiah, the weeping prophet, who said, *"The heart is deceitful above all things and beyond cure. Who can understand it? I the Lord search the heart and examine the mind, to reward a man according to his conduct, according to what his deeds deserve."* (Jeremiah 17: 9-10) It is very clear here that God consistently and continually searches our hearts; He knows exactly what motivates us, where our dreams and goals point, the innermost thoughts of our being. It is impossible to hide from God what we think, say and do. Am I conscious of that on a daily basis? Or do I, foolishly and futilely, like the poet, say "I fled him down the nights and down the days, I fled him down the labyrinth of my own mind"? (The Hound of Heaven)

There are numerous Scriptures that issue the challenge to give our whole heart to God. Here are some of them: *"Hear, O Israel: The Lord our God, the Lord is one. Love the Lord your God with all your heart and with all your soul and with all your strength. These commandments that I give to you today are to be upon your hearts."* (Deuteronomy 6: 4-6) *"So if you faithfully obey the commands I am giving you today – to love the Lord your God and to serve him with all your heart and with all your soul – then I will send rain on your land in its season, both autumn and spring rains, so that you may gather in your grain, new wine and oil. I will provide grass in the fields for your cattle, and you will eat and be satisfied. Be careful, or you will be enticed to turn away and worship other gods and bow down to them. Then the Lord's anger will burn against you, and he will shut the heavens so that it will not rain and the ground will yield no produce, and you will soon perish from the good land the Lord is giving you. Fix these words of*

Will the Real Christians Please Stand Up!

mine in your hearts and minds; tie them as symbols on your hands and bind them on your foreheads. Teach them to your children, talking about them when you sit at home and when you walk along the road, when you lie down and when you get up. Write them on the door frames of your houses and on your gates, so that your days and the days of your children may be many in the land that the Lord swore to give your forefathers, as many as the days that the heavens are above the earth." (Deuteronomy 11: 13-21) "*Blessed are they whose ways are blameless, who walk according to the law of the Lord. Blessed are they who keep his statutes and seek him with all their heart.*" (Psalm 119: 1-2) "*Trust in the Lord with all your heart and lean not on your own understanding; in all your ways acknowledge him, and he will make your paths straight.*" (Proverbs 3: 5-6) "*You will seek me and find me when you seek me with all your heart.*" (Jeremiah 29: 13) "*Even now,*" *declares the Lord,* "*return to me with all your heart, with fasting and weeping and mourning. Rend your heart and not your garments. Return to the Lord your God, for he is gracious and compassionate, slow to anger and abounding in love, and he relents from sending calamity*" (Joel 2: 12-13) "*Do not store up for yourselves treasure on earth, where moth and rust destroy, and where thieves break in and steal. But store up for yourselves treasures in heaven, where moth and rust do not destroy, and where thieves do not break in and steal. For where your treasure is, there your heart will be also.*" (Matthew 6: 19-21) "*'No servant can serve two masters. Either he will hate the one and love the other, or he will be devoted to the one and despise the other. You cannot serve both God and money.' The Pharisees, who loved money, heard all this and were sneering at Jesus. He said to them, 'You are the ones who justify yourselves in the eyes of men, but God knows your hearts. What is highly valued among men is detestable in God's sight.'*" (Luke 16: 13-15) "*Moses describes in this way the righteousness that is by the law: 'The man who does these things will live by them.' But the righteousness that is by faith says: 'Do not say in your heart, 'Who will ascend into heaven?' (that is, to bring Christ down) or 'Who will descend into the deep?' (that is, to bring Christ up from the dead). But what does it say? 'The word is near you; it is in your mouth and in your heart,' that is, the word of faith we are proclaiming: That if you confess with your mouth, 'Jesus is Lord,' and believe in your heart that God raised him from the dead, you will be saved. For it is with your heart that you believe and are justified, and it is with your mouth that you confess and are saved."* (Romans 10: 5-10.

These powerful Scriptures about the heart, straight from God as His revealed truth, show us that there is a definite relationship between the words "all" and "heart." In other words, for the real Christian there can be no middle ground, no compromise. We are called to give all to God – all our life, every thought, word and deed, every dream and hope, every talent and skill. For the Christian, the personal life mission statement must include and have as its very foundation the desire to put God first in all things. Anything that gets in the way of that is an idol, and anything and everything can be an idol – a career, a place of work, a hobby, a recreation, a person, an illness that causes self-focus instead of God-focus, a church when the focus is on attendance for the sake of attendance, on programs, numbers, a building. Anyone and anything can become an idol if it puts God – Father, Son and Holy Spirit – in the background and if it detracts from total service and commitment to the Christian walk.

When we consider spiritual warfare, the persistent onslaught by Satan and his demonic hordes to cause focus on world and self rather than God, we once again find the heart as a Biblical theme. Much of the history of the Old Testament is also a spiritual teaching on spiritual warfare (try reading the Psalms this way, when reference is made to destruction of foes). In Exodus 9-10, when Moses repeatedly confronted Pharaoh and there were signs and wonders done by God through Moses and Satanic ones permitted by God through Pharaoh's priests, we read time after time that *"Pharaoh's heart was hardened."*

"Hardening the heart," a commonly used phrase in our own vernacular, has a specific spiritual meaning in the Bible. It indicates success by the forces of evil in turning attention away from God's love and grace. We also find this in the New Testament, when we read that Satan hardened the heart of Judas – to the point that he betrayed his Master with a kiss and then committed suicide following realization of what he had done. In Ephesians 6, where we find the symbolism of putting on armor in the war against Satan, the instructions include putting on the "breastplate of righteousness" and standing firm. The breastplate protects the heart. It is crystal clear, therefore, that only righteousness – meaning a life of holiness, doing what is right, living totally committed to God – will protect the heart. And, of course, none of this is possible without God's grace. We are actually engaged in a life and death struggle, and it is all over the heart! To state it differently, and more positively: It is only by having the mind and heart of Jesus that we can stay true to our high calling; and unless our own hearts burn to be that close to Jesus, God's grace will not be able to penetrate, anoint, and guide.

I once saw someone wearing a tee shirt. The question on the front was "Do you have a hole in your heart?" On the back was the answer that "holes in the heart" are caused by abuse (by others or by self through, for example, drugs). How about it? Do you have a hole in your heart? Were you an abused child, are you an abused spouse? Have you been hurt by one you trusted and loved? Do you find yourself unable to forgive or are you consumed with jealousy? Have you been torn asunder by a divorce? Are you given to gossip, or backbiting? Do you have a sin in your past that you just do not think can be forgiven? If any of these examples, or similar ones, are true, then you need "open heart surgery", performed by Jesus and the Holy Spirit. There is absolutely nothing that cannot be forgiven (unless we refuse forgiveness); there is nothing that has happened that has to leave festering wounds or permanent scars. There is nothing, in other words, that has to build a wall separating us from a full life in and with God and with others. Satan tries to lie to us, tries to harden our hearts, tries to tell us that there is irreparable heart damage – but it is all just that, a lie. I can absolutely guarantee, based on my own experience with God's amazing grace and on the infallible Word of God, that Jesus walks the road with you right now, seeking to open your heart to Him and His saving truth and love and to fill you with joy unspeakable both now and for all eternity.

Psalm 22 is one of the great prophecies of the Bible: *"I am poured out like water, and all my bones are out of joint. My heart has turned to wax; it has melted away within me. My strength is dried up like a potsherd, and my tongue sticks to the roof of my mouth; you lay me in the dust of death. Dogs have surrounded me; a band of evil men has encircled me, they have pierced my hands and my feet. I can count all my bones; people stare and gloat over me. They divide my garments among them and cast lots for my clothing."* (Psalm 22: 14-18)

This amazing and poignant passage is a clear, detailed and specific description of the crucifixion of Jesus, written ages before it happened. Note the reference to the heart, as a powerful description of Jesus' suffering and agony on Golgotha. And, further, in John's account of the Passion, he writes that *"...when* (the soldiers) *came to Jesus and found that he was already dead, they did not break his legs. Instead, one of the soldiers pierced Jesus' side with a spear, bringing a sudden flow of blood and water.* (John 19: 33-34) The Lord Jesus, having loved us with every fiber of His being, gave His very last drop of blood, His heart literally and figuratively broken by our sins so that we might have life. Jesus never hardened His heart; He totally gave Himself to the Father and to us because we had hardened ours. We still harden them, but the grace of the Cross remains with us.

Can we ignore so great a love? The answer is yes. Thus, we must seek the Holy Spirit, the living Love of God, to soften our hearts and bring us to our knees. Let's make David's prayer our own: *"Create in me a pure heart, O God, and renew a steadfast spirit within me. Do not cast me from your presence or take your Holy Spirit from me. Restore to me the joy of your salvation and grant me a willing spirit to sustain me."* (Psalm 51: 10-12)

SUMMARY FOR REFLECTION AND DISCUSSION:

A real Christian:

1) Truly and genuinely seeks to have the heart and mind of Jesus Christ – to think, talk, and act like Him – this should be the consuming passion of the Christian life, more important than any other pursuit.
2) Has a repentant heart consistently, recognizing that we are all

sinners; even when we are temples of the living God, we still fail and fall short.

3) Never equates religiosity with spirituality – that is, never assumes that the center and essence of the Christian life is church programs or activities, never considers herself or himself better than others, always seeks to have a deeper relationship with Jesus and through Him with the Father and the Holy Spirit, never has the mind set of having "fully arrived" during this life but sees life as a journey of hearts turned toward God so that God can touch others through each Christian's life.

4) Has a "burning heart" when reading the Word of God and when entering into prayer time (not always a felt emotional high, but a distinctive act of the will seeking to know and love God ever more fully).

5) Has a deep yearning for revival in the Church, the Body of Christ, beginning with one's self (from the inside out), so that the Church may better show the love of Jesus to a hungry and thirsty world.

SCRIPTURES FOR JOURNALING:

1) Luke 24 (Emmaus)
2) Jeremiah 17: 9-10 and Jeremiah 29: 13 (and check for related Scriptures in Jeremiah and other prophets)
3) Deuteronomy 6: 4-6 (and compare with Matthew 22: 34-40)
4) Matthew 6: 19-21
5) Romans 10: 8-10 (and check for related Pauline Scriptures)
6) Ephesians 6
7) Psalm 22 and 51
8) John's Gospel, beginning with Chapter 17 to the conclusion

REFLECTION 12:

SEEKING JESUS

Ready for a Biblical brain teaser? OK, here it is: What is the relationship between Genesis 32: 22-30 and Luke 24: 13-32? Take some time now to read these powerful passages of Scripture. Remember, for a real Christian, seeking to be guided by the Holy Spirit in the reading of the Bible as in all things, there are amazing and never-ending insights into the relationship between the Old and New Testaments.

In Genesis 32, we have the somewhat mysterious account of Jacob spending the night wrestling with a "man." At daybreak the man asked Jacob to let him go, but Jacob refused until he received a blessing. Jacob was no fool; he knew that this person was really an angel, or perhaps even God Himself disguised in human form. Jacob knew that he was accurate when the mysterious person refused to share his name. However, the heavenly visitor did change Jacob's name that morning; from that time on, Jacob became Israel, which means "he struggles with God," or "prince with God prevails/rules as a prince." Jacob, now Israel, named the location of the wrestling match Peniel, which means "face of God." His reason: *"It is because I saw God face to face, and yet my life was spared."* This event took place while Jacob was on his way to meet his brother, Esau. They had been estranged ever since Jacob deceived their father and received dad's choicest blessing. Jacob was fearful, and probably feeling some guilt, and he was seeking guidance from God as to how best to handle the situation. That prayer resulted in what was surely the strangest encounter between God and man recorded in the Old Testament.

In Luke 24 (a return to the "burning heart" Scripture), we read about the meeting between the risen Jesus and the two disciples on their way to the village of Emmaus. They did not recognize Him and were very downcast over the recent events in Jerusalem that had resulted in the crucifixion of the Man they had hoped was the Messiah. Jesus began sharing the Scriptures that foretold His coming and His manner of death as they walked along the dusty road. This was therefore the first Bible study recorded under the New Covenant, which began when Jesus died and then rose triumphantly from the grave. And what a Bible Teacher! They had the living Word interpreting the Word! When He entered their house at their invitation to dine with them, He revealed Himself in the breaking of the bread. When He then disappeared from their sight, they exclaimed, *"Were not our hearts burning within us while he talked with us on the road and opened the Scriptures to us?"*

Well, where are the similarities? First, in both cases human beings had a personal encounter with God. Second, in both cases the humans were deeply affected and sought to continue the encounter. Third, and most important, Jacob and the men on the road to Emmaus burned with a desire to know God, receive His blessing, learn about Him and His revelation – in short, to be with Him intimately.

Let's return to Emmaus and our Bible teacher. Emmaus teaches us that the Bible is a God-given way to find Him, understand His teaching and direction, and relate to Him. I find it very confirming that two modern spiritual retreats have had a powerful impact on the relationship between thousands of Christians and God Almighty. Both are based on similar premises and processes; one is called "Cursillo" and the other "Walk to Emmaus." In the Luke account, Jesus makes it clear the Scriptures of the Old Testament clearly pointed to Him as the Messiah (clear, at least, to all who are willing to have totally open minds and hearts). People who really penetrated the Word and relied primarily on God for understanding

Will the Real Christians Please Stand Up!

saw the truth. They became Jesus' apostles and disciples, even though many had their faith shaken when Jesus died in such a humiliating and excruciating way. The two disciples on the road were obviously torn in their belief – wanting to see Jesus as the Messiah but also influenced by the prevalent teaching of the Jewish scholars and teachers of that time, who believed that the Messiah would be a powerful and anointed political/religious leader who would free Israel from bondage to Rome. The real truth was right there in the Old Testament writings; but even with regard to Scripture people tend to hear what they want to hear.

Emmaus also tells us that the Bible is not just a way to read about God, not just a history lesson. Rather, the Word is alive; it is actually God speaking at the time of our reading. This is what makes the Bible so radically different than another book. The Bible is a key opening the door into relationship and communication with God the Father, God the Son, and God the Holy Spirit.

Now open your hearts and minds wide for what follows: It was only when the two disciples begged Jesus to stay with them and teach them more that they were fully blessed by seeing Him for whom He really was. In other words, it is only when we hunger and thirst to know God, only when it is the single most important and burning passion in our lives that God can fully reveal Himself, His love, and His presence to us. Therefore, a sign of being a real Christian is having this goal/objective/life-focus – to know God, while realizing that we can never fully plumb the depths of the Trinity.

In Deuteronomy the future trials of the Chosen People are prophesied, with some very powerful words: *"The Lord will scatter you among the peoples* (because of their falling into idolatry), *and only a few of you will survive among the nations to which the Lord will drive you. There you will worship man-made gods of wood and stone which cannot see, hear, eat or smell. But if from there you seek the Lord your God, you will find him if you look for him with all your heart and with all your soul."* (Deuteronomy 4: 27-29) The prophet Jeremiah said something very similar centuries later: *"This is what the Lord says: 'When seventy years are completed for Babylon, I will come to you and fulfill my gracious promise to bring you back to this place. For I know the plans I have for you,'* *declares the Lord, 'plans to prosper you and not to harm you, plans to give you hope and a future. Then you will call upon me and come and pray to me, and I will listen to you. <u>You will seek me and find me when you seek me with all your heart.</u>'"* (Jeremiah 29: 10-13)

I believe in the Word of God. I believe that those words written and spoken thousands of years ago are living words being spoken to us now; for the Bible, again, is the <u>living</u> Word. I also believe in the truth of the Word of God. Both Deuteronomy and Jeremiah record that God fully responds when people seek Him with all their heart – not part of the heart, not their Sunday heart, not their heart when they happen to need Him in "really important" things of life such as job success or handling a crisis. Rather, in every moment, every breath of life, when we put God first, when our hearts are turned to Him in and before everything else, then God can truly open the storehouse of His spiritual riches. Only then does our life take on its intended fullness and meaning. It is all or nothing, says God. It is focus on faith. It is seeking an ever deeper relationship of love with Jesus and, through Him, with the Father and the Holy Spirit.

Let's look at this "seeking" topic in a somewhat different way. 1 Chronicles 15 and 16 record the bringing of the Ark of the Covenant to Jerusalem under the leadership of David. This was prior to the building of the Temple; the Ark, which traveled with the Jewish people, was the symbol and, more, the sign of God's presence. Listen:

> *"So David and the elders of Israel and the commanders of units of a thousand went to bring up the Ark of the Covenant of the Lord from the house of Obed-Edom, with rejoicing. Because God had helped the Levites who were carrying the Ark of the Covenant of the Lord, seven bulls and seven rams were sacrificed. Now David was clothed in a robe of fine linen, as were all the Levites who were carrying the Ark, and as were the singers and Kenaniah, who was in charge of the singing of the choirs. David also wore a linen ephod. So all Israel brought up the Ark of the Covenant of the Lord with shouts, with the sounding of rams' horns and trumpets, and of cymbals, and the playing of lyres and harps. As the*

Ark of the Covenant of the Lord was entering the City of David, Michal, daughter of Saul, watched from a window, and when she saw King David dancing and celebrating, she despised him in her heart. That day David first committed to Asaph and his associates this psalm of thanks to the Lord: 'Give thanks to the Lord, call on his name; make known among the nations what he has done. Sing to him, sing praise to him; tell of all his wonderful acts. Glory in his holy name; let the hearts of those who seek the Lord rejoice. Look to the Lord and his strength; seek his face always. Remember the wonders he has done, his miracles, and the judgments he pronounced, O descendants of Israel his servant, O sons of Jacob, his chosen ones.'" (1 Chronicles 15: 25-29 and 16: 7-13)

Folks, David got excited about the presence of God! And so did most of the people. Michal, unfortunately, did not, and she represents the churchy, stuffy people who think it is either undignified or foolish to get excited about God. David did not care what people thought (but neither were his actions inappropriate). He and the people sang, played music and danced in their joy, gratitude and awe that the Lord God Almighty would dwell in their midst. Psalm 42: 1 proclaims an intense desire to be in the presence of God: *"As the deer pants for streams of water, so my soul pants for you, O God."* And Psalm 84: 1-2: *"How lovely is your dwelling place, O Lord Almighty! My soul yearns, even faints, for the courts of the Lord; my heart and my flesh cry out for the living God."*

We do not have the Ark of the Covenant. We, the people of the New Covenant, are living temples, and God dwells with us and within us. I ask myself, if that is true, how is it that I could sit in my chair, jump up, yell and wave my arms (while terrifying the dog) while I watched some years ago the Buffalo Bills come back and win a football game with a reserve quarterback and in the process overcome a points deficit never achieved before or after – and be calm and cool and even nonchalant about Jesus Christ, the King of Kings and Lord of Lords, living right here with me, the God-Man who overcame the greatest deficit the world has ever known, sepa-

Will the Real Christians Please Stand Up!

ration from God because of sin?! When we think of Jesus walking this earth, when we contemplate Jesus at the right hand of the Father in heaven, when we recognize by faith that He is also right here with us, what prevents us from falling down in humble adoration before Him?

In the early Church, the Acts Church, Christians were on fire. In Acts 4, for example, after the Jewish religious authorities released Peter and John, the believers praised God and asked for strength to preach the Word:

> *"...they raised their voices together in prayer to God. 'Sovereign Lord,' they said, 'you made the heaven and the earth and the sea, and everything in them. You spoke by the Holy Spirit through the mouth of your servant, our father David: 'Why do the nations rage and the peoples plot in vain? The kings of the earth take their stand and the rulers gather together against the Lord and against his Anointed One.' Indeed, Herod and Pontius Pilate met together with the Gentiles and the people of Israel in this city to conspire against your holy Servant Jesus, whom you anointed. They did what your power and will had decided beforehand should happen. Now, Lord, consider their threats and enable your servants to speak your word with great boldness. Stretch out your hand to heal and perform miraculous signs and wonders through the name of your holy Servant Jesus.' After they prayed, the place where they were meeting was shaken. And they were all filled with the Holy Spirit and spoke the word of God boldly."*

Because their hearts were on fire, because they sought God fervently, because to know and share Him was foremost in their lives, they received an outpouring of the Holy Spirit. God has given us so much – life here, and life eternal through the shedding of the blood of the innocent One, Jesus Christ, God Incarnate. That wondrous reality is what should cause the joy and longing to fill our hearts and minds and spirits and come bubbling out in lives of service. Listen to the prophet Hosea, chapter 10, verse 12: *"Sow for yourselves righteousness, reap the fruit of unfailing love, and break up your unplowed ground; for it is time to seek the Lord, until he comes and showers righteousness on you."*

O God, show us the unplowed ground of our lives, those aspects of life not totally turned over to You. We want to be real Christians, ones who put You and keep You Number One. Fill us with a burning desire to know You more clearly, love You more dearly and follow You more nearly. We praise You, Lord God. Thank You. Forgive us for our hardness of heart and our insensitivity. Come, Lord, take all of us and give us all of You, now and forever. Amen.

SUMMARY FOR REFLECTION AND DISCUSSION:

A real Christian:

1) Believes in the Bible as the living Word of God, as God speaking in the here and now both in His Word and directly within our spirits;
2) Goes beyond the written and spoken Word to encounter the living Lord through recognition of the privilege of being living temples in which the Trinity dwells;
3) Puts God first in all things, in all of life's circumstances, and before any other person or possession;
4) Has as a personal mission a life of yielded love and service.

SCRIPTURES FOR JOURNALING:

1) Genesis 32: 22-30 and Luke 24: 13-32 (seeking depth of meaning within each and in comparison with each other);
2) Deuteronomy 4: 27-29 and Jeremiah 29: 10-13 (the meaning of "seeking with all one's heart" – also consider a word search of "seek");
3) Psalm 42 and Psalm 84 (longing for God's courts);
4) Acts 2-4 (discuss the life of the early Christian Church).

PART III:

SPIRITUAL WARFARE IN SCRIPTURE AND IN THE CHRISTIAN LIFE

This series of reflections hits head on a reality that modern society often scoffs at – including some elements of the Church. To many Satan is some medieval myth; and that is exactly the way he wants it to be.

A real Christian is a soldier, engaged on the front lines of a vicious war. It is terrorism against followers of Jesus; its proponents are spiritual beings far more intelligent than we are, and with a much better knowledge of Scripture than we have. But we have at our disposal weapons against which Satan and his demonic hordes cannot stand; they are ultimately defeated. In the meantime, they constantly seek to obtain souls for their eternal home, called Hell. And they also seek to make God's people ineffective through temptations and oppression.

We ignore this warfare at our own peril and we place other people in eternal jeopardy if we do not recognize when and how God seeks to use us to reach them. His grace and love are all-powerful. That is the good news; the challenge is for us to let that grace and love fill us and flow through us.

The summaries and Scriptures for journaling will provide opportunities for personal meditation and sharing of ideas, concerns and insights with others.

REFLECTION 13:

SPIRITUAL WARFARE

As we try to consistently walk in the Spirit, conscious of the presence of God with us and within us, He speaks to us in the quiet of our hearts – regularly, consistently, moment by moment – and He can quietly direct our steps and guide us onto the right paths according to His will. There is no question that we all miss much because of our human tendency to listen to ourselves; but when we consciously direct our hearts toward Him, He gently and lovingly reestablishes contact. As we flow more in His grace and presence, we begin to realize that what appear to be coincidences are manifestations of the guiding and loving hand of God. For every real Christian this life is a regular series of miracles – a miracle defined as the intervention of supernatural power and presence resulting in the altering of the shape and direction of natural events. We live not only in the natural, we live in the supernatural, with spiritual beings and events all around us. It is only by faith and spiritual discernment through the operating of the Holy Spirit that we can consciously walk in this realm.

To share an example from my own life: I was sitting on a picnic bench, participating in an outdoor work meeting. My mind wandered (sorry, boss!), and I looked around at the beautiful landscape of the Ozarks. The trees surrounding me were sporting their fall finery and filled my eyes with hues and shades of green, gold, red, orange and brown. As I marveled at the breathtaking beauty, God spoke to me, not with an audible voice, but deep within my spirit. He pointed out to me that the beauty of those leaves lies in their dying! It was that insight that helped me fashion the reflection on sacrifice, on dying to self. I realized that it is only in dying to self-will and selfish ambitions that the Divine Artist can bring out the spiritual beauty in my redeemed spirit – because I am made in the image and likeness of God and am washed in the blood of the Lamb. But God was not finished with the lesson. He directed my gaze downward, to the ground. The area around me was carpeted with the brown, already decomposing, leaves that had fallen from the trees. I looked up again, and I saw the leaves on those trees in a different light. Gazing carefully, I could see that many were close to death, almost ready to fall, turning brown and waiting for a wind strong enough to finally tear them from their life support system. I then looked down again and saw literally thousands of dead leaves on the ground. God pointed out to me that those leaves, on the trees and on the ground, represent human souls. There are so many people around the world who are lost and dying, desperately needing new life and buffeted by the winds of selfishness, sin and Satan's unceasing attacks. It is called spiritual warfare. The reality of it is becoming ever more dulled in the modern world, even scoffed at – including in many churches. The fact is that if real Christians, living members of the Body of Christ, do not put on their armor and let the power of God work through them, God's saving love cannot reach those people caught in Satan's grip.

Along with the concept of sacrifice, the belief of good versus evil is integral to almost all religions. Jews and Christians are blessed to have access to God's revelation of Himself, Christians the fullness of His plan for the world, and both the drama of personalized good versus personalized evil lived out in the world and in the heavenly realm. Our common source book is the Bible.

In the Old Testament, let's take a look at Genesis, Job and Zechariah.

Genesis, chapter 3, describes the fall of mankind into sin. Along with Adam, Eve and God there is another principal character in the drama – Satan. *"Now the serpent was more crafty than any of the wild animals the Lord God had made. He said to the woman, 'Did God really say, 'You must not eat from any tree in the garden?' The woman said to the serpent, 'We may eat fruit from the trees in the garden, but God did say, 'You must not eat fruit from the tree that is in the middle of the garden, and you must not touch it, or you will die.' 'You will not surely die,' the serpent said to the woman. 'For God knows that when you eat of it your eyes will be opened, and you will be like God, knowing good and evil.'"* (Genesis 3: 1-5)

Job 1: 6-7: *"One day the angels came to present themselves before the Lord, and Satan also came with them. The Lord said to Satan, 'Where have you come from?' Satan answered the Lord, 'From roaming through the earth and going back and forth in it."*

Zechariah 3: 1-2, 8-9: *"Then he showed me Joshua the high priest standing before the angel of the Lord, and Satan standing at his right side to accuse him. The Lord said to Satan, 'The Lord rebuke you, Satan! The Lord, who has chosen Jerusalem, rebuke you!'...'Listen, O high priest Joshua and your associate seated before you, who are men symbolic of things to come; I am going to bring my servant, the Branch...and I will remove the sin of this land in a single day.'"*

These are but a few of the references to Satan. He is not just an allegory, not just a figure of speech, not some poet's flight of fancy – he is real. He is the adversary of God and of the heavenly angels and of all human beings.

In the New Testament the presence of Satan is even more clearly identified and proclaimed. In fact, the apostle John in his first Letter writes, *"the reason the Son of God appeared was to destroy the devil's work."* (1 John 3: 8) After Jesus went up to John the Baptist at the beginning of the Lord's public ministry and received John's baptism, the Holy Spirit descended upon Him. Immediately thereafter the Holy Spirit led Jesus into the desert for a time of praying and fasting. Following that forty-day period, Jesus, still in the desert, encountered Satan face to face. (Obviously this was something that Jesus described to His apostles after the fact.) Satan tested Jesus with materialism, with pride and presumption, with self-seeking and self-will. (Matthew 4: 1-11) The Word of God teaches us through this event that just as Jesus, the Incarnate Second Person of the Trinity, experienced temptation (for Jesus in His human nature was like us in all things, except for sin), so will every other man and woman. In Mark's Gospel, Jesus, very early in His ministry, encountered a demon-possessed man right in the synagogue. The evil spirit cried out, prophetically, *"What do you want with us, Jesus of Nazareth? Have you come to destroy us? I know who you are – the Holy One of God!"* (Mark 1: 24) Matthew quotes Jesus as saying, *"...If I drive out demons by the Spirit of God, then the Kingdom of God has come upon you."* (Matthew 12: 28) These are all very clear descriptions of spiritual warfare in the Kingdom, where all true Christians live.

Consider some of the other references to Satan in the New Testament: The healing by Jesus of demon-possessed people on frequent occasions, including one instance where the demon said, *"My name is legion, for we are many."* (Mark 5: 9) Do not be led astray by some modern theologians, who find it "medieval" to believe in Satan and demonic forces. They say that the Gospel accounts are really describing various kinds of mental or emotional illnesses. Nonsense! There are too many indicators of spiritual warfare in the Bible to dismiss it as allegory or parables. Jesus was Himself accused by the religious leaders of being under the influence of Satan; by that they showed their own awareness of the existence of personalized evil. (Luke 11: 15) That same section in Luke goes on to provide a teaching of Jesus who said that a demon, once cast out, can return with others if the person's heart is not right with God. John states that Satan entered into Judas prior to his betrayal of Jesus. (John 13: 27) In the Acts of the Apostles, Peter confronted Ananias and his wife, Sapphira, when they lied and kept some possessions for themselves instead

Will the Real Christians Please Stand Up!

of sharing them with others. Peter said, *"Ananias, how is it that Satan has so filled your heart that you have lied to the Holy Spirit?"* (Acts 5: 3) Paul, writing to the Church at Thessalonica, said that he had wanted to visit them, but Satan stopped him. (1 Thessalonians 2: 18) Paul, again, writing to the Ephesians, described spiritual warfare graphically and very precisely. He uses military language in encouraging Christians to do battle against spiritual dark forces. He describes the armor that Christians must wear in order to be victorious. (Ephesians 6: 10-17) Peter writes (1 Peter 5: 8) that the devil is a roaring lion going about and seeking whom he may devour; and Peter is writing to Christians. Of course, the good news is that Satan is ultimately defeated through the perfect sacrifice of Jesus Christ on the cross. The Word also tells us to resist the devil and he will flee. (James 4: 7) The Book of Revelation describes in the most vivid way the great battles going on, and those to come. Revelation also proclaims the final victory of God and His people.

In the meantime, to return to the analogy, the leaves are falling off the trees. People are dying without knowing Christ. There is a tremendous urgency to spread the Good News about salvation through Jesus. The horror of hell (also a reality, not a myth) is not just flames and fire and chaos. It is also darkness, total isolation, eternal hopelessness, and raging fury and despair. If you are a Christian and are a member of a church that never talks about spiritual warfare, or, worse, speaks of it as a fable, take heed! Once I went to a large mainline denomination church to teach about the dangers of the New Age Movement (we will look closely at this danger in a later reflection). I told the group, an adult Sunday School class, that they would not understand what I was about to teach unless they believed in spiritual warfare. After the class a small group came up to me and told me something that caused my mouth to fall open. They said they had a new pastor, who told them that not only did he not believe in Satan, he went through his entire seminary preparation without once having a teaching on Satan or spiritual warfare. That is not only shocking; it is alarming.

I urge you to arm yourselves with the Word of God and prayer, and go in love to pastors and ministry leaders who do not teach about or believe in Satan. I frankly seriously question whether such leaders are capable of providing rounded Biblical teaching and guidance. I believe that a person who denies the existence of Satan is a spiritual fool, duped by the very spiritual being that he refuses to acknowledge. Foolish, too, is the Christian who does not put on the battle armor and put Satan to flight. The presence and power of Jesus Christ, the Holy Spirit and the Father, residing in the living temples that real Christians are, constitute a living force that can defeat demons and bring victory to the Kingdom of God – now, not just at the end of time. Also, let's not forget the heavenly angels. The Bible clearly describes their battles with demonic forces, with angels just like themselves who had defied God and had been cast out of heaven. When we pray, we arm the angels and they come to protect and defend God's people.

SUMMARY FOR REFLECTION AND DISCUSSION:

A real Christian:

1) Clearly recognizes the presence of supernatural spiritual forces, both good and evil, in daily life;
2) Believes firmly in the existence of Satan and demons, as fallen angels;
3) Understands that Jesus' earthly life and mission were not an allegory of good versus evil, but rather a real life and death struggle for everything that God and Christians stand for;
4) Knows that Satan and his minions have no power in the presence of Jesus Christ. The Christian is foolish to ignore Satan but is also unwise to attribute to him powers that cannot stand before the Persons of Father, Son and Holy Spirit.

SCRIPTURES FOR JOURNALING:

1) Genesis 3, Job 1, Zechariah 3;
2) 1 John 3: 8, Acts 5: 3, 1 Thessalonians 2: 18, 1 Peter 5: 8,

Will the Real Christians Please Stand Up!

James 4: 7;

3) Ephesians 6: 10-17 (spend time on each defensive weapon and the one offensive weapon;

4) Matthew 4: 1-11, Mark 1: 24, Mark 5: 9, Matthew 12: 28, Luke 11: 15-26;

5) John 13: 27 (and do a search of other references to spiritual warfare).

REFLECTION 14:

SPIRITUAL WARFARE APPLIED

"Spiritual warfare" is a term that has been used, abused, misunderstood, and often ignored. At one end of the spectrum, some people so focus on Satan and his power that they appear to tremble before him or at least lose sight of the power, victory and presence of Jesus Christ. At the other end of the spectrum, a growing number of people cross Satan off as a medieval myth, a spook used by the clergy to keep the Christian peasants in line. There is also the relatively and absolutely incredible phenomenon of portraying Lucifer (Satan) as a victim of persecution and seeking to restore him to his rightful place at the top of the hierarchy of angels (as taught by some New Age adherents). Finally, there appear to be those who not only recognize his existence but actually worship him. A wealthy California playboy who found God and eventually became a Catholic priest, Father John Corapi, tells the story of when he was on an airplane. He was having a conversation with a lady seated next to him and was sharing his faith. He eventually told her that he was going to have some private prayer time; she said that she would do the same – but that she was a witch and was going to be praying for the destruction of Christians. Father Corapi also relates that during the years when he was not only a drug user but a drug dealer, he saw firsthand a major drug supplier bring in Satanists and/or witches to "pray" over the drugs before they hit the street.

So each of us has a choice to make: Either we believe in Satan's existence or we do not. And if we do believe, then our choice is whether to believe that he is totally impotent and not a player on the world stage or that he is actively seeking to destroy spiritual lives. If you have decided that he does not exist or that he is utterly powerless – in other words, if you pride yourself on being a modern, sophisticated Christian who does not need "bogeymen" to keep your motivation properly directed, then this reflection means nothing to you and you may find it simplistic and even humorous. You are free to believe as you will. The trouble is – and I am being deliberately personal here – if you deny Satan's existence or his potential to inflict terrible harm, you are a deluded fool. You are playing right into Satan's plan; and, frankly, you are not a real Christian. A real Christian follows Jesus Christ, and Jesus Christ always recognized the devil and demons as living beings (unless, of course, you are also deluded into believing that the Bible itself is a storybook not to be taken as true, that the conflicts recorded in the Gospels are not historically accurate but are mere allegories). If you believe that, we do not have a common ground for reflection; for I, with awe, gratitude and eagerness, accept God's Word as His revelation – even though I also believe that we must be guided by the Holy Spirit in understanding the context and the meaning of the Word. At the conclusion of His sojourn in the wilderness and the temptations He experienced there, Jesus said to Satan, *"Away from me, Satan! For it is written, 'Worship the Lord your God, and serve him only.'"* (Matthew 4: 10) And also note the very next verse: *"Then the devil left him, and angels came and attended him."* Of course, there are those who deny the existence of heavenly angels also. I believe with all my heart that there are angels all around us, serving and protecting us in ways that we will only understand when we are with God in heaven. Consider, too, the following New Testament Scriptures:

> *"The seventy-two returned with joy and said, 'Lord, even the demons submit to us in your name.' Jesus replied, 'I saw Satan fall like lightning from heaven.'"* (Luke 10: 17-18) *"The coming of the lawless one* (the Antichrist) *will be in*

accordance with the work of Satan displayed in all kinds of counterfeit miracles, signs and wonders." (2 Thessalonians 2: 9) *"When anyone hears the message about the kingdom and does not understand it, the evil one comes and snatches away what was sown in his heart."* (Matthew 13: 19) *"You belong to your father, the devil, and you want to carry out your father's desire. He was a murderer from the beginning, not holding to the truth, for there is no truth in him. When he lies, he speaks his native language, for he is a liar and the father of lies."* (John 8: 44) *"The great dragon was hurled down – that ancient serpent called the devil, or Satan, who leads the whole world astray."* (Revelation 12: 9) *"And the devil, who deceived them, was thrown into the lake of burning sulphur, where the beast and the false prophet had been thrown. They will be tormented day and night forever and ever."* (Revelation 20: 10)

The remainder of this reflection proceeds from the base of belief in Satan. He is a fallen angel, and many thousands fell with him; they are called demons. Satan was the mightiest and most beautiful of the angels before pride did him in. As an angel, he has an intellect far beyond ours. He is shrewd, crafty and your and my archenemy. His goal is our destruction and/or our ineffectiveness as instruments used by God for the salvation of others. That is the bad news. The good news is that Jesus came to destroy the works of the devil, to cast out the prince of this world. The death and Resurrection of Jesus Christ give to those who believe in Him and unite themselves to Him the very power of Almighty God; and that makes us infinitely more powerful than Satan or any demon as long as we are walking in the Spirit. Though Satan is ultimately defeated because of the cross and the Resurrection and the Lord who reigns and will come again in glory, he is still at work against the Church which seeks to bring light – and Satan wants to lure as many souls as possible to his kingdom of eternal darkness. In short, Satan is the very embodiment of sin, hate, death and darkness – in direct contrast to God who is Holiness, Love, Life and Light. This means that someone who is in love with God, really in love, will have absolutely nothing to do with Satan or his ways, except to go into battle with him. Rather than minimize his power, the true Christian will be constantly on guard to avoid walking into situations that give Satan opportunities to exercise his sadistic seductiveness.

So, now, let's get practical. There is only one true religion, for God only established one. It is the Judaeo-Christian religion. Both Jews and Christians believe in the one, true God (though the Jewish people who have not accepted Jesus as the Messiah do not see beyond God the Father to God the Son and God the Holy Spirit – one God, three Persons). It stands to reason, therefore that one major strategy of Satan would be to deceive people into establishing and practicing false religion – and so they have done, throughout the history of mankind. Though Christians should never judge individuals, regardless of their beliefs – only God sees the heart – Christians should never fall into the trap of a false ecumenism that teaches the "all roads lead to heaven" theology, another Satanic deception. Real Christians do not dabble in pagan religious practices, do not embrace elements of Eastern religions, for example, because they seem to work. Let me put it this way, bluntly: Anything that detracts from or substitutes for the presence, power and love of Jesus Christ must be branded as false and avoided at all costs.

Please keep in mind that one of Satan's most significant strategies is to desensitize people. If I lose spiritual awareness of the horror of sin and of the evil that is personified in Satan and his demons, of the reality of hell and that people are lost and dying, if I become dulled to those things it becomes quite easy for me to unwittingly adopt the practices of the world and think nothing of it. In that process I play right into Satan's hand. He has always had some followers; but there is a far greater number of people who are duped into not taking him seriously. Brothers and sisters, we as Christians must neither overestimate nor underestimate Satan. When we tremble in fear at the thought of him, we overestimate him, because he simply cannot stand before the glory of God. When we do not see his presence, with the spiritual eyes of grace given us by the Holy Spirit, we perceive no need to put on and keep on the armor described in Ephesians 6.

The early Christian Church faced the wiles of Satan in many

ways – persecutions, heresies, ridicule and condemnation by the pagan people around them. One of the Fathers of the early Church, Cyril of Jerusalem, wrote the following as part of a reflection on the Lord's Prayer: "'And lead us not into temptation:'...Does entering into temptation mean being overwhelmed by temptation? Temptation is like a winter storm, difficult to cross. Those who are not overwhelmed by temptations pass through, showing themselves to be excellent swimmers, who are not swept away by the tide. Those who are of the other sort enter into the temptations and are overwhelmed...'But deliver us from evil:'...Now 'evil' is our adversary, the devil, from whom we pray to be delivered."

So, fellow Christians, let's take courage! Pray for a renewed sense of urgency. Put on the armor and go into battle with courage. Satan is truly ultimately defeated; he knows his time is short. Therefore, he is furiously active in the world trying to claim as many souls as he can for his own eternal kingdom – one of utter darkness.

Jesus is the Light. And Jesus seeks to shine through His followers. When we live as yielded and obedient servants, the Holy Spirit can use us in ways to show others the light and pull them from the darkness. We will be doing our part toward the coming of that day described in Revelation 12: 10-11:

> *"Now have come the salvation and the power and the kingdom of our God, and the authority of his Christ. For the accuser of our brothers, who accuses them before our God day and night, has been hurled down. They overcame him by the blood of the Lamb and by the word of their testimony; they did not love their lives so much as to shrink from death."*

SUMMARY FOR REFLECTION AND DISCUSSION:

A real Christian:

1) Recognizes that Satan and his demonic hordes, though ultimately defeated, are very much alive and active in the world;

Will the Real Christians Please Stand Up!

2) Sees spiritual warfare present in many of the vicissitudes and difficulties of life;
3) Puts on the spiritual armor daily and seeks to walk by the Holy Spirit in all circumstances of life;
4) Does nothing to glorify Satan, treat him lightly, or minimize his evil influence in the world;
5) Is committed to a life of intercession, as a prayer warrior, recognizing by grace that this is a powerful way to attack and defeat Satan.

SCRIPTURES FOR JOURNALING:

1) Ephesians 6: 10-18 (focus on each of the defensive pieces of armor and the one offensive one);
2) Matthew 4: 1-11 (the significance of Satanic attack on Jesus as He began His public ministry);
3) Luke 10: 17-18 (and search other Gospel Scriptures that reference Satan)
4) Job 1 and Zechariah 3
5) Revelation 12-13 and 19-20

REFLECTION 15

THE EFFECTS OF SIN

There are many familiar events recorded in the first eleven chapters of the first book of the Bible – Genesis. We read about the Garden of Eden, the first sin, the promise of Redemption, Cain and Abel, Noah, the Tower of Babel. But, once again I received a fresh insight (for me, at least) from the Holy Spirit. I just very strongly believe that whenever we read God's Word with faith and with open minds and hearts, the Holy Spirit will speak to us, each of us, deep within our spirits. This is yet another example of how personal God's love is for each of us.

In the Garden of Eden, we find a description of a beautiful intimacy between God and His people created in His image and likeness. Even after Adam and Eve sinned, we have this amazing account of the relationship: *"Then the man and his wife heard the sound of the Lord God as he was walking in the garden in the cool of the day, and they hid from the Lord God among the trees of the garden. But the Lord God called to the man, 'Where are you?'...The Lord God made garments of skin for Adam and his wife and clothed them."* (Genesis 3:8-9, 21) God intended an intimate family relationship with Him – a sharing of the divine life of Father, Son and Holy Spirit. As time went on, the awareness of God dimmed. We read in Genesis 6: *"The Lord saw how great man's wickedness on the earth had become, and that every inclination of the thoughts of his heart was only evil all the time. The Lord was grieved that he had made man on the earth, and his heart was filled with pain."* (Genesis 6: 5-6) And note Genesis 11: *"Now the whole world had one language and a common speech. As men moved eastward, they found a plain in Shinar and settled there. They said to one another, 'Come, let's make bricks and bake them thoroughly.' They used brick instead of stone, and tar for mortar. Then they said, 'Come, let us build ourselves a city, with a tower that reaches to the heavens, so that we may make a name for ourselves and not be scattered over the face of the whole earth.' But the Lord came down to see the city and the tower that the men were building. The Lord said, 'If as one people speaking the same language they have begun to do this, then nothing they plan to do will be impossible for them.' So the Lord scattered them from there over all the earth, and they stopped building the city. That is why it was called Babel – because there the Lord confused the language of the whole world. From there the Lord scattered them over the face of the whole earth."* (Genesis 11: 1-9)

So, what is the insight here? I discovered a pattern: A moving from intimacy to dulled spiritual senses, from a keen awareness of God to an almost exclusive focus on self. We see vividly here the effect of sin! A Scriptural definition of sin is "falling away from or missing the right path." Mankind walked its own way, moved away from the path which God planned and on which, figuratively speaking at least, God Himself walks. What does this mean for you and for me? I believe that it means a call to utter honesty about our current walk with God. It is one of those times to be willing to be utterly transparent before the Holy Spirit. So, let's begin with a prayer – Psalm 139:

"O Lord, you have searched me and you know me. You know when I sit and when I rise; you perceive my thoughts from afar. You discern my going out and my lying down; you are familiar with all my ways. Before a word is on my tongue you know it completely, O Lord. You hem me in – behind and before; you have laid your hand upon me. Such knowledge is too wonderful for me, too lofty for me to attain. Where can I go from your Spirit? Where can I flee

from your presence? If I go up to the heavens, you are there; if I make my bed in the depths, you are there. If I rise on the wings of the dawn, if I settle on the far side of the sea, even there your hand will guide me, your right hand will hold me fast. If I say, 'Surely the darkness will hide me and the light become night around me,' even the darkness will not be dark to you; the night will shine like the day, for darkness is as light to you. For you created my inmost being; you knit me together in my mother's womb. I praise you because I am fearfully and wonderfully made; your works are wonderful, I know that full well. My frame was not hidden from you when I was made in the secret place. When I was woven together in the depths of the earth, your eyes saw my unformed body. All the days ordained for me were written in your book before one of them came to be. How precious to me are your thoughts, O God! How vast is the sum of them! Were I to count them, they would outnumber the grains of sand. When I am awake, I am still with you...Search me, O God, and know my heart; test me and know my anxious thoughts. See if there is any offensive way in me, and lead me in the way everlasting."

We cannot hide anything from God, so let's explore what this might mean in our lives. First though, please permit an "editorial comment", one that does not directly pertain to the topic at hand: How is it that a Christian (or a Jew, for that matter) can read Psalm 139 and support abortion? Read the Psalm again and focus on what the Holy Spirit says about life in the womb. No excuses, please; either the Word of God is true or it is not. The minute I start rationalizing or picking and choosing, I cease to be a real Christian in the fully intended meaning of the term. Abortion is snuffing out life created by God – period. Actually, as I reflect further, this editorial comment is really not that far off the topic after all; for this reflection is about how our spiritual senses become dulled. And how much more dull can they become than when we justify the taking of a precious and innocent life, no matter how the conception happened to take place?

The Bible, as we have seen, frequently uses the image of the heart to describe the motivation of people – hearts turned toward God or to self and the things of this world, hearts turning away from or turning back to the Creator and Lord of the universe. Indeed, one could summarize the basic drama of the entire Bible through the hearts of people in relationship to God and His love. God creates in love; God's righteous anger burns over sin; God forgives when people repent – with the culmination of God's love seen in the Incarnation of the Second Person of the Blessed Trinity. Attractions to the world dull the fire of the heart for God; the Holy Spirit seeks to inflame the heart with love for God and a passion to tell others about Him and His incredible gifts of love.

So, the heart has the choice of embracing God or self – one or the other. Jesus tells us that we cannot serve both God and the world; we must make a conscious choice. But there are many other Scriptures that have as their theme the turning of the heart toward or away from God – and the turning away is always a result of sin dulling the spiritual senses and becomes itself a sin. Here are some of those Scriptures:

"Cursed is the one who trusts in man, who depends on flesh for his strength and whose heart turns away from the Lord...The heart is deceitful above all things and beyond cure (without the grace of God). *Who can understand it? I the Lord search the heart and examine the mind, to reward a man according to his conduct, according to what his deeds deserve."* (Jeremiah 17: 5, 9-10) *"Therefore say: 'This is what the Sovereign Lord says: I will gather you from the nations and bring you back from the countries where you have been scattered, and I will give you back the land of Israel again. They will return to it and remove all its vile images and detestable idols. I will give them an undivided heart and put a new spirit in them; I will remove from them their heart of stone and give them a heart of flesh. Then they will follow my decrees and be careful to keep my laws. They will be my people, and I will be their God. But as for those whose hearts are devoted to their vile images and detestable*

idols, I will bring down on their own heads what they have done, declares the Sovereign Lord.'" (Ezekiel 11: 17-21) *"'Even now,' declares the Lord, 'return to me with all your heart, with fasting and weeping and mourning. Rend your heart and not your garments. Return to the Lord your God, for he is gracious and compassionate, slow to anger and abounding in love, and he relents from sending calamity.'"* *(Joel 2: 12-13) "Create in me a pure heart, O God, and renew a steadfast spirit within me. Do not cast me out from your presence or take your Holy Spirit from me."* (Psalm 51: 10-11) (Note here the relationship between the heart and the Holy Spirit. It would take the revelations of the New Covenant for the Person and role of the Holy Spirit to take full bloom in our minds and spirits. Nevertheless, the Spirit here inspires the psalmist to cry out that the greatest of all tragedies would be for God to remove His Spirit – His living Love – and that the remedy is a new heart, purged from self and sin, and dedicated to serving the living God.)

Before we explore some more Scriptures on this theme of the effect that sin has on the heart and its relationship with God, I offer two thoughts for your reflection:

1) I recently rented a movie classic, "The Ten Commandments." Even though the special effects bear no comparison with what modern technology can achieve, the story is timeless and is a powerful representation of major events in Salvation History – the freeing of the people of Israel from bondage in Egypt, the giving of the Ten Commandments and the preparation of the Jewish people to enter the Promised Land. My spirit actually grieved when the people built the golden calf while Moses was up on Mt. Sinai. They forgot Moses and God and entered into a frenzy of idol worship and carousing. How could they? They had witnessed their miraculous deliverance from Egyptian might, they had escaped Pharaoh and his army through the parting of the sea, and they had come to the mountain of God. As I watched the drama unfold, even

Will the Real Christians Please Stand Up!

though I was quite familiar with the theme and knew in advance what was going to happen, I recognized a living example of what this reflection is all about. Not only had the Hebrews been in bondage for hundreds of years, many of them had lost a keen sense of awareness of who God was and what His promises were. Moses himself had been raised as a member of Egyptian royalty and had no knowledge of the Hebrew God – until the day of the burning bush. He foresaw that if he obeyed God and went back to Egypt as the deliverer of the people, they would ask him who was the God who had sent him. So Moses asked for a name. The response: "I AM." Because the people had wandered far from a relationship with God, their spiritual senses were dulled. Though they saw amazing signs of God's power, they quickly reverted to selfish thinking – and they worshipped an idol, following the example of the Egyptians, rather than trust God and worship Him. The fact that God forgave them (because of Moses' intercession) is an awesome example of God's patient love. Throughout the history of the Chosen People and throughout the history of the Christian Church, when our spiritual senses become dulled by the pleasures and the trials of the world, we turn away from God and to ourselves. When we are open to the moving of the Holy Spirit within us, our hearts become renewed and we recognize the dangers of temptation and the horror of sin.

2) David was the inspired author of many of the Psalms and was a foreshadowing of the coming of the great King, Jesus. David was a man, like us, in need of Redemption. David, like us, was a sinner. In fact, David sinned grievously. He not only committed adultery, he then caused the husband to be killed so that David would not be found out as the father of the child that Bathsheba was bearing as a result of their adulterous union. It was this two-fold sin that led David to write Psalm 51. The Holy Spirit used David's sorrow to guide him in the writing of this magnificent penitential Psalm. Now, we recognize that the Chosen People in

David's time did not have a clear understanding of the nature of God; the doctrine of the Trinity was not revealed until Jesus came. So, in David's mind, when he wrote "Take not Your Holy Spirit from me," he undoubtedly was thinking of God's presence. Regardless, I find it highly significant that the Holy Spirit would inspire David to pray that His presence not be taken from him. I believe that there is the seed of an important teaching here: I believe that, even though I have accepted God's free gift of justification and that I am a member of the Kingdom of Heaven because of what God has done, not because of what I have done, I am also called to <u>live</u> as a disciple of Jesus. I must choose to serve God or self. I have the awesome calling to bear fruit for the Kingdom of God – and if I do not daily allow the Holy Spirit to nourish my spiritual life through prayer, fellowship, meditation on and study of God's Word, then my spiritual senses can indeed become dulled, and I can sin, and then become more dull – and I can thereby become ineffectual. God is a God of love and mercy, as well as a God of justice, and is ready to forgive us when we repent of our sins. I just never want to presume that I "have it made." Remember our reflection on spiritual warfare? Paul talked about being in a race; Peter wrote to Christians about being aware of the devil who as a roaring lion seeks whom he may devour; Jesus said that by our fruit we will be known as disciples. The gift of an intimate relationship with God the Father, God the Son and God the Holy Spirit is a truly awesome and freely bestowed treasure. My prayer is that my life preserve that union and that God's grace work within me and through me day by day, so that one day I can hear "Well done, good and faithful servant. Enter into the joy of your Lord." I like the way I heard one pastor put it: "I am an adopted child of God, sharing God's family life, and I am a pilgrim in this world on the way to eternal salvation in Heaven."

Well, back to Scripture now: *"My son, pay attention to what*

I say; listen closely to my words. Do not let them out of your sight, keep them within your heart; for they are life to those who find them and health to a man's whole body. Above all else, guard your heart, for it is the wellspring of life." (Proverbs 4: 20-23) *"...I will strike her (Jezabel's) children dead. Then all the churches will know that I am he who searches hearts and minds, and I will repay each of you according to your deeds."* (Revelation 2: 23) *"Blessed are the pure of heart, for they will see God."* (Matthew 5: 8) *"For where your treasure is, there your heart will be also."* (Matthew 6: 21) *"...This is the meaning of the parable: The seed is the word of God. Those along the path are the ones who hear, and then the devil comes and takes away the word from their hearts, so that they may not believe and be saved. Those on the rock are the ones who receive the word with joy when they hear it, but they have no root. They believe for awhile, but in the time of testing they fall away. The seed that fell among thorns stands for those who hear, but as they go on their way they are choked by life's worries, riches, and pleasures; and they do not mature. But the seed on good soil stands for those with a noble and good heart, who hear the word, retain it, and by persevering produce a crop."* (Luke 8: 11-15) (Note that in this familiar parable the heart is referred to twice – once when the devil takes the word away from the hearts, and again when those with a good heart produce good fruit. So the heart is key to the spiritual life.)

Psalm 139, which we prayed earlier, speaks eloquently of how God truly knows our inmost thoughts – our hearts. Where is our heart directed? Or, to ask it another way, what are we slaves to? Let's ask the question honestly and seek God's answer. Look at God's Word:

"Don't you know that when you offer yourselves to someone to obey him as slaves, you are slaves to the one whom you obey – whether you are slaves to sin, which leads to death, or to obedience, which leads to righteousness?" (Romans 6: 16) *"...They promise them freedom, while they themselves*

are slaves of depravity – for a man is a slave to whatever has mastered him." (2 Peter 2: 19) *"If we claim to be without sin, we deceive ourselves and the truth is not in us. If we confess our sins, he is faithful and just and will forgive us our sins and purify us from all unrighteousness."* (1 John 1: 8-9)

Is it possible that the following words of Jesus apply to you or to me? *"You hypocrites! Isaiah was right when he prophesied about you: 'These people honor me with their lips, but their hearts are far from me. They worship me in vain; their teachings are but rules taught by men."* (Matthew 15: 7-9)

And then there is the fascinating account relating the aftermath of the fall of Jericho in Joshua 6 and 7. Joshua 7: 1 states that *"...the Israelites acted unfaithfully in regard to the devoted things."* What an apt description: "Devoted things." The Israelites were ordered to destroy everything, to take nothing with them out of Jericho. But a few did. They took treasure in the form of idols or other objects used in pagan worship. God's anger burned against not just them but against all the people because of them. Yes, God's anger burned; more, God punished by death those who disobeyed Him. God has not changed. He still hates sin, though He loves the sinner; the God of mercy is indeed also a God of judgment. Note how the sins of a few affected many people. When I sin, I negatively impact the entire Body of Christ. Direct, conscious sin is one thing; but what about when we become slowly dulled by "little sins" and are not acutely aware of how our actions and our very lives drag others down and block God's grace, which is intended to work and move through yielded and obedient hearts?

A sin can lead to repentance, but a series of sins can lead to loss of even the awareness of sin, much less the ugliness and horror and effect of sin. We shall all one day stand before Him, and our hearts will be bare. Now is the time to ask ourselves if there is any "devoted thing" in our lives that keeps us from hearing and responding to God, from living totally committed to Him. Is there a sin or an occasion of sin that I just cannot seem to let go of? If so, I am playing with fire. Is there something in my life that in itself is harmless but takes so much of my time, energy and attention that I do not have quality time to spend with the Lord?

SUMMARY FOR REFLECTION AND DISCUSSION:

A real Christian:

1) Asks to understand the horror and impact of sin on the Christian life;
2) Asks to spiritually see personal sins and tendencies to sin and to have the courage to flee from occasions of sin;
3) Recognizes and combats the tendency, while living in the midst of a materialistic society, to develop a permissive mentality that dulls the spiritual senses.
4) Cries out with a burning desire to love, not offend the All Holy and All Loving God.

SCRIPTURES FOR JOURNALING:

1) Joshua 6-7 (focus on obedience and "devoted things");
2) Genesis 3, 6, 11;
3) Psalm 139 (as a deeply personal prayer);
4) Psalm 51 (the great Psalm of repentance);
5) The Beatitudes in Matthew 5 as a way to live the Christian life without sin.

REFLECTION 16:

WHY ME, LORD?

This reflection is somewhat different, in one major respect. In the others, as I have stated earlier, I wrote primarily from notes and outlines used for messages on Sunday mornings in the Wilderness Church at Silver Dollar City. But, for now, I refer to no notes; I only pour out my heart to you. Most likely, all of what I write here I allude to and/or repeat in other ways elsewhere. But I want to focus on a topic that, I believe, is critical to real Christians and to everyone who wants to grasp the ways of God.

My inspiration for this reflection is my precious wife, Barbara (and, indeed, she serves as an inspiration throughout this book). She is a true and loving mate, friend, spiritual counselor, and a beacon showing the pure and uncompromising love of God in my life. She is without question, from a human perspective, the wind beneath my wings. Barb is not well physically. In fact, she has been ill for almost all of our married life, over 37 years now. She is in pain all of the time and almost unbearable pain a good part of the time. I do not know how she has the strength to go on; but go on she does. As if total body Fibromyalgia were not enough, she has also now developed neuropathy in both feet, slowly moving up her legs, and the pain is often agonizing. I have shared some of her thoughts about pain and suffering earlier; now I want to hit the subject head-on.

There are many people, Christians included, who fall into

despair when tragedy of one type or another strikes. They lose their joy and hope; they become purveyors of gloom and doom; they forget our glorious inheritance and they forget that all things on this earth are passing. I do not judge; I know that I could not endure with patience and hope what Barb goes through. But when any of us succumb to suffering by losing our spiritual direction, we do not represent the true essence of the Christian life and the walk with Jesus Christ that we are called to live during our time on earth.

Then there are those Christians who see all pain and suffering as totally unnecessary and even contrary to the Christian walk. They proclaim that Jesus took it all on the Cross and that therefore no true Christian living by faith should ever have to endure illnesses or other sufferings – except persecution. I have seen well-intentioned people tell Barb that her problem is a lack of faith. One of her friends some years ago told her that her problem is the presence of a demon in her life. That same friend, a good and well-meaning one, lost her life to cancer a few short years later. We had lost contact, and I wonder how she dealt with her situation; I certainly hope that her deep hope and love gave her and her family strength at the end. I have seen others pray for Barb one time only, and then refuse to visit her because they did not want to acknowledge the continuation of illness and pain and thereby show some kind of lack of faith in the efficacy of their prayers.

But I have also seen others show her deep love and empathy and understanding. Rather than judge her, they reach out with sensitive and caring hearts. They do not tear down; they build up.

No one knows my wife better than I do, including our children. I see the amazing depth of her faith, her desire to turn her sufferings into prayer for others, her will to keep going when it would be so much easier to just give up. She has continued to love me, our children, and others, when by all human standards she should have just withdrawn into a shell.

I have a confession to make: I want to react in anger when I hear a particular Scripture terribly misused, and I have heard it many times in some of the services we used to participate in: *"By his stripes you are healed."* It is found in Isaiah 53: 5 and in 1 Peter 2: 24. There are people who proclaim that Scripture verse and then say, in effect, "God said it, and His Word is true; therefore, He must do it – you are truly healed if you believe, even though the healing may not have manifested itself yet." That kind of thinking, well-intentioned though it is, is, in my judgment, totally contrary to the mind and heart of God. I am embarrassed for Christianity when I see the ballyhoo of some TV evangelistic healing services that focus more on material blessings (including health) than spiritual ones ("and keep those donations coming in, folks!") Don't misunderstand me: I believe in the Word of God, and I believe in healing. With regard to healing, Barb, our sons John and Mike, and I experienced the power of God at a crusade many years ago. Barb and I received immense spiritual blessings, and our younger son, Mike, just 4 years old, received an immediate healing of a visual perception problem. I have seen God touch other people physically, including a lady healed of cancer through the instrumentality of Barb's touch. But I have also seen many, many more not healed. Jesus healed many, many people. But He performed those signs and wonders as ways to show people that He was the Messiah, the Son of God. I have seen many, many more people healed, touched, spiritually through the love of Christians permitting God's grace to work through them; and that is a far greater and more important miracle than any physical healing.

Let's return to Scripture for a moment. I believe with all my heart that Jesus' suffering and death on the Cross opened anew the gates of heaven for those who accept Him as Lord and Savior. If one studies the two Scriptural references to healing through His stripes, it becomes clear that the inspired author is writing about spiritual healing – the healing of the spirit, which is the greatest of all possible healings. This is evident from the context of the Scriptural quotes. Isaiah and Peter are writing about spiritual cleansing and spiritual wholeness made available through the death and Resurrection of Jesus Christ. Does God want this type of healing for every person on the face of the earth? Absolutely yes! It is a miracle when it occurs, because no human being can do it by herself or himself; it takes a supernatural intervention by God – and that is what a miracle is. Does God also at times heal physically, mentally, emotionally? Yes! Sometimes He does it instantaneously;

Will the Real Christians Please Stand Up!

sometimes it happens gradually; sometimes, in fact most often, it happens when we pass from this life to the Kingdom of Heaven – where there will be no more pain or sorrow or suffering for all eternity. God always hears; God always cares; God always has our best interests at heart. It is just that His ways are not always or even usually our ways.

Many non-believers point to the existence of pain and suffering as "proof" that God does not exist – or that a loving, caring, and personal God does not exist. Unfortunately, the wrong beliefs, the blarney and the unrealism of many Christians make Christianity look too often like a blustering, out-of-touch, old-fashioned relic. Following is a summary of my beliefs about the "problem" of pain and suffering. I only ask that you prayerfully consider this.

Only God is perfect. Therefore, all of creation, by its very essence, is imperfect. Further, there is an enemy called Satan who is the prince of this world. He is evil personified. Moreover, when God created people in His image and likeness, He gave us intellects and wills, minds and eternal spirits. The central fact of true love, any true love, is that it must be free. God places imperfect creatures with the ability to choose in an imperfect world, ruled by Satan for a time. God gives us the freedom to choose Him or ourselves; He provides His grace, while Satan pushes and pulls in a direction opposite of grace. Satan, the mighty angel Lucifer, fell because he, too, had a choice. He chose himself, and he seeks now to influence us to do the same. To choose anyone or anything other than God is the very definition of sin. When mankind first sinned, the result was a fallen human nature, not only of our first parents, but also of everyone who followed. Also, when we sinned, we lost the intimate relationship with God and the total beauty of creation as God intended. In that context and reality, we find the beginnings of suffering, sickness, sorrow and pain.

It is clear from the first chapters of the Book of Job in the Old Testament that Satan seeks to bring harm to people – disasters, tragedies, sickness, and death. Note that in this case God specifically permits Satan to wreak havoc on Job and his family; but God remains in control. This is not to suggest that every calamity is the result of a Satanic attack. No, because of original sin, we live in an imperfect environment, prone to problems and disasters. Our ongoing sinfulness certainly adds to this. But it would be absolutely contrary to the Word of God and to what we know about God through His revelation of Himself to conclude that sickness and other problems are always or even frequently the result of an individual's particular sinfulness. This, in fact, is what the "name it and claim it" adherents wind up proclaiming: If I am sick, even after prayer, then there must be something wrong with me. Conclusions like that please Satan, for he is justifiably fearful of the person who turns suffering into prayer for others.

To recognize that Jesus healed, that early Church leaders were instruments for healing, that God touches people miraculously today is a far cry from saying that every sickness, from colds to cancer, every financial problem, every difficulty of any kind has absolutely no place in the life of the New Covenant Church. Even in the early Church, people were sick after prayer for healing. Not everyone in Jesus' time on earth was healed. More to the point, as we faithfully and openly study the Word of God, it is clear that Jesus' message and mission focused on the forgiveness of sins, the healing of souls, the establishment of relationships between God and people.

Here is my assessment of what has happened in our time (and this insistence on health and healing is primarily a modern phenomenon). Too many people have found a clever way to use the Word to ensure an abundance of material blessings; they thereby place more emphasis, whether knowingly or unknowingly, on worldly success than on living a yielded and obedient life of love and service. The person who lives in a wheelchair or in a bed and yet praises God and turns the affliction into prayer is actually a much more powerful witness than the person who "names it and claims it,", than the person who in effect tries to turn God into a puppet by pulling the strings of Scripture quotes and demanding immediate results, than the one who points to the luxury car in the garage and the lack of any illness as true signs of God's favor and living in His will. Does God bless His people? You bet He does! But the moment I start evaluating those blessings by the standards of the materialistic world I live in, I have at that moment prostituted the Gospel. I have developed myopic vision. I have inadvertently become like Judas who was more concerned with the amount of money in Jesus' treasury than with the treasure that was Jesus.

We do not want to hear this, but the fact is that God permits us to go through trials, including illness, financial problems, and other situations, as a means of building our trust, our faith, our hope and our strength. The crucible in which gold is purified is not only persecution, the sole form of suffering acceptable to the name it and claim it people. We live in the midst of imperfection, and God has chosen not to preserve us from difficulties, because they are intended for our personal spiritual growth and as an opportunity to pray for others.

So, should we wallow in our problems and have a good old pity-party? God forbid! Should we deny that God can bring much good through trial and difficulty as long as we turn it into, by His grace, joy, prayer, and service? God forbid! Should we measure the success of our Christian life by the amount of money that we have, the number of cars, the amount of physical strength and energy? God forbid! But, at the other end of the spectrum, should we avoid taking care of our bodies and not be good stewards of the resources God has given us? Once again, God forbid!

Thank you for letting me pour out my heart a bit. If you are infirm and this has given you hope, praise God! If you are insensitive to infirmity in others and judge others because of it and if this has opened the eyes of your heart even a little bit, praise God! Please pray with me: Father, I beseech You to give me the mind and heart of Jesus Christ, who set His face resolutely toward Jerusalem and the Cross, because He wanted above all things to do Your will. Give me that same resolute courage to seek You above and before all else. Give me, I pray, your Holy Spirit to teach me about Jesus, to give me wisdom and strength, and to enlighten my path. If I encounter trials and deliverance from them that can glorify You, so be it! If You want me to walk through the trials with my eyes on You and turn it into prayer for others, with your grace I will do that and will do it with joy. Above all, Lord, help me see that time on this earth is short and passing. Help me to use my circumstances to glorify You and serve You as You will, not as I will. Help me to see that intercession for others through pain and suffering is just as much a ministry and a mission as preaching the Gospel in a far-off land. Help me fill each moment of my life with the radiance of Your love and presence, so that everyone with whom I come into contact will see a purpose in my life, a joy that the world cannot explain, a light shining through me that draws others to You, the eternal Light. Thank You for creating me; thank You for redeeming me; thank You for living within me; thank You for caring about me; thank You for letting me and helping me to walk through the sufferings of this life, for truly – as Your Word says – they cannot be compared with the glory that is to come. Thank you for letting me—as Paul says—make up in my life what is lacking in the sufferings of Christ. And please help me be like Him who gave up heaven to become a Servant and to die the humiliating death of a criminal, though He was the Innocent and Pure One. Help me to see that He did this because He, and You, and the Holy Spirit love me so much and want me to be with You forever. Help me remember, Lord, that when I appear before You, You will not ask me how often I was sick or how much money I have in the bank. Rather, You will ask me how faithfully I lived each moment, how lovingly I served, how joyfully I lived in hope, how much I glorified You by my thoughts, my words, and my actions. I praise You and glorify You, Lord God. Amen.

SUMMARY FOR REFLECTION AND DISCUSSION:

A real Christian:

1) Sees every circumstance in life as an opportunity to love, to serve and to pray for others;
2) Does not measure success by anything other than growth in union with and love of God, and genuine service from the heart to all who cross the path of life;
3) Seeks to have the fruit of the Holy Spirit operative in daily life — love, joy, peace, patience, goodness, kindness, gentleness, faithfulness, self-control;
4) Keeps eyes and heart fixed on the vision of eternal joy to come, seeking to use every moment now to serve the Lord,

following Jesus, whether from a missionary campsite or from a bed or wheelchair;

5) Seeks to see the presence of God in all circumstances of life, believing that God will always give the strength to walk through; and that God has the desire and power to turn every situation into an opportunity for ministry and joyful service – even if He is the only one who sees it.

SCRIPTURES FOR JOURNALING:

1) Isaiah 50; 52: 13-53: 12
2) 1 Peter 1-2
3) Romans 8: 17-8; 1 Peter 5: 10
4) Philippians 2-3
5) Revelation 21: 4

REFLECTION 17:

THE DANGER OF THE NEW AGE MOVEMENT

During one of the early times that I was reviewing the material in this series of Biblical reflections, I realized that something was missing. In many ways, what is written here is a personal testimony of my journey with the Lord. It is quite clear to me – and to people who really know me – that the description of a real Christian, which is the overall theme, is something that I am striving to achieve in my life. I fall and fail often, but the grace of God raises me up each time. As I read somewhere, "Fall down seven times and get up eight."

An important aspect of my journey is a theme that is critical for Christians in modern times. We must both understand and confront the New Age Movement. Why? Because it brings clearly into focus the tensions that the world and the Church are experiencing, the spiritual warfare that is raging, the battle to cloud and mask what true Christianity is all about. Moreover, the New Age Movement is important for me to write about, because I was caught up in it at one time; my deliverance from it is a critical aspect of my journey.

Two preliminary statements about the New Age Movement: First, it is not some off the wall, esoteric, kooky belief system that is out of touch with the mainstream of life. It would be a serious error to ignore its impact and importance in the panorama of salvation history. Second, it is not new. It is as old as the Garden of Eden. It is a modern manifestation of the ultimate temptation; it is at its roots one of Satan's basic weapons.

Let's take a brief journey into the intricacies of the New Age Movement. There are many fine books that deal with this subject in greater depth; I urge every Christian to become knowledgeable – we must be able to recognize the enemy. The following synopsis and summary will look at the New Age Movement from two perspectives: Its teachings, and its tentacles. The teachings are pretty straightforward; the tentacles constitute the true insidiousness of the New Age Movement, for they have snaked into the very life of the Church in too many ways. So, let's begin.

Look at a very familiar Scripture, Genesis 3: 1-5. *"Now the serpent was more crafty than any of the wild animals the Lord God had made. He said to the woman, 'Did God really say, 'You must not eat from any tree in the garden'?' The woman said to the serpent, 'We may eat fruit from the trees in the garden, but God did say, 'You must not eat fruit from the tree that is in the middle of the garden, and you must not touch it, or you will die.' 'You will not surely die,' the serpent said to the woman. 'For God knows that when you eat of it your eyes will be opened, and you will be like God, knowing good and evil.'"* Genesis 11: 1-8, a description of people at a later time when they once again, after the flood, repopulated the earth and had largely forgotten the one true God, points out the same sinful theme: *"Now the whole world had one language and a common speech. As men moved eastward, they found a plain in Shinar and settled there. They said to one another, 'Come, let us build ourselves a city, with a tower that reaches to the heavens, so that we may make a name for ourselves and not be scattered over the face of the whole earth.' But the Lord came down to see the city and the tower that the men were building. The Lord said, 'If as one people speaking the same language they have begun to do this, then nothing they plan to do will be impossible for them. Come, let us go down and confuse their language so they will not understand each other.' So the Lord scattered them from there all over the earth, and they stopped building the city. That is why it is called Babel – because there the Lord confused the language of the whole world. From there the Lord scattered them over the face of the whole earth."* Compare this sin of pride with the account in Acts 2 describing the birthday of the Church on the Jewish Feast of Pentecost. There, by the power and presence of the Holy Spirit, the living Love of God, people of different languages all understand what Peter was saying. God unites; people trying to be God are ultimately extremely divisive and destructive.

Well, what Satan was doing in the garden and what the people at Babel were doing is going on today. It is the sin of seeking to be like God, indeed, to be God. That is what the New Age Movement is all about. It is actually quite difficult to pinpoint the New Age. There is no world headquarters, no common logo. But there is a phenomenon occurring, and it has not diminished even though there is not as much discussion about it as there was some years ago. Small groups, large groups, individuals with no direct contact with one another are springing up and uniting, all with the common thread of a belief system. It is truly supernatural in nature, unexplainable by coincidence. The teachings of the New Age Movement, as we shall see, are certainly not rooted in God's revealed truth; so, the supernatural aspect must have its source in Satan – a supernatural being. There is a common misperception – namely, that Satan wants people to be atheists. But, no, not at all. People are looking for supernatural answers to life's questions; they are seeking signs and wonders. In fact, when the Antichrist comes (and we do not know when that will be), he will perform signs and wonders to lead people astray. Though Satan is certainly not upset about atheists and agnostics, he appears to be focusing much attention on people who have a spiritual hunger. The danger is that he seeks to satisfy that hunger with a false and deadly spirituality.

There is no question that we live in very tumultuous and dangerous times. The words of Paul to Timothy in 2 Timothy 3: 1-5 certainly apply to these days:

"But mark this: There will be terrible times in the last days. People will be lovers of themselves, lovers of money, boastful, proud, abusive, disobedient to their parents, ungrateful,

unholy, without love, unforgiving, slanderous, without self-control, brutal, not lovers of the good, treacherous, rash, conceited, lovers of pleasure rather than lovers of God – having a form of godliness but denying its power."

This passage describes by and large our world, and far too often it describes the Church, or rather, "religious Christianity." At the same time, the world is seeking some type of renewal; people are thirsting for meaning in their lives. But they frequently do not see it in the form of Christianity that is paraded before secular eyes. So, enter the New Age Movement to try to slake the thirst.

Satan fell because he tried to set himself up as an equal to God; and the ultimate temptation that Satan uses now is to get others to do the same. Sometimes it is subtle, sometimes it is blatant. The New Age Movement makes it quite blatant.

The first and most basic teaching of the New Age is that mankind is ultimately divine – that we are truly God, but we just do not recognize it. The New Age has its roots in Hinduism and in other ancient eastern religions. The roots also include a belief in "monism" (all matter is one) and "pantheism" (all things are god). That may sound hokey, but it is striking a chord in people all over our planet. The seed of sin is in us, and sin in its ultimate and most basic form is pride – setting myself up as god-like. The New Age just takes this to its ultimate expression.

What is needed, says the New Age, is a paradigm shift, a basic change in outlook, in order to see the divinity in myself and in others. New Age devotees encourage us to raise our sights and at the same time to look deep within ourselves, and thereby find the spark of divinity that is struggling to emerge. "Harmonic convergence" will hasten that awareness, as people elevate their consciousness and let the energy of united thought and awareness open our minds to the glory of our divinity. By the way, one can find in the teaching of the most dedicated New Age leaders a need for a cleansing, a purging, in order to remove blocks to this much needed paradigm shift. Who is doing the blocking? Among others, they are committed Christians who try to live and share what the Bible and the Body of Christ really offer and teach (in other words, real Christians – not the churchy, religious ones, for they play right into the hands of Satan as he orchestrates the growth of the New Age, as we shall see shortly).

The New Age draws on Hinduism and teaches "karma" and "reincarnation." Karma is a type of impersonal judgment, a cleansing process. Reincarnation gives people the opportunity to return after death – hopefully, in progressively higher states of consciousness, ever more pure, until at last they become totally aware, free and "ascended." Such teaching flies directly in the face of Scripture. Hebrews 9: 27-28 tells us that *"Just as man is destined to die once, and after that to face judgment, so Christ was sacrificed once to take away the sins of many people; and he will appear a second time, not to bear sin, but to bring salvation to those who are waiting for him."*

With regard to Christ, the New Age believes that Jesus was a great teacher, a Messiah or Christ, but not the Christ. Sometimes the language used by New Agers is very clear in its deviation from Christian truth, but at other times it is subtle and potentially deceiving. For example, some years ago I went into a New Age bookstore to do some research. A pleasant, bubbly lady was at the counter. I requested if I could ask her a question and I inquired if she believed in Jesus Christ. Beaming her infectious smile at me, she replied, "Why certainly! I believe in the Christ-consciousness in all of us." "No," I said, "that is not what I asked. Do you believe in Jesus Christ the Second Person of the Blessed Trinity, who became Man, suffered, died, and rose from the dead?" "Oh, no," she responded, "that is where we differ." I told her that I would pray for her, and she said that she would pray for me, too. As an aside, my wife, Barbara, had entered the store with me and had just sat quietly in a corner. In the car on our way home, I noticed that she was crying. When I asked her what was the matter, she shook her head and said, "My Jesus, my Jesus, what have we done to You?"

Yes, the New Age believes that Jesus is a Christ – along with Buddha, Krishna, and others. But "the true and complete Christ" is yet to come, and he will usher in a new world order. (Perhaps what these people are describing is whom we call the Antichrist.) The New World Order will include a one-world government and a one-world religion. It sounds very good; it proclaims the way to peace and happiness – but it is straight out of the pit of hell.

Since, according to New Agers, we are all god, and since really everything is god, then belief in a personal God must go by the wayside for the sake of "a new and higher reality." And, since the only real "sin" is ignorance of our divinity, then there is no need for forgiveness, no need for redemption; the Cross and salvation by the shed blood of Jesus Christ are silly, medieval teachings.

Then there is channeling. This has taken the place of the old séances. A lot of people consider it fakery, just a clever way to get into the pockets of naïve people – and some of it undoubtedly is just that, but I firmly believe that not all of it is. I believe that in many cases channeling is truly taking place, people are truly making contact with the spirit world. The problem is, they are not "ascended masters;" they are demons. The same is true through the use of crystals; the assumed use of crystalline "energy" is a dabbling with the dark side of the supernatural.

The bottom line is that to the New Ager, traditional Christianity has failed. There is little world peace; there is hunger; the environment is in serious difficulty. The New Age Movement calls for the full release of the true potential of the world and of all its human-potentially-divine inhabitants. Put the Bible and faith in Jesus Christ on the shelf, and find the beauty of divinity residing within each of us.

These ideas represent the primary teachings of the New Age Movement. They are relatively straightforward, and should not in any way be shrugged off as just crazy ideas proposed by crazy people. New Agers are very serious and highly determined people.

Before we investigate the tentacles of the New Age Movement, which represent, in my judgment, the most dangerous aspect of this worldwide movement, carefully read two Old Testament Scripture passages.

First, Isaiah 14: 12-15: *"How you have fallen from heaven, O morning star, son of the dawn! You have been cast down to the earth, you who once laid low the nations! You said in your heart, 'I will ascend to heaven; I will raise my throne above the stars of God; I will sit enthroned on the mount of assembly, on the utmost heights of the sacred mountain. I will ascend above the tops of the clouds; I will make myself like the Most High.' But you are brought down to the grave, to the depths of the pit."*

Ezekiel 28: 12-17: *"This is what the Sovereign Lord says: 'You were the model of perfection, full of wisdom and perfect in beauty. You were in Eden, the garden of God; every precious stone adorned you: Ruby, topaz and emerald, chrysolite, onyx and jasper, sapphire, turquoise and beryl. Your settings and mountings were made of gold; on the day you were created they were prepared. You were anointed as a guardian cherub, for so I ordained you. You were on the holy mount of God; you walked among the fiery stones. You were blameless in your ways from the day you were created till wickedness was found in you. Through your widespread trade you were filled with violence, and you sinned. So I drove you in disgrace from the mount of God, and I expelled you, O guardian cherub, from among the fiery stones. Your heart became proud on account of your beauty, and you corrupted your wisdom because of your splendor. So I threw you to the earth.'"*

These are Scripture passages referring to the fall of Lucifer, who became Satan. It is clear that pride brought him down. So is it not logical to conclude that what he knows best is pride, and that what he tries to bring us down with is ultimately pride? The Word upholds this.

Let's now explore the tentacles of the New Age Movement. It is here where Satan's shrewdness manifests itself, and where true discernment through the power of the Holy Spirit working within us is essential.

The first and most critical tentacle has to do with Jesus Christ. It is now sadly common and even fashionable in many theological circles to water down the basic Christian doctrine of the divinity of Jesus Christ. And that plays right into the hand of the New Age. Let me state it bluntly: The divinity of Jesus Christ, as the Second

Person of the Blessed Trinity Incarnate, is a bedrock belief of Christianity. If a "Christian" does not proclaim that Jesus is God made Man, that person is not really a Christian at all. This is a hard saying, but it needs to be shouted from the church roofs! What better way could there be for Satan to weaken his archenemy than to have the Church waver in its beliefs?

Another tentacle is the diminished emphasis on the Cross, on the blood of Jesus shed for our Redemption, and on sin. It is not very acceptable to many in the pews today to hear preaching and teaching about these elements of Christian faith. Too many people prefer to be fed on milktoast.

Also, the inerrancy and infallibility of the Bible are under attack. I was in this camp once, and it was a major reason why I strayed so far from God and was able to rationalize all kinds of sin. I now humbly accept the Bible as the revealed Word of God. I also believe that we must understand the Word in its context, not just in its pure words, though there are indeed many, many Scriptural passages that should be literally interpreted. Even the contextual approach holds firmly that the Bible is absolutely true and inerrant. We should be grateful to Biblical scholars, who give us so much insight into Scripture and ensure accurate translations. But the endless arguing and theologizing from one's pet perspective play right into Satan's hand. It is really simple: The Holy Spirit is the author; the Holy Spirit is God; the Holy Spirit worked through human instruments; the result is the revealed, awesome, eternal Word of God. To doubt this or to become overly intellectual is to become entwined by a tentacle of the New Age Movement, which sees Scripture as gibberish and is thrilled when Christians argue over it or water it down.

Then there is ecumenism. Now it is surely admirable for Christian sects to strive to find their common ground and to pray and work together for unity. It is quite another thing to take the position that all sects, indeed all religions and all faiths, are quite acceptable — we are all going to the same place, just by different routes. This is misleading; it is dangerous, and it diminishes the true faith. I believe that God looks at the heart, so I have no right to judge any person of any faith or no faith. But I do have the responsibility as a Christian to proclaim Jesus as the Way, the Truth and the Life, and the Light of the world, and that He said the gate to salvation is narrow. To glibly proclaim that everything is alright, that we are all on the right path, is to promote a glib, sweet-sounding ecumenism that is very much in keeping with the New Age goal of a one-world religion.

Now let's consider psychology. I quickly state that psychology is a science and provides positive services to human knowledge and understanding. Further, there are many sound Christian psychologists (as long as they, as professed Christians, are Biblical in their counseling). But, take a close look at the approach used by the majority of psychologists: The focus is all on the self, the ego – self-worth, self-esteem, self-fulfillment, self-actualization. Think about it. It is considered really strange and out of touch with modern reality to question the "all important" self-esteem. This focus on self is taught in schools, in businesses, and even in churches. This is perfectly in keeping with New Age teaching, which is all self-focused, up to and including the proclamation of each person's latent divinity. As I study the life of Jesus Christ, I find a teaching and a personal emphasis on selflessness, an emptying of oneself in order to be filled with Him. The only esteem that a Christian should have is one based on union with Jesus Christ. In Him we live and move and have our being.

Finally, consider the prosperity gospel, or "name-it-and-claim-it." I have addressed this perversion of the Gospel elsewhere. Actually, I have addressed most if not all of the tentacles in one way or another. It is so very critical for us to understand the New Age Movement. Its insidious tentacles seek to squeeze the very life-blood out of the Church and out of individual members of the Body. The prosperity gospel was fanned into flame by modern TV evangelism – rather by those few who have given evangelists a bad name among so many people. After all, what better way for these out-of-balance evangelists to keep the donations coming in than to promise health, wealth and happiness to those who will just plant seeds of faith by contributing, and contributing, and contributing. At the same time, though, we should not place full blame on these spiritual marketers. No, the real foundation lies in a misplaced and misinterpreted faith in God's Word. "Name it and claim it" uses Scripture to obtain whatever we want by turning God into a puppet. He said it, He wrote it, I speak it, and so it must happen. From health to riches to whatever my heart desires, I just have to pray for it, believe in it, and if it does not come to pass there must be something wrong with my faith or some sin in my life.

What this belief system really does is turn people away from being humble, yielded, other-worldly Christians seeking only what God wants in our lives and seeking to serve and glorify Him in and through every circumstance. Thus, this perversion plays right into Satan's master plan.

Teachings or tentacles, the New Age is a basic adversary of what true Christianity stands for. Every real Christian must understand what the New Age is all about, must combat it, must pray for true revival and awakening in the Church. Only the Holy Spirit can expose and overcome this type of spiritual warfare; and the Holy Spirit can only work in hearts that are repentant, humble and pure in their search for truth and a servant's life.

To end this search, and this warning, focus on the Word of God:

"Dear friends, although I was very eager to write to you about the salvation we share, I felt I had to write and urge you to contend for the faith that was once for all entrusted to the saints. For certain men whose condemnation was written about long ago have secretly slipped in among you. They are godless men, who change the grace of our God into a license for immorality and deny Jesus Christ our only Sovereign and Lord." (Jude 3-4) Just as heresies began to spring up in the early centuries of the Church, such as Gnosticism, which has similarities to the New Age, so the supreme liar and deceiver, Satan, along with his fallen hordes, has been at work from the beginning trying to destroy or blunt God's work and plan of salvation: *"Concerning the coming of our Lord Jesus Christ and our being gathered to him, we ask you, brothers, not to become easily unsettled or alarmed by some prophecy, report or letter supposed to have come from us, saying that the day of the Lord has already come. Don't let anyone deceive you in any way, for that day will not come until the rebellion occurs and the man of lawlessness is revealed, the man doomed to destruction. He will oppose and will*

Will the Real Christians Please Stand Up!

exalt himself over everything that is called God or is worshiped, so that he sets himself up in God's temple proclaiming himself to be God. Don't you remember that when I was with you I used to tell you these things? And now you know what is holding him back, so that he may be revealed at the proper time. For the secret power of lawlessness is already at work; but the one who now holds it back will continue to do so till he is taken out of the way. And then the lawless one will be revealed, whom the Lord Jesus will overthrow with the breath of his mouth and destroy by the splendor of his coming. The coming of the lawless one will be in accordance with the work of Satan displayed in all kinds of counterfeit miracles, signs and wonders, and in every sort of evil that deceives those who are perishing. They perish because they refuse to love the truth and so be saved. For this reason God sends them a powerful delusion so that they will believe the lie and so that all will be condemned who have not believed the truth but have delighted in wickedness." (2 Thessalonians 2: 1-12) Finally, the beloved disciple, John, writes in his first Letter, Chapter 4, verses 1-6 and 19-21*: "Dear friends, do not believe every spirit, but test the spirits to see whether they are from God, because many false prophets have gone out into the world. This is how you can recognize the Spirit of God: Every spirit that acknowledges that Jesus Christ has come in the flesh is from God, but every spirit that does not acknowledge Jesus is not from God. This is the spirit of the Antichrist, which you have heard is coming and even now is already in the world. You, dear children, are from God and have overcome them, because the One who is in you is greater than the one who is in the world. They are from the world and therefore speak from the viewpoint of the world, and the world listens to them. We are from God, and whoever knows God listens to us; but whoever is from God does not listen to us. This is how we recognize the Spirit of truth and the spirit of falsehood – We know that we the children of God, and the whole world, are under the control of the evil one. We know also that the Son of God has come and has given us understanding, so that we may know him who is true. And we are in him who is true – even in his Son, Jesus Christ. He is the true God and eternal life. Dear children, keep yourselves from idols."*

SUMMARY FOR REFLECTION AND DISCUSSION:

A real Christian:

1) Does not waver in fundamental Christian beliefs:
   a) The divinity of Jesus Christ;
   b) Redemption by the shed blood of the Risen Savior;
   c) The Christian life fully described as following Jesus, with a servant's yielded and obedient heart;
   d) Scripture as the revealed and inerrant Word of God;
2) Avoids the world's fetish on the glorification of "self";
3) Does not demand anything of God, but seeks His will in all things;
4) Recognizes the presence of spiritual warfare and engages in battle.

SCRIPTURES FOR JOURNALING:

1) Genesis 3 and 11; compare with Acts 2;
2) Isaiah 14: 12-15; Ezekiel 28: 12-17; Revelation 12-13, 19-20;
3) Jude 3-4; 2 Thessalonians 2: 1-12; 1 John 4: 1-6, 19-21
4) John 15-17

PART IV:

THE CALL TO SALVATION AND RELATIONSHIP

It may seem out of place to deal with the topic of salvation and relationship so far into this book of reflections. However, it is a thread throughout the book; the intent here is to zoom in on these themes, which are so critical to the genuine Christian life.

Again, our guide is the Word of God. We will be exploring who God is and who we are as His creatures —made in His image and likeness to be sure, but His creation nonetheless.

We will return to a hopefully familiar topic – that of the real meaning of "personal relationship" and of the central place of Jesus in the true Christian's life.

The summaries and Scriptures for journaling should be seen as opportunities for, as springboards to, an open and deep examination of just how personal and alive our relationship with Jesus Christ is.

REFLECTION 18:

"MY LORD AND MY GOD!"

I would appreciate your exploring with me a Scripture passage. It is the account of Saul's conversion – the Saul who later became Paul and the greatest missionary of all time. Instead of focusing on the initial account in Acts 9, let's go to Paul's own telling of what happened, in an address to an angry crowd in Jerusalem, as recorded in Acts 21: 40-22: 21:

> *"Having received the commander's permission, Paul stood on the steps and motioned to the crowd. When they were all silent, he said to them in Aramaic: 'Brothers and fathers, listen now to my defense.' When they heard him speak to them in Aramaic, they became very quiet. Then Paul said, 'I am a Jew, born in Tarsus of Cilicia, but brought up in this city. Under Gamaliel I was thoroughly trained in the law of our fathers, and was just as zealous for God as any of you are today. I persecuted the followers of this Way to their death, arresting both men and women and throwing them into prison, as also the high priest and all the Council can testify. I even obtained letters from them to their brothers in Damascus, and went there to bring these people as prisoners to Jerusalem to be punished. About noon as I came near Damascus, suddenly a bright light from heaven flashed*

around me. I fell to the ground and heard a voice say to me, 'Saul! Saul! Why do you persecute me?' 'Who are you, Lord?' I asked. 'I am Jesus of Nazareth, whom you are persecuting,' he replied. My companions saw the light, but they did not understand the voice of him who was speaking to me. 'What shall I do, Lord?' I asked. 'Get up,' the Lord said, 'and go into Damascus. There you will be told all that you have been assigned to do.' My companions led me by the hand into Damascus, because the brilliance of the light had blinded me. A man named Ananias came to see me. He was a devout observer of the law and highly respected by all the Jews living there. He stood beside me and said, 'Brother Saul, receive your sight!' And at that very moment I was able to see him. Then he said, 'The God of our fathers has chosen you to know his will and to see the Righteous One and to hear words from his mouth. You will be his witness to all men of what you have seen and heard. And now what are you waiting for? Get up, be baptized and wash your sins away, calling on his name.' When I returned to Jerusalem and was praying at the temple, I fell into a trance and saw the Lord speaking. 'Quick!' he said to me. 'Leave Jerusalem immediately, because they will not accept your testimony about me.' 'Lord,' I replied, 'these men know that I went from one synagogue to another to imprison and beat those who believe in you. And when the blood of your martyr Stephen was shed, I stood there giving my approval and guarding the clothes of those who were killing him. Then the Lord said to me, 'Go; I will send you far away to the Gentiles.'"

What can we learn from this? Many things! For example: Saul was a very religious man and very zealous in the expression of his faith. Saul knew about Jesus, and he hated His followers. But Saul had never met Jesus personally, and he never expected to, since Saul obviously did not believe in Jesus' Resurrection or His divinity. But meet Him he did, that fateful day on the road to Damascus. Saul became blind; he really had to, for the Holy Spirit had to begin blotting out the influence of a very strong anti-Christian past. Saul

Will the Real Christians Please Stand Up!

had to become blind to religion as he knew it – Judaism, the directional signal which for centuries had been pointing to the coming of the Messiah but had made a wrong turn in its expectations of just who and what the Messiah would be. Saul had to change his religious bearings, his prejudices and his world-view. Then Saul received new sight, not just physical, but most importantly spiritual, and he was baptized. We discover in Galatians 1: 16 that Paul apparently did not spend a long time consulting men; instead he went into solitude for three years in order to listen to Jesus and to the Holy Spirit and to become firmly grounded in the truth.

Why do I share this? Well, I once had a beautiful but sobering experience. I was given that wonderful opportunity to be an instrument in leading someone to the Lord. What is interesting is that another Christian had done the same thing with this person a few days previously! There had been tears, an emotional high, but also confusion. The supposed convert did not understand the Trinity, the Incarnation, or that Jesus is God – either before the initial conversion experience or after it (even after growing up in a large church). So, the Holy Spirit guided me to return to the basics. That is what all we Christians need to do periodically – go back to the basics and test the strength and solidity of our faith. A key question, in addition to ensuring proper doctrinal belief, is whether our faith is truly spiritual, or only religious. Paul was religious; he apparently had no genuine spiritual relationship with God.

When we share our faith with others, I believe that first and foremost we must proclaim the divinity of Jesus Christ. This, as we have already seen, is becoming more and more unfashionable in some theological circles, and doubting who Christ is becomes a major weapon of Satan. After all, the proclamation of Jesus Christ as God Incarnate is the very cornerstone of Christianity. What better way to attack the edifice of the Church than by weakening, even trying to destroy, its foundation? We had best check our own spiritual walk. Have I had a "Damascus experience?" Have I been knocked off my high horse and encountered the living King of Kings and Lord of Lords? Have I made Him Lord of my life and not just mouthed some words of acceptance or gone through some rite of initiation? Has my Damascus experience brought me so close to Jesus that I can speak passionately from my heart as Paul did to that crowd in Jerusalem and as he did from prison years later, for example in the Letters to the Philippians and the Colossians?

"If you have any encouragement from being united with Christ, if any comfort from his love, if any fellowship with the Spirit, if any tenderness and compassion, then make my joy complete by being like-minded and having the same love, being one in spirit and purpose...Your attitude should be the same as that of Christ Jesus: Who, being in very nature God, did not consider equality with God something to be grasped, but made himself nothing, taking the very nature of a servant, being made in human likeness. And being found in appearance as a man, he humbled himself and became obedient to death – even death on a cross! Therefore God exalted him to the highest place and gave him the name that is above every name, that at the name of Jesus every knee should bow, in heaven and on earth and under the earth, and every tongue confess that Jesus Christ is Lord, to the glory of God the Father." (Philippians 2: 1-11) *"He is the image of the invisible God, the firstborn over all creation. For by him all things were created; things in heaven and on earth, visible and invisible, whether thrones or powers or rulers or authorities; all things were created by him and for him. He is before all things, and in him all things hold together.. See to it that no one takes you captive through hollow and deceptive philosophy, which depends on human tradition and the basic principles of this world rather than on Christ. For in Christ all the fullness of the Deity lives in bodily form, and you have been given fullness in Christ, who is the head over every power and authority."* (Colossians 1: 15-17; 2: 8-9)

In the Gospel accounts of Jesus' life, many people met Jesus personally and found new life. Matthew was sitting at his money-changer's table when Jesus looked at him and invited him to follow. Zacchaeus was up in the tree when Jesus saw him and told him to come down. The lady at the well had a conversation with

Will the Real Christians Please Stand Up!

Jesus, and her life changed forever.

Then there was Thomas: *"Now Thomas (called Didymus), one of the Twelve, was not with the disciples when Jesus came. So the other disciples told him, 'We have seen the Lord!' But he said to them, 'Unless I see the nail marks in his hands and put my finger where the nails were, and put my hand into his side, I will not believe it.' A week later his disciples were in the house again, and Thomas was with them. Though the doors were locked, Jesus came and stood among them and said, 'Peace be with you!' Then he said to Thomas, 'Put your finger here; see my hands. Reach out your hand and put it into my side. Stop doubting and believe.' Thomas said to Him, 'My Lord and my God!' Jesus told him, 'Because you have seen me, you have believed; blessed are those who have not seen and yet have believed.'"* (John 20: 24-29)

In these days of confusion and doubting, of so much theological pomposity and empty cynicism, real Christians – those who have had a personal encounter with the living Jesus – are compelled to cry out regarding the Person they have met with the spiritual eyes of faith, "My Lord and my God!"

Remember the person I mentioned when this reflection began? After pronouncing faith in His divinity (and saying, "Now it all makes sense, if I believe He is God"), there was suddenly a wondrous facial expression as we were sitting on a picnic bench at work, and I heard these unforgettable words: "Oh, I hear the birds singing! I haven't heard them singing in such a long time!"

My prayer is that we as Christians, believing in the wondrous truth of an Incarnate, Risen and Glorified God, have the same zeal as that of Paul just before his final voyage to Rome and ultimately to his death:

"'So then, King Agrippa, I was not disobedient to the vision from heaven. First to those in Damascus, then to those in Jerusalem and in all Judea, and to the Gentiles also, I preached that they should repent and turn to God and prove their repentance by their deeds. That is why the Jews seized me in the temple courts and tried to kill me. But I have had God's help to this very day; and so I stand here and testify to

small and great alike. I am saying nothing beyond what the prophets and Moses said would happen – that the Christ would suffer and, as the first to rise from the dead, would proclaim light to his own people and to the Gentiles.' At this point Festus interrupted Paul's defense. 'You are out of your mind, Paul!' he shouted. 'Your great learning is driving you insane.' 'I am not insane, most excellent Festus,' Paul replied. 'What I am saying is true and reasonable. The king is familiar with these things, and I can speak freely to him. I am convinced that none of this has escaped his notice, because it was not done in a corner. King Agrippa, do you believe the prophets? I know you do.' Then Agrippa said to Paul, 'Do you think that in such a short time you can persuade me to be a Christian?' Paul replied, 'Short time or long – I pray God that not only you but all who are listening to me today may become what I am, except for these chains.'" (Acts 26: 19-29)

Amen! So let it be!

SUMMARY FOR REFLECTION AND DISCUSSION:

A real Christian:

1) Believes in the divinity of Jesus Christ and, more, proclaims that He is Risen, spiritually present and will come again;
2) Relies on the faith expressed by "My Lord and my God!" during times of trial and difficulty – in the valley as well as on the mountain top;
3) Reflects on the personal "Damascus experience" and readily shares it with all who will listen.

SCRIPTURES FOR JOURNALING:

1) Acts 9; Acts 21: 40-22: 21; Acts 26: 19-29;
2) Philippians 2-3; Colossians 1-2;
3) John 20-21

REFLECTION 19:

NEW CREATION

I watched a TV show once about a father and son who had been estranged and were trying to rebuild their relationship. To do this, they set off on a crosscountry motorcycle trip. Along the way, they had a minor accident outside a small town in Missouri. A local resident, an aging farmer named Oscar, stopped to help them. Oscar offered them a room while their cycle was being repaired.

As the story unfolded, it turned out that Oscar was quite a character. His farm was much older than he was, and Oscar was old. The homestead had deteriorated, and Oscar appeared unperturbed about its condition. He had some cows that he called "his girls." Oscar had no use for the townsfolk, calling them "the town of the living dead", and they in turn viewed him as an old and eccentric fool. To top it all off, Oscar had a large and beautiful sailboat that he was in the process of building, in his barn! Oscar's dream – apparently for a long time by now – was to finish the boat, transport it through town to a nearby river while thumbing his nose at the townsfolk, leave his old farm behind, and sail down the river to the sea – thereby transforming into a sailor for the remaining years of his life.

Dad and son decided to help Oscar finish his boat since they were not on any particular schedule for their bonding trip. So, they worked every day for hours on end, all the while patiently waiting for the motorcycle parts to arrive. Finally, ahead of their motorcycle repair completion, they and Oscar put the finishing touches on the admittedly sleek and seaworthy vessel.

Then it began raining. It not only rained; it poured, and the torrential downpour continued relentlessly for days. The water rose, and with it Oscar's hopes. He drove to the river and saw it rising, easily able to handle the large sailboat. Oscar's new friends encouraged him to go ahead and realize his dream. Oscar smiled, saw the rain as a true sign (probably envisioning himself as a modern day Noah!), and said, "Yep, I am going to do it!"

Oscar quickly made arrangements for the "girls" to be cared for and concluded whatever personal arrangements were left to accomplish. By now the father and son were deeply sharing Oscar's dream, were excited for him and for the fact that their help had also achieved their personal goal of a renewed relationship. They helped Oscar hitch the boat to his old pickup and drove the truck through the town toward the river, with Oscar standing proudly in the bow. The final scene of the TV show is a graceful boat, sails billowing, making its way down the swollen river into whatever the future might hold for Oscar – and father and son, standing side by side, seeing a new future for them as well.

For all three of the characters in this story, they found rejuvenation; in a real way, a new world opened for them. With this story (as a parable) in mind, reflect on 2 Corinthians 5: 17-21 and on Colossians 3: 10-11:

> *"Therefore, if anyone is in Christ, he is a new creation; the old has gone, the new has come! All this is from God, who reconciled us to himself through Christ and gave us the ministry of reconciliation – that God was reconciling the world to himself in Christ, not counting men's sins against them. And he has committed to us the message of reconciliation. We are therefore Christ's ambassadors, as though God were making his appeal through us. We implore you on Christ's behalf. Be reconciled to God. God made him who had no sin to be sin for us, so that in him we might become the righteousness of God."..."...and have put on the new self, which is being renewed in knowledge in the image of its*

Creator. Here there is no Greek or Jew, circumcised or uncircumcised, barbarian, Scythian, slave or free, but Christ is all, and is in all."

These two Pauline passages express in inspired words a divine truth that is almost too awesome and wonderful to comprehend; and it is a truth that every real Christian participates in.

In the Book of Exodus in the Old Testament we find the magnificent account of the liberation of the people of Israel from bondage in Egypt. God reached down with a mighty arm, rocked the earth's most powerful nation of the time back on its heels and said, in effect, "Let My people go!" Following the sparing of the first born of the Hebrews through the placing of lamb's blood on their doorposts (a wonderful type and sign pointing to the Redemption of mankind by the shedding of the blood of the Lamb many centuries later), Moses and Aaron led the people to the shores of the Red Sea. There God performed one of the mightiest miracles recorded in the Old Testament (in spite of the objections of some modern scholars who try to "water this down" through other explanations – such as Moses really leading the people through some shallow, reedy water that resulted in Pharaoh's chariots bogging down in the muck). The sea parted, and the people of Israel crossed on dry land. One reason for sticking to our guns regarding this event is that it is yet another type of the future – the cleansing waters of Baptism.

Yet, the people took baggage with them through the waters – not just the physical baggage of personal possessions and animals, but also emotional and spiritual baggage. They grumbled continually, they doubted, they even longed for the more secure days that had experienced as slaves in Egypt. They tested Moses' patience, and God's. Time and time again, Moses became the intercessor, pleading with God to forgive and spare His people (which, of course, He knew from all eternity that He would do). Because the people did not totally yield to God (including even Moses on one occasion), most did not enter the Promised Land. Joshua became the designated leader when the Hebrews at last crossed the Jordan River (with another miraculous parting of the waters).

So the Word is telling us that it is not enough to just "go through the waters". Regardless of the various denominational beliefs of the meaning and efficacy of Baptism, all Christians listening to the Holy Spirit recognize that the new creation requires at some point a personalization of the process – the recognizing and accepting of Jesus as Savior and Lord. It is His shed blood that makes possible the miracle of new creation, from spiritual death to spiritual life; it is Jesus as the Great High Priest and the Mediator at the right hand of the Father who parts the waters for us to enter into new life. It is one thing to accept Jesus as Savior; it is quite another to make Him the Lord of my life. And even that requires a conscious choice. Jesus Himself told us that it is not enough to call Him "Lord, Lord," but to do His will – to commit to a life of yielded service and obedience to the King of Kings and Lord of Lords.

Now reflect on Ezekiel 37, the well-known and often sung account of the dry bones. God told Ezekiel to prophesy to a bunch of dead and scattered bones in the desert. But, prophets were frequently doing things that seem very, very strange to most other people. So, Ezekiel obeyed God. But it was only when Ezekiel obeyed a second command and prophesied to the breath that breath entered into the rearranged bones and they became living beings. This amazing Old Testament account is again a prefiguring – a type, a foreshadowing – of what was to transpire under the New Covenant following the death and Resurrection of the Messiah, Jesus the Christ. I encourage a reading and meditating on the entire 37th chapter of Ezekiel. Reading about the dry bones reminds us that the new creation is really a two-step process: 1) Recognizing who Jesus, the Savior, is and who we are – sinners in need of Redemption. Accepting Him as that in our lives is the first step. 2) We also need the Holy Spirit, the living "Breath," the living Love of God, to infuse and transform us and to lead us to and through lives dedicated to Jesus our Lord. Without the Holy Spirit there is no true life, there is no real Christian.

But let's focus now on the new creation itself. It is so awesome a gift that we can actually go through life without grasping what it truly means. Unfortunately, some people also conclude that it is so grand that it could never be theirs. Both problems are the direct result of Satan's strategic plan. If he can dull or divert our minds, he

Will the Real Christians Please Stand Up!

will. If he can convince us that we could never really be part of such a wonderful life, he will. What kind of baggage, if any, do I carry around? Do I think that I have to somehow "earn" entrance into this wonderful new life of union with God, and know that I never could? Well, the latter part of that statement is indeed true! We can never do anything to merit or earn it. It is a gift, pure and simple, to be received with joy, humility, and the totality of my spirit. It was the sin of the first Adam that took away our intimate family life with God. It is the new Adam, Jesus Christ, who, by His Incarnation, death and Resurrection reopened the possibility for that family life. We enter the new spiritual life through accepting an offer to cross the bridge to that life; it is not a toll bridge, for Jesus paid the toll. He invites us, and all we have to do is accept the invitation. Some denominations teach that Baptism is the way to that life; for churches who perform infant Baptism that is a necessary conclusion, as infants do not have the ability to make a conscious choice. But even in those cases, at some point each person must ratify Baptism by making spirituality a conscious choosing of relationship with the living Jesus, and, through Him, with the Father and the Holy Spirit. The Lord then asks us to follow Him, commit our lives to Him and, through grace, bear fruit for the Kingdom.

The new creation means that I have been raised with Christ to live with Him in the heavenly realms, even now in a mysterious way. (Ephesians 2: 6). The new creation means that I have been transformed from a life of darkness into the Kingdom of light (Colossians 1: 13) – with Jesus, who is the Light of the world. What Adam and Eve lost through sin – intimacy with God – Christ restored by "becoming sin" and offering Himself as the ultimate sacrifice on the Cross. He then rose triumphantly, He ascended into heaven, and He will return one day for His Church and to judge the living and the dead. When we accept the gift of new life, we rise with Him – washed, transformed, with an inner beauty of spirit that puts angels in awe.

When we become new creatures in Christ, we are marked – marked with the NAME of Jesus. Isaiah proclaimed: *"The nations will see your righteousness, and all kings your glory; you will be called by a new name that the mouth of the Lord Jesus will bestow.*

You will be a crown of splendor in the Lord's hand, a royal diadem in the hand of your God." (Isaiah 62: 2-3) John, seeing and writing down the great revelation by God of the reality of heaven, quotes Jesus, who said: *"...I will write on him the name of my God and the name of the city of God, the new Jerusalem, which is coming down out of heaven from my God; and I will also write on him my new name."* (Revelation 3: 12)

A true Christian walks with the awareness that she/he does not just use the name "Christ" but it truly marked with that name. It is a glorious privilege and a weighty responsibility, to walk with the name of Christ imprinted on us and showing it and Him to everyone we see by the lives we live.

There is cause for great rejoicing! *"...those who hope in the Lord will renew their strength. They will soar on wings like eagles; they will run and not grow weary, they will walk and not be faint."* (Isaiah 40: 31) *"Sing to the Lord a new song, his praise from the ends of the earth; you who go down to the sea, and all that is in it, you islands, and all who live in them."* (Isaiah 42: 10) *'I waited patiently for the Lord; he turned to me and heard my cry. He lifted me out of the slimy pit, out of the mud and mire; He set my feet on a rock and gave me a firm place to stand. He put a new song in my mouth, a hymn of praise to our God."* (Psalm 40: 1-3)

So, walk renewed! Walk with hope and conviction and awareness of all that is yours. As Paul writes, *"Do not conform any longer to the pattern of this world, but be transformed by the renewing of your mind. Then you will be able to test and approve what God's will is – his good, pleasing and perfect will."* (Romans 12: 2) Paul also writes in Corinthians, *"Therefore we do not lose heart. Though outwardly we are wasting away, yet inwardly we are being renewed day by day. For our light and momentary troubles are achieving for us an eternal glory that far outweighs them all. So we fix our eyes not on what is seen, but on what is unseen. For what is seen is temporary, but what is unseen is eternal."* (2 Corinthians 4: 16-18)

In Colossians, Paul exhorts us, *"Since, then, you have been raised with Christ, set your hearts on things above, where Christ is seated at the right hand of God. Set your mind on things above, not on earthly things. For you died, and your life is now hidden with Christ in God. When Christ, who is your life, appears, then you also will appear with him in glory.*" (Colossians 3: 1-4) But take note! Right after these verses, Paul gets very specific as to what living the new creation means: "*Put to death, therefore, whatever belongs to your earthly nature: Sexual immorality, impurity, lust, evil desires and greed, which is idolatry. Because of these, the wrath of God is coming. You used to walk in these ways, in the life you once lived. But now you must rid yourselves of all such things as these: Anger, rage, malice, slander, and filthy language from your lips...Therefore, as God's chosen people, holy and dearly loved, clothe yourselves with compassion, kindness, humility, gentleness and patience. Bear with each other and forgive whatever grievances you may have against one another. Forgive as the Lord forgave you. And over all these virtues put on love, which binds them all together in perfect unity. Let the peace of Christ rule in your hearts, since as members of one body you were called to peace. And be thankful. Let the word of Christ dwell in you richly as you teach and admonish one another with all wisdom, and as you sing psalms, hymns and spiritual songs with gratitude to God. And whatever you do, whether in word or deed, do it all in the name of the Lord Jesus, giving thanks to God the Father through him.*" (Colossians 3: 5-10, 12-17)

Living in the new creation results in this kind of life, not as a response to a command, but as a supernatural joyous overflowing – a desire to love and serve Father, Son and Holy Spirit who have given such a tremendous and eternal gift. Come, Holy Spirit; show us, in the very depths of our minds and hearts, what the new creation really is.

SUMMARY FOR REFLECTION AND DISCUSSION:

A real Christian:

1) Has a vision and is goal-oriented;
2) Has heaven as the ultimate vision and goal;
3) Has the interim vision and goal of doing all and only what the Lord wants – is a yielded servant;
4) Sees in every line and word of Scripture true Revelation from God;
5) Rejoices in the gift of having direct communication with Father, Son and Holy Spirit;
6) Rejoices in the wondrous truth of salvation and the awesome personal love of God;
7) Seeks to grow in and share with others the meaning of the gift of new creation.

SCRIPTURES FOR JOURNALING:

1) 2 Corinthians 5: 17-21 and Colossians 3: 10-11;
2) Ezekiel 37;
3) Ephesians 2: 6 and Colossians 1: 13;
4) Isaiah 62: 2-3 and Revelation 3: 12;
5) Isaiah 40: 31 and 42: 10 and Psalm 40: 1-3;
6) Romans 12: 2; 2 Corinthians 4: 16-18; Colossians 3: 1-10 and 12-17.

REFLECTION 20:

PERSONAL RELATIONSHIP

There is a "shaggy dog" story about Sammy. Have you ever heard of him? Sammy is the man who knew everyone famous – or so he said. He told that to a friend, who decided to challenge Sammy to prove what he so boastfully, and outrageously, claimed. Sammy began by saying that he knew the President personally. So, he wrote to the White House, and a week later back came a chummy note from none other than the President of the United States! Then Sammy said he knew an all-star baseball player. So, Sammy and his friend went to the ballpark and Sammy sent a message to the dugout. The next thing you know, Sammy and friend were invited to sit with the players! And on and on it went. (I will spare you the shaggy dog treatment and not give you the endless scenarios; I will get right to the point.) Finally, the friend said, in total exasperation, "I can name someone famous you don't know – the Pope; to prove it, I am going to buy airline tickets to Rome." So he did, and on the next Sunday they were in St. Peter's Square. The Square was filled with thousands of people waiting for the Pope to come out on the balcony of his apartment and give his blessing. Sammy's frustrated, but now hopeful, friend then upped the stakes. He said, "Sammy, I want you to appear on the balcony with "your good friend" the Pope," knowing that it is all but impossible to make one's way through the many obstacles to even reach, much less enter, the Pope's living quarters.

(I know, because I tried once!) The noon bells rang and the Pope, resplendent in his white cassock, came out on the balcony to the cheers of the multitude. Sammy's friend looked closely, and then his mouth fell open. There, standing next to the Pope, waving to the crowd, was Sammy! Just then a man standing next to the dumbstruck companion of Sammy tapped him on the shoulder and asked him, "Excuse me, but may I ask you a question? Can you please tell me, who is that up there standing next to Sammy?"

Well, that is absurd, right? To use a different, but almost as absurd, example: I have been a Human Resources person for many years. In that capacity I had occasion to review many, many resumes. After awhile, one develops a knack for spotting exaggerations and discrepancies. So, if I were to receive a resume listing as personal references the Pope, the President, and a few famous sports and entertainment figures, I would obviously suspect the veracity of the resume (though I would probably contact the person, just out of curiosity!).

This rather bizarre introduction may help you understand the reaction of listeners to Jesus of Nazareth when He made statements like the following:

"I am one who testifies for myself; my other witness is the Father, who sent me...You do not know me or my Father...If you knew me, you would know my Father also." (John 8: 19) *"The miracles I do in my Father's name speak for me, but you do not believe because you are not my sheep. My sheep listen to my voice; I know them and they follow me. I give them eternal life, and they shall never perish; no one can snatch them out of my Father's hand. I and the Father are one."* (John 10: 25-30) *"I am the Way and the Truth and the Life. No one comes to the Father except through me. If you really knew me, you would have known my Father as well. From now on, you do know him and have seen him...Anyone who has seen me has seen the Father. How can you say, 'Show us the Father'? Don't you believe that I am in the Father, and that the Father is in me? The words I say unto you are not just my own. Rather, it is the Father,*

living in me, who is doing his work. Believe me when I say that I am in the Father and the Father is in me; or at least believe on the evidence of the miracles themselves." (John 14: 6-11)

The claims of Jesus were not only extraordinary, they were blasphemous to pious religious ears of the time. That is why they accused Him of being possessed by Satan; that is why they threatened to stone Him; and that is why they finally had Him executed. Knowing some famous person is absolutely nothing compared to knowing personally and intimately Almighty God – at least the way Jesus was describing the relationship.

This Biblical word, "know," is fascinating. John used it 107 times in the New Testament Books he wrote under the inspiration of the Holy Spirit. Paul used it 81 times in his Letters. So, let's take a brief look at some Scriptural events that give meaning to this word.

When Jesus selected His twelve apostles, He obviously knew them. He called them by name; He had spent time praying for them; He knew their strengths and weaknesses when He said, *"Come, follow me"* to them. It was a personal call based on personal knowledge. When some of the apostles were fishing after the Resurrection, and the Man on shore told them where to throw their nets – after they had been fishing without success all night – John cried out, *"It is the Lord!"* Peter immediately swam to shore, because he wanted to see his Lord and Master. (John 21: 7) After Jesus healed the man born blind from birth, and the man had been thrown out of the synagogue by the religious leaders because of his testimony regarding the healing, Jesus found the man and asked, *"Do you believe in the Son of Man?"* The passage (John 9: 36-39) goes on: *"'Who is he, sir?' the man asked. 'Tell me, so that I may believe in him.' Jesus said, 'You have now seen him; in fact, he is the one speaking with you.' Then the man said, 'Lord, I believe,' and he worshiped him. Jesus said, 'For judgment I have come into this world, so that the blind will see and those who see will become blind.'"*

Jesus is speaking of the true meaning of knowing – looking below the surface, finding the real person and having a true personal encounter. We have already explored the conversion of Saul; let's revisit it briefly. Saul, to become Paul, also came to know Jesus. Unlike the man born blind from birth, Paul, in his Damascus experience, was struck blind for a short time – to give him time to reflect on the magnitude of what he had heard: "I am Jesus, whom you are persecuting." That event totally changed Paul's life; the zeal for persecuting Christians was transformed by grace into a lifelong zeal to see everyone he met become a Christian. Another example is the Samaritan woman at the well. Early in His ministry, Jesus changed the life of a sinful woman by exposing her to, well, to herself as she really was. Then she saw Jesus as He really was. She came to know Him in a very personal and saving way. She also became God's instrument for touching the hearts of other people in her town. They said, *"We no longer believe just because of what you said; now we have heard for ourselves, and we know that this man is the Savior of the world."* (John 4: 42) Earlier even than that, John the Baptist met Jesus. John had spent his entire life in prayer and self-discipline, becoming prepared to be the precursor of the Messiah. When Jesus came to the Jordan to be baptized along with many others, John recognized Him and cried out, *"Behold the Lamb of God who takes away the sins of the world."* (John 1: 29) In the pivotal 16th chapter of the Gospel according to Matthew, Jesus, prior to setting His face toward Jerusalem for the final time, asked the apostles whom others said He was and then asked them personally who He was. Peter spoke up, *"You are the Christ, the Son of the Living God."* (Matthew 16: 16) Peter knew Jesus. So did Judas: At that terrible meeting in the Garden of Gethsemane, Jesus looked at Judas and asked him, *"Judas, do you betray the Son of Man with a kiss?"* (Luke 22: 48) Yes, Judas knew Jesus, but unlike Peter, who repented after he denied his Lord, Judas despaired and committed suicide.

What all of this means is that **Christianity is a personal religion**. It is truly sad that so often the words "personal" and "religion" become contradictions. Far too often religious behavior focuses on the impersonal; true Christian spirituality is founded on, nourished by and expressed through a deep personal relationship of love with God the Father, God the Son and God the Holy Spirit. To delve into this further, let's look at two New Testament Scriptures:

First, John 7: 37-39: "On the last and greatest day of the Feast,

Jesus stood and said in a loud voice, "'If anyone is thirsty, let him come to me and drink. Whoever believes in me, as the Scripture has said, streams of living water will flow from within him.' By this he meant the Spirit, whom those who believed in him were later to receive. Up to that time the Spirit had not been given, since Jesus had not yet been glorified." This powerful passage emphasizes quite clearly that the Holy Spirit is integral and critical to knowing God and living a life of personal relationship and service. The Holy Spirit is the living Love of God, and it is love that molds relationships.

The second Scripture is John 6. This oft debated and misunderstood chapter is one of the most significant events in the life and teaching of Jesus Christ. Jesus chose very specific words to describe His desire for intimate relationship. The listening Jews were horrified, as Jesus was describing the eating of His flesh and drinking of His blood in a way that sounded like cannibalism. Now note a critical stage in the communication process: John writes that from that day many of Jesus' disciples walked with Him no longer – we already know that the religious leaders were infuriated with Him, but His disciples shocked to the point of walking away?! This is key. Jesus did not modify His position; He did not say to the disciples that He was just using an example to graphically describe the intimacy of union that He desired and desires with His followers. He simply looked at the Twelve and asked if they were going to walk away as well. Peter, again speaking for them, replied, "Lord, to whom shall we go? You have the words of eternal life." The vast majority of the Protestant world sees the description of eating Jesus' Body and drinking His Blood as symbolic. The Roman Catholics, the Orthodox Churches, and a few others take it very literally. The very essence of spiritual life and worship for them is a belief that the bread and wine, when consecrated, truly and literally become the Body and Blood of Jesus Christ. Regardless, though, of the theological differences in interpretation, it should be clear to any thinking and seeking person that Jesus is inviting His followers to the greatest possible life of intimacy with Him. And Jesus is God!

So, Jesus at this very moment is looking at you, looking at me. He is asking us whether we want, really want, what He is offering. He is asking if we choose to just go through the religious motions

Will the Real Christians Please Stand Up!

of a personal relationship or if we yearn for it with all of our being. Do I define my Christianity by my religious practices or by the depth of my relationship with God? Do I have a burning, passionate desire to become ever more closely united with Jesus Christ, having His mind and heart, and letting His light and His life shine through me to a world in darkness? The answer to that question has eternal significance, for each of us and for others who cross our path during our life on earth.

Further, just as religious practice by itself is no substitute for personal relationship, so, too, does so-called "private religion" or "private spirituality" have no place in the true Christian life. I have a deep and personal relationship with my wife. I am excited about having Barb as my wife, and I look for every opportunity to tell others about how wonderful she is and how blessed I am to have her as my spouse. So, too, someone who really knows Jesus –not as just some name, not just some historical figure, not some distant, divine Person on a throne, but as a living and present Person, closer to me than anyone else is or could be – has a burning desire to share the Beloved with others and have all the world experience the joy of a personal relationship with Jesus Christ – and through Him, with the Father and the Holy Spirit. May our prayer be that of Paul: *"I want to know Christ, and the power of his Resurrection and the fellowship of sharing in his sufferings."* (Philippians 3: 10)

SUMMARY FOR REFLECTION AND DISCUSSION:

A real Christian:

1) Has been "knocked off his/her horse" like Paul, and has personally and powerfully experienced the risen Jesus;
2) Has a daily relationship with Jesus Christ that is as real and intimate – even more so – than the closest possible human relationship;
3) Actively seeks the guidance of the Holy Spirit, thirsting to know the Lord Jesus ever more deeply;
4) Avoids the trap of defining Christianity by the degree of adherence to religious rites, rituals, programs, practices or social activities.

SCRIPTURES FOR JOURNALING:

1) John 6 (the entire chapter, and compare it with Matthew 26: 17-29);
2) John 4, John 7: 37-39, John 8: 19, John 9: 36-39, John 10: 25-30 and John 14: 6-11;
3) Find and reflect on favorite Scriptures in the New Testament describing relationship with Jesus Christ.

REFLECTION 21:

WE WANT TO SEE JESUS

From time to time I have shared my testimony at a variety of Christian prayer meetings. It is fascinating to me that, while the essential testimony of every Christian is the same, the path that God takes each individual on is unique. I am also discovering that testimonies change, as the Holy Spirit continues to teach and direct hearts willing to yield to Him. What do I mean by the statement that "the essential testimony of every Christian is the same"? Occasionally I begin my testimony with reading a section of Scripture, and stating that every true Christian can proclaim the words as her/his own. The Scripture is part of Ephesians 1 and 2. What follows is the New Living Translation, and I am deliberately changing to the first person singular. Please read it prayerfully:

"How I praise God, the Father of my Lord Jesus Christ, who has blessed me with every spiritual blessing in the heavenly realms because I belong to Christ. Long ago, even before he made the world, God loved me and chose me in Christ to be holy and without fault in his eyes. His unchanging plan has always been to adopt me into his own family by bringing me to himself through Jesus Christ. And this gave him great pleasure. So I praise God for the wonderful kindness he has poured out on me because I belong to his dearly

loved Son. He is so rich in kindness that he purchased my freedom through the blood of his Son, and my sins are forgiven. He has showered his kindness on me, along with all wisdom and understanding. God's secret plan has now been revealed to me; it is a plan centered on Christ, designed long ago according to his good pleasure. And this is his plan: At the right time he will bring everything together under the authority of Christ – everything in heaven and on earth. Furthermore, because of Christ, I have received an inheritance from God, for he chose me from the beginning, and all things happen just as he decided long ago...And when I believed in Christ, he identified me as his own by giving me the Holy Spirit, whom he promised long ago. That Spirit is God's guarantee that he will give me everything he promised and that he has purchased me to be his own. This is just one more reason for me to praise our glorious God...Once I was dead, doomed forever because of my many sins. I used to live just like the rest of the world, full of sin, obeying Satan, the mighty prince of the power of the air. He is the spirit at work in the hearts of those who refuse to obey God. I used to live that way, following the passions and desires of my evil nature. I was born with an evil nature, and I was under God's anger just like everyone else. But God is so rich in mercy, and he loved me so very much, that even while I was dead because of my sins, he gave me life when he raised Christ from the dead. (It is only by God's special favor that I have been saved!) For he raised me from the dead along with Christ, and I am seated with him in the heavenly realms – all because I am one with Christ Jesus. And so God can always point to me as an example of the incredible wealth of his favor and kindness, as shown in all he has done for me through Christ Jesus. God saved me by his special favor when I believed. And I can't take credit for this; it is a gift from God. Salvation is not a gift for the good things I have done, so I can't boast about it. For I am God's masterpiece. He has created me anew in Christ Jesus, so that I can do the good things he planned for me long ago."

What a beautiful and powerful statement! And it is a truth that every real Christian can joyfully proclaim. I find it highly noteworthy that in this passage there are sixteen references to life in and through Christ. It is only in Jesus Christ that life has any true meaning, only in Him that we can live in God now and can look forward to an eternity of happiness. (I once read a "Family Circus" cartoon that defined heaven as a "great big hug that lasts forever.")

There is a song that describes the longing of the Christian to know and love Jesus: "Open our eyes, Lord, we want to see Jesus, to reach out and touch Him, to say that we love Him. Open our ears, Lord, and help us to listen. Open our eyes, Lord, we want to see Jesus." There is a much more recent song that goes like this: "You are the air I breathe, Your very Presence living in me. You are my daily bread, Your holy Word spoken to me. And I am desperate for You; and I am lost without You." Let's have the courage right now to test our relationship with Him; let's test where our hearts really dwell.

When we read the drama of the Gospels, we are prompted by the Holy Spirit to see Jesus as He was and is, the eternal Son of God; and to cry out because of the blindness and deafness of so many with whom He came into contact. But what about the drama of today? Do we really see Him with eyes of faith? Do we really hear Him, daily talking to us in the depth of our spirits? Do we really care whether we do or not? If it is not the consuming passion of our lives, we have not grasped what it means to be a Christian.

Listen to God speaking to the prophet Zechariah, and know that this living Word is just as applicable today: *"'When I called, they did not listen; so when they called, I would not listen,' said the Lord Almighty. 'I scattered them with a whirlwind among the nations, where they were strangers. The land was left so desolate behind them that no one could come or go. This is how they made the pleasant land desolate.' Again the word of the Lord Almighty came to me. This is what the Lord Almighty says: 'I am very jealous for Zion; I am burning with jealousy for her.' This is what the Lord says: 'I will return to Zion and dwell in Jerusalem. Then Jerusalem will be called the City of Truth, and the mountain of the Lord*

Almighty will be called the Holy Mountain.' This is what the Lord Almighty says: 'Once again men and women of ripe old age will sit in the streets of Jerusalem, each with cane in hand because of his age. The city streets will be filled with boys and girls playing there.' This is what the Lord Almighty says: 'It may seem marvelous to the remnant of this people at that time, but will it seem marvelous to me?' declares the Lord Almighty. This is what the Lord Almighty says: 'I will save my people from the countries of the east and the west. I will bring them back to live in Jerusalem; they will be my people, and I will be faithful and righteous to them as their God.' This is what the Lord Almighty says: 'You who now hear these words spoken by the prophets who were there when the foundation was laid for the house of the Lord Almighty, let your hands be strong so that the Temple may be built.'" (Zechariah 7, 13: 8-9)

Keep in mind that when we read the Bible, Old or New Testament, we are not just reading history – we are reading the eternal living Word of God. The passage from Zechariah speaks of God's great love for His people, His burning anger when they turn away from Him, and the resulting consequences of sinful actions, His great penchant for forgiveness, His saving of a remnant, and His call to build and restore the Temple. The temple of today, the Church of Jesus Christ (not any one denomination, but the Body of true believers cutting through all denominational and non-denominational lines) needs building and restoration. Further, so does the temple of today that is each true Christian – filled with the very presence of God – as we seek to live ever more pure and holy lives in and through Christ, guided by the Holy Spirit, for the glory of the Father.

Proverbs 8: 34-36 states it well: *"Blessed is the man (and woman) who listens to me, watching daily at my doors, waiting at my doorway. For whoever finds me finds life and receives favor from the Lord. But whoever fails to find me harms himself; all who hate me love death."* Actually, Proverbs 8 (I urge you to read all of this masterpiece) refers to the Holy Spirit. It is the Holy Spirit who seeks to tell us about Jesus and the ways of the Trinity and the life of God with and within us. But we must desire to listen in order to hear, and we must desire to act in order to yield, obey, and find the fullness of life.

The miracles performed by Jesus are also quite symbolic for us

Will the Real Christians Please Stand Up!

today. For example, explore Mark 7: 31-35 and 8: 22-25:

"Then Jesus left the vicinity of Tyre and went through Sidon, down to the Sea of Galilee and into the region of the Decapolis. There some people brought to him a man who was deaf and could hardly talk. They begged him to place his hand on the man. After he took him aside, away from the crowd, Jesus put his fingers into the man's ears. Then he spit and touched the man's tongue. He looked up to heaven and with a deep sigh said to him, 'Ephphatha' (which means, 'be opened'). At this, the man's ears were opened; his tongue was loosened; and he began to speak plainly...They came to Bethsaida, and some people brought a blind man and begged Jesus to touch him. He took the blind man by the hand, and led him outside the village. When he had spit on the man's eyes and put his hands on him, Jesus asked, 'Do you see anything?' He looked up and said, 'I see people; they look like trees walking around.' Once more Jesus put his hands on the man's eyes. Then his eyes were opened, his sight was restored, and he saw clearly."

I am deaf, I want to hear Jesus; I cannot speak well, I want to be able to proclaim Jesus; I am blind, I want to see Jesus. It takes courage and motivation to walk out from among the crowd, approach Jesus, and ask Him to touch us. In Jesus' healing of the blind man, notice that the healing occurred in two stages. Now, certainly Jesus was able to heal completely the first time. It may be that there was some shaky faith and trust, and perhaps Jesus was asking him to yield completely. It may be also that the Holy Spirit is trying to teach us something today. Here is what it means to me: There are distinct stages at the beginning of the Christian life. First, there is repentance and the asking of Jesus Christ to be my personal Savior. Second, there is making Him the Lord of my life, accompanied by the seeking of the guidance of the Holy Spirit and the grace to walk daily in and by the Holy Spirit. It is this second stage that separates the real Christian from the "card-carrying" and uninvolved type – you know, the lukewarm ones whom God wants to vomit from His mouth. (Revelation 3: 16)

So, seek and find the Jesus of the Gospels, the same Jesus alive and among us today and yearning to be an intimate part of our lives. Jesus wept when He saw the grief over the death of Lazarus. Jesus asked His closest friends why they could not stay awake and watch with Him during His terrible agony in the Garden of Gethsemane. Jesus asked His apostles if they would go away, too, when many of His disciples left Him because of His radical teaching. Jesus said to come and follow Him. Jesus reached out in love and forgiveness to the sinful woman at the well, and to the one caught in adultery. John wrote in his Gospel that on the night before He died, Jesus was about to show the full extent of His love. Jesus spoke to fiery Saul about his persecuting of the Messiah, and it totally changed his life.

That same Jesus is right here, right now, as you read this. He loves you. He is ready to forgive anything and everything. He weeps when you ignore Him. He wants to be your close friend. Peter, the forgiven one, wrote the following in his first Letter to the early Church – can you and I say it and mean it? *"Though you have not seen him, you love him; and even though you do not see him now, you believe in him and are filled with an inexpressible and glorious joy, for you are receiving the goal of your faith, the salvation of your souls."* (1 Peter 1: 8-9)

Open our eyes, Lord, we want to see Jesus, to reach out and touch Him, and say that we love Him. Open our ears, Lord, and help us to listen. Open our eyes, Lord, we want to see Jesus. Lord, You are my daily bread, Your holy Presence living in me; You are the air I breath, Your very Word, spoken to me.

Will the Real Christians Please Stand Up!

SUMMARY FOR REFLECTION AND DISCUSSION:

A real Christian:

1) Quite simply, and quite profoundly, knows that the Jesus of the Gospels is the Jesus who is alive today, in our hearts and in our worship and in the daily life of service to Him and others;
2) And, with just as much conviction, knows that every word and sentence of the Bible is God speaking today, guided by the Holy Spirit;
3) Seeks with all her/his heart to hear Jesus, to heed Jesus, to follow Jesus whenever He calls, to listen to the prompting and guidance of the Holy Spirit.

SCRIPTURES FOR JOURNALING:

1) Ephesians 1-2 – personalizing the chapters;
2) Zechariah 1, 7, 8;
3) 1 Peter 1-2.

REFLECTION 22:

WE WANT TO SEE JESUS, CONTINUED

When I gave the message in the Wilderness Church that resulted in the previous reflection, I had planned to end with a tape recording playing that beautiful chorus, "Open our eyes, Lord." But the recorder did not work! After I fumbled around for a minute or so and realized that I was losing any potential impact of the moment, I asked the congregation if anyone knew the song and would be willing to sing it or lead it (I am definitely not gifted in knowing how to pick opening notes of a song!). A visitor to the Park raised his hand and offered his services. Well, he sang it, to be sure; but the tune was completely different than anything I had ever heard, and the voice was of a quality that was definitely not going to bring the young man fame and fortune. But through his openness, his simplicity, and his evident passionate love of God, the Holy Spirit ministered to us all far better than He could have through my planned conclusion. While driving home after that experience, I was thanking the Lord for His faithfulness and guidance, and I began thinking about possible topics for the following Sunday. Then He said, through that quiet, inner voice that He normally uses when He talks with His people, "I'm not finished with this topic yet." Well, that was pretty exciting, for a couple of reasons: First, it is always thrilling to hear from God and learn about His Word and revelation. Second, it certainly confirmed that these messages and reflections are not mine; they are His, and I seek to be a vessel He can use to touch people's lives.

So, I then waited to hear more from Him, since I had no idea what continuation of the theme meant. As is common when the Holy Spirit gets involved, on that same day I happened to hear an evangelist referring to Matthew 20: 29-34. And, yes, it is another Gospel passage about the healing of the blind! Then the Holy Spirit began directing my attention to the text and to the verses before and after it, and, behold! – another message. Thank you, Lord!

Recall from the last reflection that Ephesians 1 and 2 refer again and again to life in and through Christ. The real Christian is one who lives this in a personal, loving, intimate relationship with Him. We can always grow, always deepen that relationship. I, like you, have blind spots, bouts of spiritual deafness – because we are weak, fallible creatures who just happen to be immensely loved by God. As we explore further in this reflection, let's focus in a deeper way on just what it means to see and hear Jesus.

> First, the Matthew text: *"As Jesus and his disciples were leaving Jericho, a large crowd followed him. Two blind men were sitting by the roadside. When they heard that Jesus was going by, they shouted, 'Lord, Son of David, have mercy on us!' The crowd rebuked them and told them to be quiet, but they shouted all the louder, 'Lord, Son of David, have mercy on us!' Jesus stopped and called them. 'What do you want me to do for you?' he asked. 'Lord,' they answered, 'we want our sight.' Jesus had compassion on them and touched their eyes. Immediately, they received their sight and followed him."*

Note that the crowd rebuked the blind men. These two beggars were probably sitting there bothering the people by their repeatedly asking for money. They were undoubtedly dirty and unkempt, and now they were daring to interfere with the crowd's impatient waiting to see the famous and controversial carpenter from Nazareth. So the crowd berated the blind men, told them to shut up, let them know that their loud voices were bothering these upright citizens lining the roadside. And so it is today. Those two men knew their need and believed with all their hearts that Jesus could restore their sight. They did not let the anger and the put-downs deter them. The true, intense, committed seekers after Jesus today – the ones who know that He is the key to the meaning of life and who want a complete relationship with Him – bother the world and, frankly, bother most religious people. The seekers appear to be fanatics, and spiritual fanatics are not popular in the secular world and the world of religion. The world lashes out because it does not believe in Jesus and/or because it is uncomfortable with His challenging message. The religious folk lash out because they do not want their apple cart upset. What apple cart? The one that gives license to just do the minimum, to just get by, to just go through the motions – to be Christian in name but not in substance, certainly not the substance that Jesus talks about, to avoid the commitment that Paul lived and wrote about, to skirt around the dynamic relationship that is the basis of the true Christian life. It is somewhat like a new worker being told by the veterans on his first day, "Now, watch and follow us; don't work too hard, don't show us up; we have this game mastered." It is like an evangelist friend who, in his youth when he was searching for the truth and questioning the laid back religious practices of his church, was told by one of the elders, "We have a good thing going here; don't rock the boat...It is like eating spinach; you'll get used to it after awhile."

Alright, let's go on. If we are willing to identify with those blind men, if we really and truly want to see – that means we, from the bottom of our hearts, want to know Him as He is and want to imitate and follow Him in our daily lives. If your desire right now is not a "from the bottom of the heart one," I urge you to stop here and ask the Holy Spirit to bring you to a personal revival in your spiritual life; to shake you up and wake you up; to fill you with a new and refreshed longing. Take however much time is necessary. Seek the Lord!

Ready? One of the beauties of the Word is that it all flows with such amazing continuity and consistency, always bringing new and fresh insights to the true seeker. What does it mean to be like Jesus, to see Him and follow Him? Well, look at the passage right before the account of the blind men:

> *"Jesus called them* (the apostles) *together and said, 'You know that the rulers of the Gentiles Lord it over them, and their high officials exercise authority over them. Not so with you. Instead, whoever wants to become great among you must be your servant; and whoever wants to be first must be your slave – just as the Son of Man did not come to be served, but to serve, and to give his life as a ransom for many.'"* (Matthew 20:25-28)

Jesus was no wimp. When He talked about being a servant, He was talking about true greatness, true courage. Our society has a hard time dealing with the servant concept. It goes against the grain of secular notions of self-assurance, self-confidence, against the idea of the self-made man and woman. But the greatest leader of all time gave the example and issued the challenge to live a life of dedicated service. And, not just when convenient – always, and in all circumstances, even and especially when we are taken advantage of. That takes guts, folks!

To show that He was willing to walk His talk, take a look at what comes right after the account of the blind men. Matthew 21: 1-11 gives us the gripping narrative of the entry into Jerusalem, His final entrance into the Holy City before He died. This mighty man of God, who was truly God Himself, the long-awaited Messiah, the living Word, entered the city to shouts of praise of people, many of whom a few days later would be shouting just as loudly for His execution. How did He enter? Oh, He could have had His disciples make a portable throne, they could have dressed Him in royal finery, He could have sat on satin cushions. But that was obviously not Jesus' way. He rode into town on a donkey, as an expression of His identification with the people and as a fulfillment of Zechariah's prophecy: *"Say to the daughter of Zion, 'See, your king comes to you, gentle and riding on a donkey, on a colt, the foal of a donkey.'"* (Zechariah 9:9) He came to serve, not to be served – and

He is our Creator!

So, if we want to see Jesus, to truly follow Him, He sets before us the challenge of a life of total service, not just when convenient but with every breath. At the same time, there is something else to see about Jesus. Read carefully what Matthew writes about what happened right after Jesus' entry into Jerusalem:

> *"Jesus entered the Temple area and drove out all who were buying and selling there. He overturned the tables of the moneychangers and the benches of those selling doves. 'It is written,' he said to them, 'My house will be called a house of prayer, but you are making it a den of robbers.' The blind and the lame came to him at the Temple, and he healed them. When the chief priests and the teachers of the law saw the wonderful things he did and the children shouting in the Temple area, 'Hosanna to the Son of David!' they were indignant. 'Do you hear what these children are saying?' they asked him. 'Yes,' replied Jesus, 'have you never heard read, 'From the lips of children and infants you have ordained praise.'?"* (Matthew 21: 12-16)

There are at least two significant facts to point out regarding this incident: First, Jesus was totally committed to truth, justice, righteousness. He absolutely refused to compromise. Though He knew that severe criticism would fall upon His head for daring to interfere with Temple activities, Jesus saw the Temple as the presence of His Father among men – a place, therefore, for reverence and worship. To see people taking advantage of the surroundings in order to turn a profit, to denigrate the holiness of the Temple, to cause distraction from prayer – all of this was an abomination in Jesus' eyes and He knew that it should have been in the eyes of the religious leaders. He took swift action by exercising His divine authority among men. This is totally consistent with being a servant. Servants give tough love. When it comes to the affairs of God, there must be no compromise. That is why Christians have a responsibility (and real Christians a burning desire) to protect the temple of the person from sin, to not permit contact with or tolerance of impurity, immorality, unethical behavior, to keep one's eyes, feet, heart away from anything that could tarnish the living temple of God. In other words, real Christians have a finely tuned sensitivity to God's holiness and to sin. Second, notice who was praising Jesus in the Temple – not the priests, not the Levites, certainly not the merchants and the moneychangers, but the children. It was this same Jesus who had said that unless we become as little children we will not inherit the Kingdom of Heaven. It is clear from this incident what He meant. It takes a child's heart to truly recognize just who Jesus Christ is. Without simplicity, without humility, without a focus of our minds and hearts on Him, we will neither see Him nor hear Him in our daily lives.

Read on; there is more. In Matthew 21: 18-19 we read: *"Early in the morning as he was on his way back to the city, he was hungry. Seeing a fig tree by the road, he went up to it but found nothing on it except leaves. Then he said to it, 'May you never bear fruit again!' Immediately the tree withered."*

Wait a minute! Does this mean that there is more to this Christian life than talking about it, than going through the motions, than just doing enough to get by and squeak into heaven? This particular Gospel account makes is clear – yes! That tree did not know when Jesus was going to pass by, and it was not ready – it did not have any fruit to show at His command. Jesus Christ is a very results-oriented person; He seeks fruit from His followers. There is work to be done; there is a field ripe for the harvest. There is intercession to be made, witnessing to do, a walking of the talk that is part and parcel of the daily life of the Christian. It is simply not enough to sin, seek God's forgiveness, go back to sin, hope for His mercy, and keep on living for self. Nor is it enough to go to church on Sunday and then live life during the week that may be productive in the world's view but is not Christ-centered. That person is only fooling himself or herself. The trappings of religion are no protection against the piercing eyes of Jesus as He looks deep within us, or against the fire of the Holy Spirit as He exposes us to ourselves as well as to Himself. The fact is, the real Christian does not worry about, or focus on, laws . The true Christian has as life's goal the bearing of fruit for the Kingdom and walks with the awareness that

Jesus is right with her and him as the journey of life goes on.

Finally, our exploration of this section of Matthew brings us to Chapter 22, verses 11-14, the parable of the wedding banquet:

"...But when the king came in to see the guests, he noticed a man there who was not wearing wedding clothes. 'Friend,' he asked, 'how did you get in here without wedding clothes?' The man was speechless. Then the king told the attendants, 'Tie him hand and foot, and throw him outside into the darkness, where there will be weeping and gnashing of teeth. For many are invited, but few are chosen.'"

It is humanly desirable to pass quickly over passages like this, or even to ignore them or at the very least to water them down by interpreting them through rationalization. But, what is written is written. What this passage means, literally, is that the invitation is not the same thing as the selection. God chooses me. I do not choose Him, meaning justification is a free gift, impossible to be earned. That is a key step, the step of faith. But what are the intended consequences of being chosen? The parable makes it clear: Do I have my wedding clothes on? In other words, have I committed myself to my King? Has my encounter with Him changed my life? Are my goals reflective of my faith and my love? Have I truly answered the call by my actions, or am I only mouthing nice-sounding words? Jesus told me to come and follow Him, not to wait or be distracted, to let the dead bury the dead, to put my hand to the plow and not look back – to follow with all my heart and all my life. (Luke 9: 60-62) The good news is that as long as I have a breath left, I can answer that call. I do not have to hang my head, look back to a fruitless life up to this point, say that it is too late. The love and mercy of God are boundless, and He is calling – right now.

What better way to close this reflection than with the Word of God? Make a combination of 2 Timothy, Hebrews and 2 Peter your personal prayer, as I make it mine.

"So do not be ashamed to testify about our Lord...But join with me in suffering for the gospel, by the power of God, who

has saved us and called us to a holy life – not because of anything we have done but because of his own purpose and grace. This grace was given us in Christ Jesus before the beginning of time, but it has now been revealed through the appearing of our Savior, Christ Jesus, who has destroyed death, and has brought life and immortality to light through the gospel." (2 Timothy 1: 8-10) *"Therefore, holy brothers, who share in the heavenly calling, fix your thoughts on Jesus, the apostle and high priest whom we confess."* (Hebrews 3: 1) *"For this very reason, make every effort to add to your faith goodness; and to goodness knowledge; and to knowledge, self-control; and to self-control, perseverance; and to perseverance, godliness; and to godliness, brotherly kindness; and to brotherly kindness, love. For if you possess these qualities in increasing measure, they will keep you from being ineffective and unproductive in your knowledge of our Lord Jesus Christ. But if anyone does not have them, he is nearsighted and blind, and has forgotten that he has been cleansed from his past sins. Therefore, my brothers, be all the more eager to make your calling and election sure. For if you do these things, you will never fall, and you will receive a rich welcome into the eternal kingdom of our Lord and Savior Jesus Christ."* (2 Peter 1: 5-11)

SUMMARY FOR REFLECTION AND DISCUSSION:

A real Christian:

1) Does not see Jesus as some sickly sweet and sentimental idealist;
2) Does not see Jesus as a purely historical figure without meaning today;
3) Sees Jesus as true Man and true God, a hero, a role model for the ages;
4) Seeks to hear and listen to Jesus through the Holy Spirit every day of his and her life;
5) Seeks to love Jesus by serving and loving others in need;
6) Is never satisfied with mediocrity, but instead recognizes and embraces the demands of the committed Christian life.

SCRIPTURES FOR JOURNALING:

1) Matthew 20-21
2) Matthew 22
3) 2 Timothy 1; Hebrews 3; 2 Peter 1.

PART V:

LIVING THE CHRISTIAN LIFE

This final section seeks to wrap everything up with a series of practical reflections on the Christian life in action. Actually, though, the intent is not for this to be the end for readers – but rather a new beginning, a fresh vision of genuine Christianity.

I encourage readers to go back through the reflections periodically. Each one contains endless opportunities for spiritual growth – not because of me but because they are based on God's Living Word.

The reflections also provide ongoing opportunities for prayer journaling with one other person or a small group.

Thank you for taking this journey with me. I have grown in the writing and reflecting; my prayer is that you have grown and will continue to grow through the reading and reflection. Peace!

REFLECTION 23:

HAVING VISION

One of the great swimmers in history was a lady named Florence Chadwick. She did the "impossible." She swam the English Channel, and she did it more than once. Florence Chadwick became an inspiration for many as she battled wind, wave and fatigue.

But Florence also had a significant failure in long distance swimming. She was unsuccessful in her bid to swim from the island of Catalina to the coast of California. Why? After all, she was experiencing warmer water, less wind and an overall much more pleasant environment. The reason is very revealing: She did not succumb to bad weather, illness, or even tiredness in and of itself. She gave up because fog rolled in; she could not see the coastline. Florence Chadwick, because she could not keep the vision of her goal physically before her, found the going too rough and she gave up.

Switching gears for a moment, imagine with me that you are having a new house built. You have carefully planned it; you designed the layout and the details, even to include the style and color of bathroom and kitchen faucets. Almost every day you go to the building site to check on progress. With growing excitement you see your dream taking shape under the skilled hands of the carpenters and other craftsmen. During the wait, you have rented a small, rather nondescript house. You are tolerating it while you look forward to moving into your dream home. Now, I ask you: Would you spend a lot of time fixing up the temporary quarters, a lot of money redecorating and refurbishing? Of course not, for something much better is coming!

What do these stories, one true and one made up, have in common? They are both examples of how we who have a personal relationship with Jesus Christ should be living and where we should be focusing our attention. If I have accepted the gift of grace enabling me to be born again, I look forward to something very special and wonderful awaiting me when this life ends. It is called heaven. But, we are creatures who live in the flesh as well as in the spirit; it is therefore difficult to keep our vision fixed on what is coming. If we do not remain fixed, if we fail to consciously recognize that all we have and all we do is passing, we can begin to flounder and, like Florence Chadwick who lost sight of her goal, we can be overwhelmed by the waves and pressures of life and lose heart. Further, we can become so preoccupied with our present dwelling that we lose sight of the glorious one that is prepared for us. We can become immersed in the worries and the pleasures of this life to the point of losing perspective and balance.

Let's consider this from a different viewpoint. Let's go to the Word. One of the greatest prophets was Elijah. He was an early prophet in the history of Israel; in his appearance and even his mannerisms he foreshadowed John the Baptist. Like all prophets, Elijah was called to remind the people of their covenant with God (the job description of a prophet). He was also a highly sensitive man; he experienced times of great fear and deep discouragement. But Elijah nevertheless was dedicated to the God who called him and loved him. I encourage you to read about this man of God who is a true inspiration for us as we journey along the Christian path of life. Read primarily 1 Kings 17 through 2 Kings 2.

In 1 Kings 19, Elijah found a man plowing a field. Elijah placed his cloak on that farmer as a sign that he would one day carry on Elijah's work. The farmer became a disciple; his name was Elisha. In 2 Kings 2 there is a powerful account of Elijah's completion of his ministry and the beginnings of Elisha's. Read with me the following excerpts from that chapter:

"When the Lord was about to take Elijah up to heaven in a

whirlwind, Elijah and Elisha were on their way from Gilgal. Elijah said to Elisha, 'Stay here; the Lord has sent me to Bethel.' But Elisha said, 'As surely as the Lord lives and as you live, I will not leave you.' So they went down to Bethel." You see, Elijah as a prophet knew that he was about to leave this earth, and in a very select way – not by dying and being buried but by being caught up by God body and soul. Elisha was also a prophet, and he sensed that something extraordinary was about to happen. It is hard to fool a prophet! Now, read on:

"The company of the prophets at Bethel came out to Elisha and asked, 'Do you know that the Lord is going to take your master from you today?' 'Yes, I know,' Elisha replied, 'but do not speak of it.' Fifty men of the company of the prophets went and stood at a distance, facing the place where Elijah and Elisha had stopped at the Jordan. Elijah took his cloak, rolled it up and struck the water with it. The water divided to the right and to the left, and the two of them crossed over on dry ground. When they had crossed, Elijah said to Elisha, 'Tell me, what can I do for you before I am taken from you?' 'Let me inherit a double portion of your spirit,' Elisha replied." Elisha was no fool! Let's not forget that Elijah was the man who did amazing things: confronted kings and queens, multiplied flour and oil, raised a boy from the dead, called down fire from heaven to prove he was a true prophet (fire that consumed the false prophets, by the way), ended a drought and now dried up the Jordan so that he and Elisha could cross. Elisha wanted twice that supernatural power! He was not on a power kick or ego trip; he was speaking as prompted by the Spirit of God and sought only to serve God and the people of Israel. Let's go on. *"'You have asked a difficult thing,' Elijah said, 'yet if you see me when I am taken from you, it will be yours – otherwise not.' As they were walking along and talking together, suddenly a chariot of fire and horses of fire appeared and separated the two of them, and Elijah went up to heaven in a whirlwind. Elisha saw this and cried out, 'My father! My father! The chariots and horsemen of Israel!' And Elisha saw him no more. Then he took hold of his own clothes and tore them apart. He picked up the cloak that had fallen from Elijah and went back and stood on the bank of the Jordan. Then he took the cloak*

that had fallen from him and struck the water with it. 'Where now is the Lord, the God of Elijah?' he asked. When he struck the water, it divided to the right and to the left, and he crossed over. The company of the prophets from Jericho, who were watching, said, 'The spirit of Elijah is resting on Elisha.' And they went to meet him and bowed to the ground before him." So Elisha carried on the work of God. He lived a life of great triumph, walking constantly and consistently in the Spirit of God. Elisha actually performed more miracles than any other prophet except Moses.

Elijah and Elisha were men who had vision, who maintained balance as they did the work of God. To be sure, they had their moments of weakness, especially Elijah. There were doubts and fears, but when all was said and done they remained faithful and walked the path God had laid out for them.

There are two further events in 2 Kings that are worth exploring, in light of the overall theme of this reflection. First, in 2 Kings 6, we read that the King of Aram, at war with Israel, was repeatedly thwarted because the Israelites always knew where he was encamped. Furious over this, and discovering that it was Elisha who was telling the King of Israel where he was, Aram sent to Dathan – where Elisha was – *"horses and chariots and a strong force. They went by night and surrounded the city. When the servant of the man of God got up and went out early the next morning, an army with horses and chariots had surrounded the city. 'Oh, my lord, what shall we do?' the servant asked. 'Don't be afraid,' the prophet answered. 'Those who are with us are more than those who are with them.' And Elisha prayed, 'O Lord, open his eyes that he may see.' Then the Lord opened the servant's eyes, and he looked and saw the hills full of horses and chariots of fire all around Elisha. As the enemy came down toward him, Elisha prayed to the Lord, 'Strike these people with blindness.' So he struck them with blindness, as Elisha had asked. Elisha told them, 'This is not the road and this is not the city. Follow me, and I will lead you to the man you are looking for.' And he led them to Samaria. After they entered the city, Elisha said, 'Lord, open the eyes of these men so they can see.' Then the Lord opened their eyes and they looked, and there they were, inside Samaria. When the king of Israel saw them,*

*he asked Elisha, 'Shall I kill them, my father? Shall I kill them?'
'Do not kill them,' he answered. 'Would you kill men you have
captured with your own sword or bow? Set food and water before
them so that they may eat and drink and then go back to their
master.' So he prepared a great feast for them, and after they had
finished eating and drinking, he sent them away, and they returned
to their master. So the bands from Aram stopped raiding Israel's
territory."* (2 Kings 6: 14-23)

The second account, shorter but just as amazing if not more so,
is recorded in 2 Kings 13: *"Elisha died, and was buried. Now
Moabite raiders used to enter the country every spring. Once while
some Israelites were burying a man, suddenly they saw a band of
raiders; so they threw the man's body into Elisha's tomb. When the
man touched Elisha's bones, the man came to life and stood up on
his feet."* (2 Kings 13: 20-21)

If you and I will only humbly and reverently accept the Word of
God, we have here some powerful testimonies of the presence and
power of God. If, however, we choose to follow those who cross
such stories off as exaggerations, as tales made up to teach the truth
of God's sovereignty and guidance, then we miss the full import of
this awesome gift of God called the Bible.

But back to the point: In these accounts of Elijah and Elisha, we
find some important truths and lessons. Elijah clearly had his eyes
fixed on God and God's eternal Kingdom, so much so that God
gave him the rare, rare privilege of being caught up body and soul
and spirit. Elisha was the given the privilege of seeing exactly what
happened (the company of prophets standing nearby did not, they
just knew that Elijah was gone). Elisha saw heaven opened; he saw
the glory of God and His angels. And what did he do? Ask to go
with Elijah? No, he took the cloak and struck the waters of the
Jordan River – and thus began his ministry. There is a close parallel
here to Acts 1: 8-11, as Jesus ascended to heaven forty days after
His Resurrection:

*"'You will receive power when the Holy Spirit comes on you;
and you will be my witnesses in Jerusalem, and in all Judea
and Samaria, and to the ends of the earth.' After he said this,*

he was taken up before their very eyes, and a cloud hid him from their sight. They were looking intently up into the sky as he was going, when suddenly two men dressed in white stood beside them. 'Men of Galilee,' they said, 'why do you stand here looking into the sky? This same Jesus, who has been taken from you into heaven, will come back in the same way you have seen him go into heaven.'"

Folks, Jesus is talking to us, not just to the apostles. He wants to give us power, in order to be His witnesses. And the angels tell us, too, not to stand around gazing into the sky, but to get to work – for Jesus is coming back.

Now let's put it all together: First, we as Christians are to have a vision of heaven, of our eternal home, promised by Jesus before He died and described by John in the Book of Revelation. It is our goal. It will last forever, while our time here on earth is short. We are called to live with our spiritual eyes on that goal, for *"eye has not seen, nor has ear heard, nor has it entered into the mind of man what things God has prepared for those who love him."* (1 Corinthians 2: 9) The pleasures and pains of this life are passing, and we are to walk with our eye on the crown to come. But, we are not called to be star-gazers. There is indeed work to be done; there are people to be saved; there is a purifying in each of our lives that needs to happen as we grow closer to our Lord and live more by the Spirit and give glory to the Father by everything we do and say. The great Christian writer, A.W. Tozer, gave us a litmus test to determine if we live with true spirituality while we are on this earth:

1) It is manifested by the desire to be holy rather than happy;
2) There is a true desire to see the glory and honor of God advanced through one's life, no matter the consequences – to gasp for God's glory as a suffocating person gasps for breath;
3) There is a desire to carry the cross through obedience to Christ and attachment to His name;
4) To see everything from God's viewpoint;
5) To prefer to die right rather than live wrong;

6) To genuinely want to see others advanced;
7) To consistently make eternity, not time, judgments;
8) To serve rather than be served;
9) To do all of this through the operation of the Holy Spirit within us.

When we die, could what happened when the dead man touched Elisha's bones happen to people in contact with us? More importantly, when we die, will people at our funeral say that we were truly men and women of God, and that they came closer to God because of our lives, our example, and our obedience to God's Spirit working within us? Do we walk so profoundly by the Spirit that when we see dangers, enemies, difficulties and trials facing us we also sense the angels of God and God Himself with us to see us through? Do we believe – do we really believe – that Jesus is speaking to each of us when He tells us to be filled with power from on high and asks us to be His witnesses?

Do we, in summary, live each day as if it were our last – full of love, joy and eagerness to serve the One who died and rose for us? Therein lies the difference between a real Christian and one who bears the name only. Please read Revelation 21 and 22, the end of the Bible. It is real; it is going on right now; it is a description of our true home. We are called to go forth and bring others home with us. As the very last words of the New Testament pronounce: *"He who testifies to these things says, 'Yes, I am coming soon.' Amen. Come, Lord Jesus. The grace of the Lord Jesus be with God's people. Amen."*

Will the Real Christians Please Stand Up!

SUMMARY FOR REFLECTION AND DISCUSSION:

A real Christian:

1) Has a spiritual mission and a vision that guides each day, each decision of life;
2) Seeks more than anything else to live a holy life, modeled on the life of Jesus;
3) Recognizes and relies on the presence and guidance of the Holy Spirit;
4) Has a passion that all be saved, that none be lost, and yearns to help.

SCRIPTURES FOR JOURNALING:

1) 1 Kings 19 and 2 Kings 2;
2) 2 Kings 6 and 13, and Acts 1;
3) Revelation 21 and 22.

REFLECTION 24:

RADICAL HOPE

Proverbs 13: 12 is a fascinating passage of Scripture: *"Hope deferred makes the heart sick, but a longing fulfilled is a tree of life."* What does this mean? Think back to that time when you were looking forward to going to the beach, or to an amusement park, or to a ball game. You bounded out of bed on the great day, looked out the window, and saw rain pouring down! Remember that hollow feeling? A friend of mine was planning a trip with his son to several major league baseball parks, one after the other. It was a long-time dream of both father and son. Then a baseball strike dashed their eager anticipation. It was especially heartbreaking for the young boy. *"Hope deferred makes the heart sick."* Have you ever had a hoped-for promotion given to someone else? Have you ever had the person whom you hoped would be your mate give her/his love to another? Have you experienced the sudden death of a loved one in the prime of life? *"Hope deferred makes the heart sick."*

So, it seems that the only real key to maintaining inner peace and joy through the vicissitudes of life is to have hope fixed on the most important thing. For a real Christian, there is only one "right thing" – as we shall see.

Let me tell you a story, a true one, about three men who lived a long time ago. They lived in Asia, and their names were Hananiah, Mishael and Azariah. They had the world by the tail. Why? Well,

Will the Real Christians Please Stand Up!

the king of the country in which they lived put out a call for some young men. The goal was to find and train personal and privileged servants for the king's court. Our three heroes were handsome; they had an aptitude for learning; they had a maturity and a wisdom beyond their years. Moreover, they had high moral standards and an impeccable value system. So, the job was theirs.

The benefits included partaking of the finest food and drink from the king's table. But they declined; their unusual religious beliefs – at least unusual in that kingdom – prohibited eating and drinking many of the delicacies. They assured their masters that they would nevertheless be as robust and healthy as the servants who ate the choice food. And they were right.

Yes, Hananiah, Mishael and Azariah had everything going for them. They were privileged subjects in the kingdom, and they had every reason to believe that they would shine in the service of the king. But then it all fell apart. The king one day decreed that an image of him be built and be worshipped by all his subjects. Every time the people heard the blast of the trumpet they were to fall down on their faces and pay homage to the king's statue. Because of their strong religious beliefs, the three youths refused to bow down. And, sure enough, someone turned them in – perhaps a person jealous of their status or a person zealous for kingly worship. The furious monarch ordered them to appear before him and to obey the decree – under penalty of death, a quite excruciating death, I might add.

Perhaps by now you have figured out who these three young men were. They are better known by their other names, given to them by an official who did not want them to keep their Jewish ones. He named them Shadrach, Meshach and Abednego. Daniel 3: 17-18 records their response to the king:

> *"We do not need to defend ourselves before you in this matter...The God we serve is able to save us...and he will rescue us from your hand, O king. But even if he does not, we want you to know, O king, that we will not serve your gods or worship the image of gold you have set up."*

Will the Real Christians Please Stand Up!

We know, of course, that God delivered them from the fiery furnace. But the amazing statement they made was not based on an absolute assurance that they would live – live or die, they determined to serve and obey God. You see, they had their hope where it belonged. That hope did not lie in their jobs or status as personal servants to the king; it lay in their commitment to being in the KING'S service! Because their hope was secure in God and His Kingdom, nothing in this world could cause them to lose their peace or deter them from their chosen course. That is radical hope! I encourage the reading of chapters 1 and 3 of Daniel for the full account of this story; and do not lose sight of the presence and influence of the "fourth man."

Romans 5: 3-5 is one of the most famous Biblical passages on the subject of hope: *"We know that suffering produces perseverance; perseverance, character; and character, hope. And hope does not disappoint us, because God has poured out his love into our hearts by the Holy Spirit, whom he has given us."* Note the order: Hope is not first, it is last – after suffering, perseverance and character. You see, suffering in and of itself is neither good nor beneficial. In fact, suffering can shrivel the human spirit and lead to bitterness and despair. But when we, through faith, see that suffering can lead to growth, we begin to have the courage to persevere. And as we persevere, our resolve and vision and strength to manage adversity grow – and so we grow in character. Then, walking by the Holy Spirit and yielding to God's will, we find hope – a gift from God, along with faith and love.

Also consider another passage from Romans: *"We know that the whole creation has been groaning as in the pains of childbirth right up to the present time. Not only so, but we ourselves, who have the firstfruits of the Spirit, groan inwardly as we wait eagerly for our adoption as sons, the redemption of our bodies. For in this hope we were saved. But hope that is seen is no hope at all. Who hopes for what he already has? But if we hope for what we do not yet have, we wait for it patiently."* (Romans 8: 22-25)

A young couple experienced the death of their child. After their time of agony, anger and confusion, the peace of the Lord came into their lives. The father said something very beautiful: "The cold, dark winter causes the roots to grow deeper." That is radical hope.

Another example of this kind of hope is my wife, Barbara, whom I have written about previously. She is truly a wonderful gift from God to me and to our children. Even though she lives in constant pain and fatigue, she wrote this (among other beautiful things): "When I began to love the pain as part of my growth, I was able to enter into a fuller relationship with the Lord; for I know that without His carrying me I would not be able to do anything. Enter into your trial, and know the Lord is the only one who can carry you through. Therefore, you can do nothing but what He wants you to do. To the world you may look a failure, but to Him you are being obedient. You will glow in your job; you will have peace; you will not be stressed about what you are doing. You will be peaceful in what you are doing, as you will know that the Lord is carrying you. Jesus is drawing you into obedience. The sick and the hurting will no longer be encouraged to go to man for their comfort, but will go directly to God. This is so important to see. The Lord showed me this; and when I stopped going to man, I went to Jesus." Barb does not imply here that we should not go to physicians; some truly great ones have helped her and continue to do so. She is referring to our spiritual journey. As Paul wrote in 1 Thessalonians 5: 8, *"But since we belong to the day, let us be self-controlled, putting on faith and love as a breastplate, and the hope of salvation as a helmet."*

This approach is so much richer and deeper than the superficial cries of Christians who lay claim to perfect healing now, on demand, because of a terrible misinterpretation of the meaning of God's Word. True hope does not say, "I know I am healed, because I speak and believe in God's Word – the healing is just not manifested yet." True hope does say, though, "I know I am a member of God's family, and that He loves me. Father, Son and Holy Spirit dwell with me and know what is best for me at all times. I yield; I trust; I seek only God. Nothing else matters."

Another benchmark passage about hope is Hebrews 11: 1: *"Now faith is being sure of what we hope for and certain of what we do not see."* Faith and hope are closely intertwined for the real Christian. Because of whom I believe in, I have hope. Because I believe, I look forward. The entire Chapter 11 of Hebrews is a powerful chronicle of faith – and hope – in action, as a number of Old Testament heroes come to life in this glorious exclamation: Noah, who was obedient to God in a seemingly ridiculous situation…Abraham, who believed and obeyed *"even though he did not know where he was going."*…Moses, who gave up his princely status and ultimately led God's people from bondage, keeping his vision on the Promised Land…The prophets and other holy people of God, *"who through faith conquered kingdoms, administered justice, and gained what was promised, who shut the mouths of lions, quenched the fury of the flames, and escaped the edge of the sword; and who became power-ful in battle and routed foreign armies…Others were tortured and refused to be released, so that they might gain a better resurrection. Some faced jeers and flogging, while still others were chained and put in prison. They were stoned; they were sawed in two; they were put to death by the sword. They went about in sheepskins and goatskins, destitute, persecuted and mistreated – the world was not worthy of them. They wandered in deserts and mountains, and in caves and holes in the ground."*

Where is our hope? Where and how do we focus our hope? If it is directed to anything other than God, then truly hope deferred will make our spirits sick. The next chapter of the great Book of Hebrews, chapter 12, following up on the narrative of faith, proclaims:

> *"Therefore, since we are surrounded by such a great cloud of witnesses, let us throw off everything that hinders and the sin that so easily entangles, and let us run with perseverance the race marked out for us. Let us fix our eyes on Jesus, the author and perfecter of our faith, who for the joy set before him endured the cross, scorning its shame, and sat down at the right hand of the throne of God."* (Hebrews 12: 1-3)

Now consider some additional Scriptures: *"Consider it pure joy, my brothers, whenever you face trials of many kinds, because you know that the testing of your faith develops perseverance. Perseverance must finish its work so that you may be mature and complete, not lacking anything."* (James

1: 2-4) *"One thing I ask of the Lord, this is what I seek: That I may dwell in the house of the Lord all the days of my life, to gaze upon the beauty of the Lord and to seek him in he Temple. For in the day of trouble he will keep me safe in his dwelling; he will hide me in the shelter of his tabernacle and set me high upon a rock."* (Psalm 27: 4-5) *"Find rest, O my soul, in God alone; my hope comes from him. He alone is my rock and my salvation; he is my fortress, I will not be shaken. My salvation and my honor depend on God; he is my mighty rock, my refuge. Trust in him at all times, O people; pour out your hearts to him, for God is our refuge."* (Psalm 62: 5-8)

Where is your hope? Is it in the things of the world, or are your eyes fixed on Jesus, the author and finisher of our faith and the source of the only true hope?

SUMMARY FOR REFLECTION AND DISCUSSION:

A real Christian:

1) Keeps spiritual eyes fixed on the great truths of revelation – including creation, redemption, the Incarnation, the Resurrection, the indwelling of the Holy Spirit, the eternal Kingdom of Heaven which is our home; in other words, fixed on the Father, on the Son and on the Holy Spirit;
2) Refuses to let the problems and trials of life dim the vision that hope provides;
3) Does not become entrapped in the flashy, empty and show biz hype of the name-it-and-claim-it-clique – people who appear to be well-grounded in the Word but are in reality and probably unconsciously better grounded in the world, using God and His Word to attempt to meet their every demand. This is not hope; this is highly offensive to the sovereign power and holiness of God;
4) Like the young men in the fiery furnace, proclaims faith in the presence and love of God and values relationship with Him greater than any earthly treasure.
5) Puts Jesus first in everything, seeking only to follow, love and serve Him – which includes radical hope in the Kingdom that is within us and the Kingdom which is to come.

SCRIPTURES FOR JOURNALING:

1) Hope Scriptures: For example, Proverbs 13: 12; Romans 5: 3-5; Romans 8: 22-25; 1 Thessalonians 5: 8; James 1: 2-4; Psalm 27: 4-5; Psalm 62: 5-8;
2) Daniel 1-3;
3) Hebrews 11-12

REFLECTION 25:

JUST "HANGIN' IN THERE"

One of the many simple rituals of life is the daily greeting. Two people, upon seeing one another, might engage in an exchange such as this: "Hi! How are you? Response (choose one!): "Okay."…"Alright."…"Just fine."…"I'm above ground."…or "I'm just hangin' in there." In most interchanges such as this, minds may be elsewhere and the words flow from long habit. To be kind, I would not call these exchanges phony; but, it is disturbing when the words flow from the mouth of a real Christian.

Picture with me the following: There is a large tree, dwarfing in size and beauty anything else on the horizon. Its branches are resplendent in green leaves; the branches extend up and down and to the left and right in majestic fashion. Toward the top of this magnificent tree there is a large platform; standing on it is Jesus Christ. A ladder extends from the ground to the platform and reaches slightly above the platform from a large hole cut in its floor. Jesus looks down through the hole and, slowly shaking His head, smiles wistfully. For there, just below the platform, is a person – perhaps you or I – holding on to a branch, legs dangling below. Jesus asks, "What are you doing?" We respond, "Just hangin' in there!" But the ladder is right next to us, leading easily to the platform and to Jesus! It would be a simple matter to just take hold of it and climb up. But instead we choose to "just hang in there."

For a true Christian, one walking in faith, hope and a relationship of love with Jesus, the response to a greeting can never be ho-hum. The question "How are you?" is an invitation and a reminder to give testimony to a wonderful reality. The only appropriate responses are (choose any one): "Wonderful!"..."Glorious!"... "Praise the Lord!"...or something similar – and regardless of problems, difficulties or even tragedies in our life. Why? Well, to use as an acronym the letters of a word that will sum it all up, join me in a brief journey through Scripture:

S = Saved

"If you confess with your mouth, 'Jesus is Lord,' and believe in your heart that God raised him from the dead, you will be saved. For it is with your heart that you believe and are justified, and it is with your mouth that you confess and are saved." (Romans 10: 9-10)

"Now if we are children, then we are heirs – heirs of God and co-heirs with Christ, if indeed we share in his sufferings in order that we may also share in his glory." (Romans 8: 17)

"But because of his great love for us, God, who is rich in mercy, made us alive with Christ even when we were dead in transgressions – it is by grace you have been saved. And God raised us up with Christ and seated us with him in the heavenly realms in Christ Jesus, in order that in the coming ages he might show the incomparable riches of his grace, expressed in his kindness to us in Christ Jesus. For it is by grace you have been saved, through faith – and this is not from yourselves, it is the gift of God – not by works, that no one can boast." (Ephesians 2: 4-9)

"Surely God is my salvation; I will trust and not be afraid. The Lord, the Lord, is my strength and my song; he has become my salvation. With joy you will draw water from the

wells of salvation." (Isaiah 12: 2-3)

H=Hope

"And when the Chief Shepherd appears, you will receive the crown of glory that will never fade away." (2 Peter 5: 4)

"For our light and momentary troubles are achieving for us an eternal glory that far outweighs them all. So we fix our eyes not on what is seen, but on what is unseen. For what is seen is temporary, but what is unseen is eternal." (2 Corinthians 4: 17-18)

"Since, then, you have been raised with Christ, set your hearts on things above, where Christ is seated at the right hand of God. Set your minds on things above, not on earthly things. For you died, and your life is now hidden with Christ in God. When Christ, who is your life, appears, then you will also appear with him in glory." (Colossians 3: 1-4)

"Now there is in store for me the crown of righteousness, which the Lord, the righteous Judge, will award to me on that day – and not only to me, but also to all who have longed for his appearing." (2 Timothy 4: 8)

"Then the righteous will shine like the sun in the kingdom of their Father. He who has ears, let him hear." (Matthew 13: 43)

A = Awe

"But the Lord is in his holy Temple; let all the earth be silent before him." (Habakkuk 2: 20)

"The Sovereign Lord is my strength; he makes my feet like the feet of a deer, he enables me to go on the heights." (Habakkuk 3: 19)

"When the Lord saw that he had gone over to look, God called to him from within the bush, 'Moses! Moses!' And Moses said, 'Here I am.' 'Do not come any closer,' God said. 'Take off your sandals, for the place where you are standing is holy ground.'" (Exodus 3: 4-5)

"When your words came, I ate them; they were my joy and my heart's delight, for I bear your name, O Lord God Almighty." (Jeremiah 15: 16)

"I will bow down toward your holy Temple and will praise your name for your love and your faithfulness, for you have exalted above all things your name and your word." (Psalm 138: 2)

"...I saw the Lord seated on a throne, high and exalted, and the train of his robe filled the Temple. Above him were seraphs, each with six wings. With two wings they covered their faces, with two they covered their feet, and with two they were flying. And they were calling to one another, 'Holy, holy, holy is the Lord Almighty; the whole earth is full of his glory." (Isaiah 6: 1-3)

L=Loved

"I have loved you with an everlasting love; I have drawn you with loving-kindness." (Jeremiah 31: 3)

"I delight greatly in the Lord; my soul rejoices in my God, for he has clothed me with garments of salvation and arrayed me in a robe of righteousness, as a bridegroom adorns his head like a priest, and as a bride adorns herself with her jewels." (Isaiah 61: 10)

"...known, yet regarded as unknown; dying, and yet we live on; beaten, and yet not killed; sorrowful, yet always rejoic-

ing; poor, yet making many rich; having nothing, and yet possessing everything." (2 Corinthians 6: 9-10)

"But God demonstrates his own love for us in this: While we were still sinners, Christ died for us." (Romans 5: 8)

"How great is the love the Father has lavished on us, that we should be called children of God! And that is what we are!" (1 John 3: 1)

O = Oyee! (Oyee is an African word that is an affirmation, meaning "Right on!" "Yes!" "Amen!")

"Though you have not seen him, you love him; and even though you do not see him now, you believe in him and are filled with an inexpressible and glorious joy, for you are receiving the goal of your faith, the salvation of your souls." (1 Peter 1: 8-9)

"About midnight Paul and Silas were praying and singing hymns to God, and the other prisoners were listening to them. Suddenly there was such a violent earthquake that the foundations of the prison were shaken. At once all the prison doors flew open, and everybody's chains came loose." (Acts 16: 25-26)

"Do not grieve, for the joy of the Lord is your strength." (Nehemiah 8: 10)

"And the ransomed of the Lord will return. They will enter Zion with singing; everlasting joy will crown their heads. Gladness and joy will overtake them, and sorrow and sighing will flee away." (Isaiah 35: 10)

M = Ministry

"Then I heard a voice from heaven say, 'Write: Blessed are

the dead who die in the Lord from now on.' 'Yes,' says the Spirit, 'they will rest from their labor, for their deeds will follow them.'" (Revelation 14: 13)

"Not many of you were wise by human standards; not many were influential; not many were of noble birth. But God chose the foolish things of the world to shame the wise. He chose the weak things of the world to shame the strong. He chose the lowly things of this world and the despised things – and the things that are not – to nullify the things that are, so that no one may boast before him." (1 Corinthians 1: 26-29)

"And if anyone gives even a cup of cold water to one of these little ones because he is my disciple, I tell you the truth, he will not lose his reward." (Matthew 10: 42)

The glorious, wondrous, heart-bursting news is that real Christians are called to share in the ministry of our Lord and Savior, Jesus Christ, who was the subject of Isaiah's prophecy:

"The Spirit of the Sovereign Lord is on me, because the Lord has anointed me to preach good news to the poor. He has sent me to bind up the brokenhearted, to proclaim freedom for the captives and release from darkness for the prisoners, to proclaim the year of the Lord's favor and the day of vengeance of our God, to comfort all who mourn, and provide for those who grieve in Zion – to bestow on them a crown of beauty instead of ashes, the oil of gladness instead of mourning, and a garment of praise instead of a spirit of despair." (Isaiah 61: 1-3)

If we are true Christians, we are SAVED, we have HOPE looking forward to a glorious eternity. We stand in AWE before a holy and mighty God and we are LOVED by Him with an undying love. We therefore cry out OYEE! We all have a MINISTRY to show forth the love of God and salvation through Jesus Christ to others we encounter during our lives. Put these first letters all together and they spell SHALOM, the Hebrew word that means "PEACE." Jesus said, *"My peace I leave you, My peace I give you."* The fruit of the Holy Spirit, dwelling within us as New Testament temples, includes peace.

This is why we, as Christians, are never, never "just hangin' in there"!

There is a story that has been frequently utilized in motivational speeches. It certainly fits here. It is a true story, and it took place many years ago in Africa. It goes like this:

An African farmer heard accounts of how some of his fellows were selling everything they had and were becoming diamond prospectors (similar to the Gold Rush in our own country). The farmer decided to do likewise. He sold out to another man and began his quest. He spent the rest of his life searching far and wide, but in vain. He ultimately threw himself into a river out of despair and ended his life. In the meantime, the man to whom the unfortunate farmer had sold his property was content with enjoying his land. One day, while walking through a dry creek bed, he discovered a large and unusually pretty stone. He took it home and placed it on the mantle above his fireplace. Some time later, a friend was visiting and noticed the stone. He remarked on its beauty and, taking it down from the mantle, examined it more closely. All of a sudden he let out a cry and told the owner that what he had in his possession was a very large diamond. It turned out to be the largest one every found up to that time in Africa. The owner, shaking his head in wonder, said that it was one of many similar stones he had seen in the creek bed. Yes, you guessed it, the original farmer had sold, in order to look for diamonds, acreage that turned out to be one of the largest and most successful diamond mines on the continent!

Are we "waiting for our ship to come home"? Are we looking for that lucky break, struggling through life's ups and downs, "just hangin' in there" – and never noticing that we are walking through acres and acres of spiritual diamonds? Is the Bible just words? Or is it a living Word, touching the depths of our minds and hearts, making us come alive with the joy that comes from the awareness that we possess all the true and lasting riches of life – and this is just a hint of what is to come for all eternity?

Jesus said, "I am with you always." And one day He will say, "Come, blessed of My Father." So, how are you? The only answer from the mouth of a real Christian is "GLORIOUS!" "OYEE!" "THE JOY OF THE LORD IS MY STRENGTH!" "PRAISE THE LORD!" "AMEN, AND AMEN!" And note: When Christians face times of spiritual dryness, when they pass through "the dark night of the soul", they are still able, by God's grace, to maintain a deep, inner peace – even without the accompanying warm feelings. That is true living by faith, and hope, and love.

SUMMARY FOR REFLECTION AND DISCUSSION:

A real Christian:

1) Has a deep and inner peace that comes from awareness of relationship with God and an eternal home to come;
2) No matter how difficult and burdensome life becomes, consistently walks with steadfast purpose and springs back from setbacks with hope and faith – and an abiding love for God;
3) Has a commitment to share that hope with others – as every real Christian is evangelistic, filled with the desire that every person be saved and desirous to share, under the guidance of the Holy Spirit, the Good News of the Gospel;
4) Lives with a spiritual awareness of the holiness and presence of God, permeating every day and giving it supreme purpose.

SCRIPTURES FOR JOURNALING:

1) Take each letter of the acronym: S. H. A. L. O. M. Refer back to the Scriptures identified and search for others relating to the same theme.

REFLECTION 26:

A CALL TO INTERCESSORY PRAYER

Read prayerfully, first Daniel and then the Psalmist:

"Now, our God, hear the prayers and petitions of your servant. For your sake, O Lord, look with favor on your desolate sanctuary. Give ear, O God, and hear; open your eyes and see the desolation of the city that bears your Name. We do not make requests of you because we are righteous, but because of your great mercy. O Lord, listen! O Lord, forgive! O Lord, hear and act! For your sake, O my God, do not delay, because your city and your people bear your Name. While I was speaking and praying, confessing my sin and the sin of my people Israel and making my request to the Lord my God for his holy hill – while I was still in prayer, Gabriel, the man I had seen in the earlier vision, came to me in swift flight about the time of the evening sacrifice. He instructed me and said to me, 'Daniel, I have now come to give you insight and understanding. As soon as you began to pray, an answer was given, which I have come to tell you, for you are highly esteemed.'" (Daniel 9: 17-23)

"Praise awaits you, O God, in Zion; to you our vows will be fulfilled. O you who hear prayer, to you all men will come.

When we were overwhelmed by sins, you forgave our transgressions. Blessed are those you choose and bring near to live in your courts!" (Psalm 65: 1-4)

In the first instance, Daniel prayed with intensity and faith, and the archangel Gabriel appeared to tell him that his prayer was heard and answered from the moment he began praying. That is an example of the power of prayer. In the second Scripture, the psalmist, under the inspiration of the Holy Spirit, describes God as the one who hears and responds to prayer – thus explaining why prayer has power.

Note that these are people of the Old Testament, under the old Covenant, and their prayers are meaningful and full of power. The exciting news is that we as Christians are the people of the New Testament, under the new Covenant, and we have the wondrous privilege of being members of the living Body of Christ. He is the Word made flesh who is the fulfillment of the Scriptures, of God's great promise of salvation.

What does this mean for the real Christian? The following four brief stories, along with a kaleidoscope of Scriptures, will explain and will make a point – a wonderful, mind-blowing point!

Story #1: Steve Brown, a pastor with an audiotape ministry some years ago, talked about the time he had been invited to give a message to a convention of youths. He prepared, prayed, and was ready to give what he believed would be an inspiring message. But, at the last minute, the convention organizer asked Steve to change his topic and give a message on missions and ministry. Steve almost objected, wanting to explain that he had given much thought, prayer and energy to his planned message; but the Holy Spirit checked him, and he agreed to meet the man's request. So, Steve sought the Spirit's guidance and gave his somewhat impromptu talk. At the end he gave an altar call. But no one, not a single youth of the hundreds in attendance, came forward. Steve was embarrassed and left as quickly as he could, convinced that on that evening he had been an abject failure. Quite a few years later, in another part of the country, a young man approached Steve and told him that he had been a participant in that youth convention. Steve thought to himself, "Oh no, the memory won't go away! I am about

Will the Real Christians Please Stand Up!

to be humbled again." Instead, the young man quietly said, "Pastor Brown, I gave my life to the Lord that night, and I am now in the seminary, preparing for the ministry." Because Steve Brown was obedient and turned the entire situation over to God, in prayer, a soul was touched – and who knows ultimately how many more.

Story # 2: Jack Calvin, a businessman and former evangelist, was at the bottom of the barrel many years ago. He had turned a very successful sales career into disaster because of alcohol and drugs. His family left him, and he went from a five figure per week salary to shoplifting in order to survive. Jack checked into a motel, fully intending to take his life. As he states in his testimony, he planned to leave that shabby inn feet first. Flopping on the bed, he flipped on the TV, and there was a preacher giving a message about the crucifixion of Jesus Christ. Quoting Jesus from the cross, the minister cried out in a loud voice, "Father, forgive them, for they know not what they do." Jack, touched to the quick by the Spirit, fell to his knees by the bed and cried out, "Lord, if You will set me free from this and save me, I will give my life to You." Years later he discovered something absolutely incredible: He learned that at the very moment he decided to turn on the TV, a cousin several times removed, far away in another State, was moved to cry out in a church service that the people needed to pray for his cousin Jack, right then, not knowing where Jack was or what he was doing, but only knowing in his heart that the Holy Spirit was urging him to pray for his cousin. Because he was obedient, because he became at that moment a yielded vessel, God used his prayers and changed Jack's life.

Story #3: Our older son, John, was at one time an assistant youth pastor in Dayton, Ohio. He sent us a letter in which he told about a teenage girl who had been in the occult, and who had given her life to Christ in a service. Several days later, John felt a strong urging to pray for her, and he asked several others to intercede with him. They prayed that she not be led into witchcraft, though they did not understand why they were praying that way. The next day they discovered, to their joy and amazement, that at the very time of their interceding, the girl was being enticed by a witch (yes, there are witches) to join her coven! She was sorely tempted, especially because of her past, but suddenly she experienced a mighty surge of spiritual power – and she walked away victorious.

Story #4: A church in England was dying. There was no real love, no zeal for souls or passion for worship – only dryness and boredom. The people were blaming the pastor; the pastor was blaming the people. Then a middle-aged woman moved into the area and began attending the church. She quietly began praying and urged others to join her. At the first prayer service she informally organized, only seven people showed up. But she prayed and sought the Lord with great fervor, and the seven joined her in interceding for the church. The seven quickly became seventy, and the number grew steadily from there. Revival began in that congregation, and the church became a powerful force for renewal in the entire neighborhood. All of this happened because a single individual said, "Let's pray."

With these stories tucked away in our minds and hearts, let's now take a brief journey through Scripture:

> *"'I looked for a man among them who would build up the wall and stand before me in the gap on behalf of the land so I would not have to destroy it, but I found none. So I will pour out my wrath on them and consume them with my fiery anger, bringing down on their own heads all they have done,' declares the Sovereign Lord." (Ezekiel 22: 30-31)*

> *"But if the watchman sees the sword coming and does not blow the trumpet to warn the people and the sword comes and takes the life of one of them, that man will be taken away because of his sin, but I will hold the watchman accountable for his blood. Son of man, I have made you a watchman for the house of Israel; so hear the word I speak and give them warning from me. When I say to the wicked, 'O wicked man, you will surely die,' and you do not speak out to dissuade him from his ways, that wicked man will die for his sin, and I will hold you accountable for his blood. But if you do warn the wicked man to turn from his ways and he does not do so, he will die for his sin, but you will have saved yourself...Say to them, 'As surely as I live,'*

declares the Sovereign Lord, 'I take no pleasure in the death of the wicked, but rather that they turn from their evil ways! Why will you die, O house of Israel?'" (Ezekiel 33: 6-9, 11)

"I have posted watchmen on your walls, O Jerusalem; they will never be silent day or night. You who call on the Lord, give yourselves no rest, and give him no rest till he establishes Jerusalem and makes her the praise of the earth." (Isaiah 62: 6-7)

"The prayer of a righteous man is powerful and effective. Elijah was a man just like us. He prayed earnestly that it would not rain, and it did not rain on the land for three and a half years. Again he prayed, and the heavens gave rain, and the earth produced its crops." (James 5: 16-18)

"Elijah climbed to the top of Carmel, bent down to the ground and put his face between his knees. 'Go and look toward the sea,' he told his servant. And he went up and looked. 'There is nothing there,' he said. Seven times Elijah said, 'Go back.' The seventh time the servant reported, 'A cloud as small as a man's hand is rising from the sea.' So Elijah said, 'Go and tell Ahab, 'Hitch up your chariot and go down before the rain stops you.' Meantime, the sky grew black with clouds, the wind rose, a heavy rain came on and Ahab rode off to Jezreel." (1 Kings 18: 42-46)

"I lay prostrate before the Lord those forty days and nights because the Lord had said he would destroy you. I prayed to the Lord and said, 'O Sovereign Lord, do not destroy your people, your own inheritance that you redeemed by your own great power and brought up out of Egypt with great power and brought out of Egypt with a mighty hand.'" (Deuteronomy 9: 25-26)

"So Peter was kept in prison, but the Church was earnestly praying to God for him. The night before Herod was to

Will the Real Christians Please Stand Up!

---

bring him to trial, Peter was sleeping between two soldiers, bound with two chains, and sentries stood guard at the entrance. Suddenly an angel of the Lord appeared and a light shone in the cell. He struck Peter on the side and woke him up. 'Quick, get up!' he said, and the chains fell off Peter's wrists. Then the angel said to him, 'Put on your clothes and sandals.' And Peter did so. 'Wrap your cloak around you and follow me,' the angel told him. Peter followed him out of the prison, but he had no idea that what the angel was doing was really happening; he thought he was seeing a vision. They passed the first and second guards, and came to the iron gate leading to the city. It opened for them by itself, and they went through it. When they had walked the length of one street, suddenly the angel left him. Then Peter came to himself and said, 'Now I know without a doubt that the Lord has sent his angel and rescued me from Herod's clutches and from everything the Jewish people were anticipating.' When this had dawned on him, he went to the house of Mary, the mother of John, also called Mark, where many people had gathered and were praying. Peter knocked at the outer entrance, and a servant girl named Rhoda came to answer the door. When she recognized Peter's voice, she was so overjoyed she ran back without opening it and exclaimed, 'Peter is at the door!' 'You're out of your mind,' they told her. When she kept insisting that it was so, they said, 'It must be his angel.' But Peter kept on knocking, and when they opened the door and saw him, they were astonished. Peter motioned with his hand for them to be quiet and described how the Lord had brought him out of prison. 'Tell James and the brothers about this,' he said, and then he left for another place." (Acts 12: 5-17)

"Do not be afraid, Daniel. Since the first day that you set your mind to gain understanding and to humble yourself before your God, your words were heard, and I have come in response to them. But the prince of the Persian kingdom resisted me twenty-one days. Then Michael, one of the chief *princes, came to help me, because I was detained there with the king of Persia."* (Daniel 10: 12-13)

It is clear from God's Word: People who pray in accordance with God's will and in obedience to His call are powerful vessels from which He pours out His blessings. It is clear, too, especially from the Daniel passage, that there is a spiritual battle going on. Prayer both causes the enemy to stir and is a key to victory for God's people. Frank Peretti's first two novels on spiritual warfare, "This Present Darkness" and "Piercing the Darkness," describe this ongoing battle in a vivid and riveting way.

Let's return now to Scripture: *"Therefore I tell you, whatever you ask for in prayer, believe that you have received it, and it will be yours."* (Mark 11: 24) This verse, and several others like it in the Gospels, have been often misused and misinterpreted by well-intentioned Christians who say in effect that since the statement is in the Word, God must honor it, and whatever I ask for God must give me in order for Him to be true to His Word. (We have exposed this before – the "name it and claim it" approach to prayer). Please, will the real Christians please stand up and be counted! God is not at the beck and call of every Christian's whim and fancy! A prayerful study of the entire New Testament places such verses as these in their proper context and reveals that the key to the prayer life of the Christian is to yield to God's will, to seek the Holy Spirit's guidance, to put on the mind of Christ, and to pray for God's perfect will to be done – with specific prayers offered as the Holy Spirit puts them in our hearts. When we pray with obedience and faith according to God's will, then, indeed, prayer will be answered. In this way God is powerfully true to His Word.

"...The four living creatures and the twenty-four elders fell down before the Lamb. Each one had a harp; and they were holding golden bowls full of incense, which are the prayers of the saints...Another angel, who had a golden censer, came and stood at the altar. He was given much incense to offer, with the prayers of all the saints, on the golden altar before the throne. The smoke of the incense, together with

the prayers of the saints, went up before God from the angel's hand." (Revelation 5: 8; 8: 3-4)

What an awesome sight this must be, going on right now in heaven! The Book of Revelation opens heaven's reality to us. In the midst of the praise, adoration and worship we discover that the prayers of the saints (that is, all people who are in the glory of their eternal home) are an integral part of heaven's activity. When Paul says in Ephesians 2 that we are somehow mystically caught up right now in the heavenly realm, the Word of God is telling us something tremendously important: Prayer is communion with God; when we pray, we are spiritually united with the hosts of heaven – the Trinity, the saints, the angels – and our prayers on earth, as those in heaven, are like incense ascending to the throne of God. Our prayers are indeed far-reaching and power-packed!

"As you come to him, the living Stone – rejected by men but chosen by God and precious to him – you also, like living stones, are being built into a spiritual house to be a holy priesthood, offering spiritual sacrifices acceptable to God through Jesus Christ." (1 Peter 2: 4-5)..."In the same way, the Spirit helps us in our weakness. We do not know what we ought to pray for, but the Spirit himself intercedes for us with groans that words cannot express. And he who searches our hearts knows the mind of the Spirit, because the Spirit intercedes for the saints in accordance with God's will."* (Romans 8: 26-27)

These two Scriptures confirm the amazing truth of our supernatural life of union and prayer. The "spiritual house", "holy priesthood" and "offering spiritual sacrifices" proclaim that the Body of Christ shares with its Head, the High Priest, the Lamb who was slain and who rose from the dead, the privilege and responsibility of making our very lives offerings of praise and intercession. The power of prayer comes from the Holy Spirit, for when we are united with Him, when we are living temples, He is active in our lives – guiding us, interceding for us, helping us to direct our prayer according to the will of the Father, showing by His actions that He is the living Love of God.

Finally, we look at a familiar Scripture, Ephesians 6, which teaches us about spiritual warfare and instructs us to put on the full armor of God. Verses 10-18 are worthy of serious study and meditation. Note what comes right after the admonition to put on the belt of truth, the helmet of salvation and the sword of the Spirit: *"And pray in the Spirit, on all occasions, with all kinds of prayers and requests."* Life is a spiritual battle; prayer is integral to that battle. And we are not alone.

So, we all share an exciting and critically important ministry if we are true Christians. We are called to pray, and to pray without ceasing. Every day, many times during the day, there will come into our minds and hearts people and situations to pray for. As we grow in sensitivity to things spiritual, we will see things we witness on TV, encounters we have at work or at home – indeed, every situation we find ourselves in – as an opportunity to pray. God puts these things in our path, because He wants us to be ministers of prayer – they are not just chance happenings. We can heed the call of the Spirit, or we can ignore it and over time grow insensitive to it. If the latter happens, we miss out on a glorious calling, and people whom God's plan places in our lives will go unaided, unless God in His mercy raises up another vessel. No matter what our limitations in education, skills, finances, and/or state in life, we can all be prayer warriors. Even though we do not always, or even usually, see the fruit of our prayer in this life, we shall see it when we enter the Kingdom of Heaven. God is calling, folks; are we responding?

SUMMARY FOR REFLECTION AND DISCUSSION:

A real Christian:

1) Knows that prayer is communication and is absolutely essential to a vibrant spiritual life. Just as communication is essential for every healthy relationship, so is communication with God both a privilege and a responsibility;

Will the Real Christians Please Stand Up!

2) Has an enduring personal passion for this communication with Father, Son and Holy Spirit. Prayer is seen not as something "required" but as the greatest joy of life;
3) Seeks time to simply be quiet and listen to God;
4) Prays not just at designated times but throughout the day, regularly lifting mind and heart to the Lord as the Holy Spirit leads;
5) Recognizes and lives out active membership in the Body of Christ, seeking to impact the world through spiritual service;
6) Sees prayer as normal as eating, drinking and even breathing; listens to God and talks to and with Him – in humility and awe but also in the joy of being God's child and heir.

SCRIPTURES FOR JOURNALING:

1) Daniel 9: 17-23 (focusing on the spiritual warfare between the enemy and the angelic forces) and Ephesians 6: 10-18;
2) Psalm 65: 1-4 and Revelation 5-8;
3) Ezekiel 33; Isaiah 62; James 5;
4) 1 Kings 18; Deuteronomy 9: 25-26 (and other instances of Moses' intercession; also, compare with Abraham's intercession for Sodom and Gomorrah in Genesis 10);
5) Acts 12 5-17 (and compare with Paul and Silas in Acts 16);
6) 1 Peter 1-2 and Romans 8.

REFLECTION 27:

THE SERVING LIFE

Stories once again introduce a reflection, two of them this time: The first story is about two elderly gentlemen in a convalescent home. Both were bedridden. One's bed was by the door, the other's by the only window in the room – a small window positioned in such a way that the man by the window could see out, but not the man by the door. After a time, as they grew more acquainted with each other, the old gent by the door asked his roommate to describe the scene outside that window. If he could not see and experience the outdoors as a shut-in, at least he could share in a description of it. So, the man in the window bed did just that. Each day he would talk about some aspect of the scene through his window. One day it was the beautiful oak and elm trees, with a lone dogwood between them. Another day it was the pond, with ducks swimming, and once he talked about the little ducklings following mama, in single file, into the water and across the pond. Yet another day the scene was one of a mother with her children, walking and playing with them in the grass. So it went, day after day, the descriptions bringing some rays of sunshine into the life of the crippled man by the door. Then, one day, quite suddenly, the man by the window died. The other senior citizen asked a charge nurse if he could change beds, so that he could see for himself the beauty of the outdoors. She looked at him strangely, but she agreed. The moment he was placed in his new bed,

Will the Real Christians Please Stand Up!

he craned his neck and looked out his window with great eagerness – and all he saw was a large, drab, gray wall of the building just next door. "But, who put that wall there?" he exclaimed with dismay, "I can't see anything!" The nurse replied that the wall had always been there, that there was nothing to see outside that window. Confused and dismayed, he began reflecting on this unexpected turn of events, and then it hit him. He suddenly realized that his partner had seen nothing but a stone wall either, but in his compassion and love he had described the beautiful scenes from his imagination, in order to bring some peace and joy into another person's life. Now the man could not wait until he had a new roommate; he wanted to describe his view of the beautiful vistas from the window of his room.

The second story is about a missionary and his wife who, as a young married couple, journeyed to a foreign mission field, a place where the Gospel had scarcely been presented. There they began their life's work of sharing Jesus and the good news of salvation with the natives of that land. The missionary lived and labored year after year, his wife by his side, but there was not a single convert to Christianity. He decided that what was needed was a church, a place of worship for attracting the people. So he built a simple chapel. Every day the couple went there to pray. Every Sunday they sang hymns and he preached a message – but only to his wife. No one came. In the course of time, they had a child, a beautiful baby boy. Their disappointment at not seeing anyone accept Christ was at least tempered by the joy of seeing their God-given son grow strong in the Lord. Then one day, when the boy was three, he was stricken with a terrible illness. Lacking the conveniences of modern medical technology, the couple could do little, and their son died. The father built a small wooden coffin and, alone with the boy's mother, carried the coffin on his shoulders to the village cemetery. One of the native leaders saw the couple and asked what they were doing. The missionary replied that their son had died and they were on their way to bury him. The native followed at a distance to watch this poignant scene. The missionary laid the coffin in the prepared grave and began to read Bible passages and to pray. Suddenly the father, overcome with grief, threw himself down on top of the tiny casket and wept bitterly. His wife, sobbing uncontrollably herself,

Will the Real Christians Please Stand Up!

tried to comfort her husband; they stood there, holding one another, and crying. Finally, he completed the task of burial. On the following Sunday, the couple went to the chapel as was their custom, fully expecting to be once again alone, and now even more than before. But the chapel was full of natives! One by one they began accepting Jesus as their Savior. After a relatively short time, almost the entire village was Christian. The missionary asked the leader what had happened. He replied, "When I saw you crying for your son, I realized that you are just like the rest of us. You are human, even though your skin is a different color; you have feelings, you suffer, you love." Many years later the missionary, now an old man, was recounting the experience to a group of students. One asked, "Do you mean to tell me that it took the death of your only son to bring those people to God?" The missionary replied, "Why is that so hard to believe? After all, my Father God experienced the same thing!" This is a beautiful and powerful example of absolute trust in God. No matter what the trial, no matter how difficult the path is, no matter how long we are asked to endure – if we yield to God, He will bring good from the experience. Think: How often have you looked back at some experience and realized God's hand and loving presence. The old saying is that hindsight is better than foresight; but for the true Christian, the foresight of faith and hope is what keeps us on the path God has chosen for us.

Jesus said, *"Blessed are you when people insult you, persecute you and falsely say all kinds of evil against you because of me."* (Matthew 5: 11) Again, *"All men will hate you because of me, but he who stands firm to the end will be saved."* (Matthew 10: 39) Yet again, *"Everyone who has left houses or brothers or sisters or father or mother or children or fields for my sake will receive a hundred times as much and will inherit eternal life."* (Matthew 19: 29)

In some ways it was even harder for the missionary couple, as they were not persecuted – they were just ignored. Year after laborious year they lived in that village – and they deeply loved the people. But that love that was for years a seed planted in the spiritual ground of that village bloomed when they journeyed on after the death of their son. What bloomed? Souls for the Kingdom of Heaven! Many times they surely asked why they were there, surely

Will the Real Christians Please Stand Up!

they were frequently tempted to pack up and go elsewhere; but they persevered, because they listened to the quiet voice of the Holy Spirit. And their faithfulness was rewarded.

We need to reflect on something very important, though quite mysterious. The real Christian believes that Jesus Christ is both God and man. (Again, do not permit any watering down or theologizing of this. People who do not proclaim this with all their hearts and souls are simply not Christians – period.) It is frankly beyond our human understanding to grasp just what Jesus thought and felt as He was born, as He grew, as He lived out His private and public life. Nor is it important to speculate on this. What we do know is this: The eternal Word of God became flesh and lived among us. He chose to be born in a cave, with poor people as mother and foster father. He came this way instead of coming as a king or prince in a palace – no red carpet for the King of Kings and Lord of Lords. He lived on the run during His infant years in a strange land – Egypt. He grew up in a tiny and scorned village and learned a trade as a carpenter. His ministry was that of an itinerant preacher – no television revenues, no Rolex on His wrist, no carefully tended hairdos and expensive clothes. Of course, He lived in a time when most of these things did not exist – but do you honestly think He would have chosen that type of approach if He were among us today? He walked many miles, often slept in borrowed beds in friends' homes or on the ground with his apostles, and he had few possessions. He was hated and feared by most, loved and followed by some, and in the end He was too much for the established Church to take. They found a way to arrest Him, put Him through a kangaroo court and have Him put to death. He was not guilty – the only Person in the history of mankind who could honestly say He was never guilty of any sin – but He died the death of the lowest criminal. The Romans stripped Him, mocked Him, flogged Him, crucified Him – but He never stopped loving. Through His death the way to heaven once again became clear and accessible. The Father and the Holy Spirit loved Him so much, yet They – and He – permitted this life and death to occur. They did it for us. This is the humanly incomprehensible extent of divine Love given to us all.

If God loved us enough to give His only-begotten Son, can we

Will the Real Christians Please Stand Up!

just ignore or take for granted or walk away from that incredible love? Well, yes, as a matter of fact we can, for God respects our free will. But one of the messages of that missionary story is that if we will just open our spiritual eyes we will see how much God wants to enter into a personal relationship with us, and how much He keeps loving and giving and guiding and protecting. Just as it took the death of a son for the people to see and understand the gift of love in their midst, so, too the essence of Christianity is the death of a Son. Let's pray that we truly see and understand and respond to this gift freely offered to us, totally unmerited by us, just there because the God of the universe loves us – and is Love itself.

Now to return to the first story: It is a story of vision. Surely the description of a true Christian includes the having and sharing of a vision of what is to come and of what is already right here in our midst. Reflect back on the life of the prophet Elisha. The man of God saw the protection of God around him, not as something symbolic but as an actual reality. The Bible is not just telling a nice and dramatic story; it is revealing the assurance and protection that comes from walking with the Lord. This is the vision that the world desperately needs. Governments are drawing up treaties, sitting around the negotiating table, spending billions on defense, redefining national boundaries, tottering on the brink of destruction. What is needed is the recognition of the supreme authority of the God who not only created us but who desires a relationship with us. In that, and that alone, can mankind find a vision of true hope. If the Christian does not exemplify that vision, it will not happen. God has chosen to work through His Church, the Body of Christ on earth. If the Christians are bogged down in materialism, in despondency, in fear and fatalism, pessimism and short-sightedness, then the world will turn away in disgust (as it is doing far too often) – seeing a lot of talk but little walk. As Jesus said, *"If your eyes are bad, your whole body will be full of darkness. If then the light within you is darkness, how great is that darkness!"* (Matthew 6: 23) Further, Hebrews encourages us to be like Moses: *"By faith he left Egypt, not fearing the king's anger; he persevered because he saw him who is invisible."* (Hebrews 11: 27) Moses had vision. So did Stephen, who, as he was being executed, *"...looked up to heaven and saw the glory of God, and Jesus standing at his right hand."* (Acts 7: 55)

The man in the bed near the window had a vision and shared it with a servant's heart. The missionary couple worked without fruit for years, even through the birth and tragic death of their only child – all because they had a vision of hope and the loving hearts of servants. The serving life describes the real Christian; it is a life based on the sacrifice of Jesus Christ and consists of a daily taking up of the cross and following Him, seeking to share His light and love with all. It is a life filled with vision, vision that is shared by how that life is lived. It is a life that reveals a light in the midst of darkness, a ray of hope in a world filled with gloom and despair – a brilliant light overshadowing the false lights of materialism and earthly glory. By quietly living in hope and faithfulness, walking and talking and making decisions only under the guidance of the Holy Spirit, the Christian becomes a lighthouse showing the way to souls adrift on the turbulent seas of life without God, without vision, without hope. It is a glorious calling; but it is only for the true followers of Jesus Christ.

Will the Real Christians Please Stand Up!

SUMMARY FOR REFLECTION AND DISCUSSION:

A real Christian:

1) Finds life's greatest happiness in bringing light and vision and hope to others, bringing a smile to another's face, sharing the very love of Jesus Christ – by living a life of genuine service;
2) Keeps on giving and serving, despite the odds, despite repeated failures or delays, seeking only to follow the guidance of the Holy Spirit;
3) Believes completely and simply, and with an unwavering conviction that Jesus Christ is the Incarnate Son of God and bases everything – every thought, every word, every action – on that belief and on the personal relationship of love that is His gift to all who will accept Him.

SCRIPTURES FOR JOURNALING:

1) Hebrews 11 – the faith and vision chapter;
2) Hebrews 12 – our response; and all based on Hebrews 11;
3) Matthew 5: 1-10 – the Beatitudes;
4) Acts 7 – Stephen;
5) Mark 14-15 – Mark's account of the Passion.

REFLECTION 28:

LOVE FOR ONE ANOTHER

In 1992, people around the nation and around the world witnessed an ugly event in American history – the Los Angeles riots. People who were there and who watched on television will long remember the fires, the constant sirens reminiscent of World War II in Europe, the looting, the beating of Rodney King some months earlier, and the trial of the policemen involved in that beating. The riots caused most of us to stop and take stock of the values of our nation, and the fine line between civility and violence.

But there was one incident that both graphically punctuated the ruthless violence and, at the same time, the strength of the human spirit that gives us enduring hope. The world watched in horror, on live TV, as a small band of men savagely attacked a truck driver who was just trying to do his job. They pulled him from the cab of his truck and then they beat him and they shot him. He lay on the ground, writhing in pain, helpless to defend himself. A few blocks away, a black woman watching the beating of this white man on her TV set, immediately left her home and went to the scene. Literally risking her life, she helped the man into his truck, got in with him, and guided him to a hospital. All but blind and barely conscious, he had to rely on this Good Samaritan to lead him. The truck driver survived, thanks to the courage and love of this woman, who, to all intents and purposes given the tensions of that day, should have been his enemy – she a black, he a honkey.

During His final journey to Jerusalem, Jesus Christ knew that He was about to die. He knew that He would be terribly beaten, mocked, ridiculed and executed as the lowest of criminals. He also knew that His friends would desert Him, that He would face this horror without their love, comfort and support – except for His mother, some caring women and the apostle John. It is John who records what Jesus had to say to His apostles on that night before His death. Here are some excerpts from John 13-17 (I urge you to prayerfully read the entire section, recognizing by faith that it is Jesus speaking to you through the living Word):

"It was just before the Passover Feast. Jesus knew that the time had come for him to leave this world and go to the Father. Having loved his own who were in the world, he now showed them the full extent of his love...He poured water into a basin and began to wash his disciples' feet, drying them with the towel that was wrapped around him...When he had finished washing their feet, he put on his clothes and returned to his place. 'Do you understand what I have done for you?' he asked them. 'You call me 'Teacher' and 'Lord', and rightly so, for that is what I am. Now that I, your Lord and Teacher, have washed your feet, you also should wash one another's feet. I have set you an example that you should do as I have done for you. I tell you the truth, no servant is greater than the one who sent him. Now that you know these things, you will be blessed if you do them...If you love me, you will obey what I command. And I will ask the Father, and he will give you another Counselor to be with you forever – the Spirit of truth. The world cannot accept him, because it neither sees him nor knows him. But you know him, for he lives with you and will be in you. I will not leave you as orphans; I will come to you...Whoever has my commands and obeys them, he is the one who loves me. He who loves me will be loved by my Father, and I too will love him, and we will come to him and make our home with him. He who does not love me will not obey my teaching...As the Father

has loved me, so have I loved you. Now remain in my love. If you obey my commands, you will remain in my love, just as I have obeyed my Father's commands and remain in his love. I have told you this so that my joy may be in you and that your joy may be complete. My command is this: Love each other as I have loved you. Greater love has no one than this, that he lay down his life for his friends...Father...I have revealed you to those whom you gave me out of the world. They were yours; you gave them to me and they have obeyed your word. Now they know that everything you have given me comes from you...I pray for them. I am not praying for the world, but for those you have given me, for they are yours. All I have is yours, and all you have is mine...I will remain in the world no longer, but they are still in the world, and I am coming to you. Holy Father, protect them by the power of your name – the name you gave me – so that they may be one as we are one. While I was with them, I protected them and kept them safe by that name you gave me...I am coming to you now, but I say these things while I am still in the world, so that they may have the full measure of my joy within them...My prayer is not that you take them out of the world but that you protect them from the evil one...For them I sanctify myself, that they too may be truly sanctified..My prayer is...that all..may be one, Father, just as you are in me and I am in you. May they also be one in us so that the world may believe that you have sent me...May they be brought to complete unity to let the world know that you sent me and have loved them even as you have loved me...I have made you known to them, and will continue to make you known in order that the love you have for me may be in them and that I myself may be in them."

Jesus makes it abundantly clear: To love Him is to obey Him, and His command is to follow His example – which was and is love in action. To quote a former President, "Let me make one thing perfectly clear": This is where the rubber meets the road in the Christian life. Show me a Christian who hates or looks down on or avoids blacks or whites or ethnic groups or nationalities; show me a Christian who has been hurt and refuses to forgive; show me a Christian who wants to nuke nations, string up individuals, clobber those who dare to differ; show me a Christian who has a lifestyle that includes gossip, backbiting, the spreading of rumors – show me "Christians" like this and I will show you someone who, regardless of pious and religious lip service to the contrary, is anything but a real Christian. I am not referring to failure and sin, for we are all subject to that and can only overcome by the grace of God. No, I am referring to a way of life and a self-righteous attitude that proclaim hate and unforgiveness and insensitivity to others as justified as long as those emotions are directed to the "bad guys." How I praise God that He does not see things that way. If He did, the crucifixion of the Son of God would have resulted in destruction – instead of redemption – for us all. We are all the 'bad guys" who nailed the Son of God to the tree.

In that same section of John, Jesus defines a disciple: *"By this all men will know that you are my disciples, if you love one another."* How sad it is that some have interpreted this as meaning we are only called to love those who share our beliefs and opinions, with whom we are united in a bond of fellowship. We are certainly called to do that – in fact, one of the great scandals of Christianity is the lack of harmony and love among Christians. But the context of this final discourse of Jesus is that the love that unites believers should strengthen and encourage us to show and give the love of God to all – as Jesus Himself did and does.

Peter was a man who learned to love the hard way. There is no doubt that Peter had great affection for the Lord. Peter often took the lead in expressions of faith and trust, and Jesus in turn included Peter in some events that most of the apostles did not participate in, such as the Transfiguration and Jesus' time of deep emotional and spiritual agony in the Garden of Gethsemane. But Peter also failed Jesus in the most difficult hours of His life, following His arrest and through the Crucifixion. Peter's courage left him; he denied that he even knew Jesus. Peter assumed – and presumed – that he loved Jesus more than himself, but in a terrible time of trial he failed the acid test. However, unlike Judas, who despaired, Peter repented.

Will the Real Christians Please Stand Up!

After the Resurrection, Jesus asked Peter three times if he loved Him. Three times Peter answered in the affirmative. Three times Jesus responded with a command to feed His sheep. Then Jesus simply said, *"Follow me."* It is clear that Jesus was saying to Peter – and He is saying to us – that if he/we truly love Him, we will follow Him; and, further, that we will serve and love others – no exceptions, no holding back, no picking and choosing. So it is that Peter could write years later, in his first Letter:

"Though you have not seen him, you love him; and even though you do not see him now, you believe in him and are filled with an inexpressible and glorious joy, for you are receiving the goal of your faith, the salvation of your souls...Now that you have purified yourselves by obeying the truth so that you have sincere love for your brothers, love one another deeply, from the heart." (1 Peter 1: 8, 9, 22)

Paul wrote more about love than anyone else in the New Testament. A man who became an apostle after Jesus' Resurrection and Ascension, a zealot who persecuted Christians until the Lord knocked him off his high horse – literally – Paul met and learned to love Jesus Christ. Paul, through prayer (much prayer – he went out into the desert for three years after his conversion) and through the inspiration of the Holy Spirit, grasped the meaning of true Christian love. In 1 Thessalonians 3: 12, he writes so fervently that it is clear he is crying out from his heart: *"May the Lord make your love increase and overflow for each other and for everyone else, just as ours does for you."* We will let Paul tell us more about love a little later in this reflection.

One of the most well known parables that Jesus used for teaching is that of the Good Samaritan. In fact, it is so well known and loved that we run the risk of missing the revolutionary teaching embodied in it. The setting was this: An expert in the Law challenged Jesus' knowledge of the Scriptures and the Law by asking Him what was necessary to inherit eternal life. Jesus, always the Teacher, turned the question around and asked the expert what he himself found in the Law. The response was Deuteronomy 6: 5, the command to love the Lord God with one's whole heart, soul, strength and might, and to love one's neighbor as oneself. Jesus complimented the Jewish leader for answering correctly. Realizing that he had been outwitted, the man tried another tack by asking Jesus just who one's neighbor is. Jesus was obviously waiting for that opening; He answered the question with the parable of the Good Samaritan. Read it in Luke 10: 30-35. The unexpected and revolutionary response contained in that parable was this: My neighbor is not just the person living next to me; not just the person who shares my political or religious beliefs; not the person I drink coffee with; no, my neighbor is anyone and everyone, even those I want absolutely no association with. Mouths must have fallen open as Jesus first described the plight of the traveler who had been robbed, beaten, left for dead by bandits and then went on to describe just who reached out and helped the poor man. Jesus very pointedly stated that the Priest passed the man by, the Levite passed the man by – and these people represented two of the most honored religious classes in Jewish society. Who stopped to help? A Samaritan! Now that word does not mean much to us in our culture. But the very use of the word caused the Jews to shrink back in revulsion. Samaritans were fellow Semites to be sure and geographic neighbors, but people who had perverted the true worship as given and directed by God and who were therefore considered to be heretics and were shunned by pious Jews. But Jesus made the Samaritan the hero of the parable! It was a direct and obvious attack on established religion. Jesus was saying in effect that following the Law, keeping the rules, and participating faithfully in worship do not in and of themselves make us pleasing in God's sight. What matters is how much we live out our worship of God by loving and serving our fellow man. It was not at all the answer the Law expert expected, and he must have winced when Jesus concluded by looking at him and saying, *"Go and do likewise."* Note the specifics of love in action in this parable: The Samaritan took pity on the man. He activated that pity by stopping his journey and going to the man's aid. He bound the victim's wounds; he took the poor man to the nearest inn and paid for his lodging out of his own pocket. The Samaritan anointed the man with oil and wine (symbolizing the

Will the Real Christians Please Stand Up!

---

love of the Holy Spirit). And then he followed up later to make sure the man was recovering. Now that is true love! And all the while the Priests, Levites and hypocritical religious folks were cutting a wide path around the despised Samaritan.

Finally, there is the great poem about love in Paul's first Letter to the Corinthians, chapter 13. Reflect on the oft-quoted words in verses 4, 5, 6 and 13:

> *"Love is patient, love is kind. It does not envy, it does not boast, it is not proud. It is not rude, it is not self-seeking, it is not easily angered, it keeps no record of wrongs. Love does not delight in evil but rejoices with the truth. It always protects, always trusts, always hopes, always perseveres...And now these three remain: Faith, hope and love. But the greatest of these is love."*

In closing, ponder some additional Scriptures and use them for meditation, for letting the Holy Spirit whisper to your innermost spirit:

> *"I have been crucified with Christ and I no longer live, but Christ lives in me. The life I live in the body, I live by faith in the Son of God, who loved me and gave himself for me."* (Galatians 2: 20)..."*But the fruit of the Spirit is love, joy, peace, patience, kindness, goodness, faithfulness, gentleness and self-control. Against such things there is no law. Those who belong to Christ Jesus have crucified the sinful nature with its passions and desires. Since we live by the Spirit, let us keep in step with the Spirit. Let us not become conceited, provoking and envying each other."* (Galatians 5: 22-26)..."*I am the vine; you are the branches. If a man remains in me and I in him, he will bear much fruit; apart from me you can do nothing."* (John 15: 5)...And, from John's first Letter: *"Anyone who claims to be in the light but hates his brother is still in the darkness...How great is the love the Father has lavished on us, that we should be called children of God! And that is what we are!...This is how we*

know who the children of God are and who the children of the devil are. Anyone who does not do what is right is not a child of God; nor is anyone who does not love his brother. This is the message you heard from the beginning: We should love one another...This is how we know what love is: Jesus Christ laid down his life for us. And we ought to lay down our lives for our brothers. If anyone has material possessions and sees his brother in need but has not pity on him, how can the love of God be in him? Dear children, let us not love with words or tongue but with actions and in truth...And this is his command: To believe in the name of his Son, Jesus Christ, and to love one another as he commanded us...God is Love. Whoever lives in love lives in God, and God in him. In this way, love is made complete among us so that we will have confidence on the day of judgment, because in this world we are like him...We love because he first loved us. If anyone says, 'I love God,' yet hates his brother, he is a liar. For anyone who does not love his brother, whom he has seen, cannot love God, whom he has not seen. And he has given us this command: 'Whoever loves God must also love his brother.'" (from 1 John 2, 3, 4)

SUMMARY FOR REFLECTION AND DISCUSSION:

A real Christian:

1) Defines spiritual life not by religious practices but by the daily imitation of Jesus Christ, who loved without measure;
2) Loves every human being, regardless of skin color, nationality, ethnicity, and even regardless of behavior and life style;
3) Forgives readily, without condoning sin;
4) Seeks the Holy Spirit's intimate presence and guidance, in order to know, love and serve Jesus as completely and consistently as possible;
5) Refuses to condone bigotry of any kind, does not participate in conversation that backbites or gossips about others or ridicules people.

SCRIPTURES FOR JOURNALING:

1) John 13-17;
2) John 21;
3) 1 Corinthians 13;
4) Luke 10: 30-35;
5) The first Letter of John.

REFLECTION 29:

BE CLOTHED WITH CHRIST

Your quiz for the day: What do Mark 14: 51-52 and the fable, "The Emperor's New Clothes," have in common? Here is your first – and only – clue: They are both about clothes, or the lack thereof. Let's look at the Mark passage: *"A young man, wearing nothing but a linen garment, was following Jesus. When they seized him, he fled naked, leaving his garment behind."* Now that is "naked fear" – pun, unfortunately, intended! Most experts believe that Mark is writing here about himself. He was not an apostle, but he was certainly a follower of Jesus and he eventually figured prominently in the life of the early Church. Mark was probably hanging around on the fringe, when Jesus was arrested in the Garden. He was watching the unthinkable happen, witnessing his Master being arrested and the apostles running away. The soldiers apparently spotted Mark, and he barely eluded their grasp by running right out of his robe and leaving it in the grasp of a would-be captor. Mark, the inspired writer of the Gospel, had just stated in verse 50 that *"Then everyone deserted him and fled."* He now punctuated that by revealing his own abject fear and terror. Now think: How afraid would you have to be to run away naked? Maybe from a burning building, maybe in an earthquake, but it would take a lot. Mark is graphically telling us how fear ruled that night among the followers of Jesus in the Garden of Gethsemane. Keep in mind that the powers of darkness were orchestrating this event (or so they thought). One of the most potent weapons of the enemy is fear. Mark felt its icy touch, and he ran.

Now we turn our attention to the emperor in the fable. This short but powerful story teaches an important lesson. Namely, it is quite possible to become so enamored of ourselves, so caught up in what we think we are and have, that we lose sight of reality. That is precisely what happened to the emperor. He actually believed his tailor's yarn (whoops, there I go again with the puns – it is a sickness; pray for me) about the exquisite quality of the thread. The emperor was convinced that he was wearing the finest set of clothes ever made; but he was totally nude as well as totally in the dark! In his excitement over his new clothes, he ordered a parade. His faithful subjects came and cheered, indulging the emperor's royal fantasies as he strutted among them.

Well, what is the point? For the answer, read with me Romans 13: 14: *"...Clothe yourselves with the Lord Jesus Christ, and do not think about how to gratify the desires of the sinful nature."* Now that is a strong statement! The Greek phrase "to be clothed with" means such things as taking upon oneself the interests of another, entering into a deep understanding and acceptance of his/her views, being wholly on another's side, imitating that person in all things. In other words, a Christian is clothed with Jesus Christ; to grasp the meaning, substitute "clothed" with each of the meanings provided in the previous sentence. These are not just nice words, pleasant expressions, or exaggerations. It is a fact, right from the Word of God, that to be a real Christian is to have Jesus Christ shine from me and be as visible as the clothes I wear to work, at home, to church, at play.

Clothes and other adornments have almost always played an important part in cultures. A sign of cultural decadence is inordinate attention paid to such finery. Think, for example, about how we are bombarded with advertisements – radio, TV, magazines, newspapers. Think about how much some people will pay for a shirt or a blouse just because it has a particular brand name or logo on it. Actually, the obsession goes back a long way. For example, Isaiah wrote about it (chapter 3, verses 18-24):

Will the Real Christians Please Stand Up!

"In that day the Lord will snatch away their finery; the bangles and headbands and crescent necklaces, the earrings and bracelets and veils, the headdresses and ankle chains and sashes, the perfume bottles and charms, the signet rings and nose rings, the fine robes and the capes and cloaks, the purses and mirrors, and the linen garments and tiaras and shawls. Instead of fragrance there will be a stench; instead of a sash, a rope; instead of well-dressed hair, baldness; instead of fine clothing, sackcloth; instead of beauty, branding." (By the way, Isaiah is not picking on the ladies; he is tough on both sexes.)

Peter was another one of those who ran away from the Garden. Worse, he even denied that he knew his best Friend. But through it, as we have seen, Peter became a much stronger and wiser man. Listen to his words in his first Letter, chapter 3, verses 3-4: *"Your beauty should not come from outward adornment, such as braided hair and the wearing of gold jewelry and fine clothes. Instead, it should be that of your inner self, the unfading beauty of a gentle and quiet spirit, which is of great worth in God's sight."*

One of Jesus' most powerful parables was that of the rich man and Lazarus. Prayerfully read Luke 16: 19-23:

"There was a rich man who was dressed in purple and fine linen and lived in luxury every day. At his gate was laid a beggar named Lazarus, covered with sores and longing to eat what fell from the rich man's table. Even the dogs came and licked his sores. The time came when the beggar died and the angels carried him to Abraham's side. The rich man also died and was buried. In hell, where he was in torment, he looked up and saw Abraham far away, with Lazarus by his side..."

You see, the world defines success by possessions and power. The rich man had luxurious clothes and an accompanying lifestyle. But it was all for naught, as he lost eternal life. Why? Because he was not caring, not gentle, not giving, because he was self-centered – because, expressed in light of the New Covenant, he was not clothed with Jesus Christ.

In the great chapter 3 of the Book of Revelation, Jesus says some very critical things, important for each of us. In verse 20 He says, *"Here I am! I stand at the door and knock. If anyone hears my voice and opens the door, I will come in and eat with him, and he with me."* Just before that He says, *"So be earnest and repent."* And just prior to that He says, *"I know your deeds, that you are neither cold nor hot. I wish you were one or the other! So, because you are lukewarm – neither hot nor cold – I am about to spit you out of my mouth. You say, 'I am rich; I have acquired wealth and do not need a thing.' But you do not realize that you are wretched, pitiful, poor, blind and naked* (sounds like the emperor!). *I counsel you to buy from me gold refined in the fire, so you can become rich; and white clothes to wear, so you can cover your shameful nakedness; and salve to put on your eyes, so you can see."* (The emperor could have used some of that salve!)

What we see described here is the salvation message and the call to live a true Christian life of discipleship. If you have not personally experienced Jesus knocking at the door of your heart and asking to come in, you have not really and fully met Him – and that relationship is key to the Christian life. Going to church will not do it. For every Christian there must be at some point a personal encounter with the living Jesus – the only exceptions are infants who die, fetuses who miscarry or are aborted (from the very moment of conception this is true), children and adults who because of age or disability are not able to make a conscious choice for relationship. Let the words of Revelation 3 settle deep within your spirit. This is the living Word. This is the Holy Spirit trying to touch us and introduce us to Jesus. If you and I do not have a burning desire to think, talk and act exactly only as Jesus would, then we have missed the point of Christianity. We may be going through the motions; but we are truly naked and run the risk of standing before the Lord one day with shame because of our nakedness.

Matthew, Mark and Luke all record the temptations of Jesus in the desert as He was preparing to begin His public ministry. I am

Will the Real Christians Please Stand Up!

sure that Jesus told His apostles and disciples on more than one occasion what happened to Him out there alone in the wilderness. He must have stressed its importance and its impact on Him. So, let's not kid ourselves. If God Incarnate was subjected to Satanic temptation, we will be, too. The Holy Spirit who led Jesus into the desert and inspired the writing of the Bible is trying to tell us something. He is outlining for us, in graphic form, demonic strategy and is giving us the tools we need to be prepared and victorious. Jesus experienced temptation in three specific ways: 1) To focus on the material rather than the spiritual; 2) to concentrate on the self; 3) to seek personal gain above all else. (Matthew 4: 1-10) It all really boils down to choosing God or choosing self. Which have I chosen? Am I sure that I am not deceiving myself? Am I totally sold out to Jesus with an accompanying sense of urgency to follow and serve Him, or am I deceiving myself and straddling the fence? Jesus did not mince words:

"Do not suppose that I have come to bring peace to the earth. I did not come to bring peace, but a sword...Anyone who loves his father or mother more than me is not worthy of me; anyone who loves his son or daughter more than me is not worthy of me; and anyone who does not take his cross and follow me is not worthy of me. Whoever finds his life will lose it, and whoever loses his life for my sake will find it." (Matthew 10: 34-39)

Do we really want to be like Him? He tells us how to do it in the famous Beatitudes: (Blessed are the poor in spirit, are those who mourn, are the meek, are those who hunger and thirst for righteousness, are the merciful, are the peacemakers, are those who are persecuted because of righteousness, are we when people insult us, persecute us and falsely say all kinds of evil against us because of Him.)

Jesus constantly sought the will of the Father, constantly sought the guidance of the Holy Spirit, constantly served others and stood steadfast for the truth. He is the hero of heroes. The reason, in my judgment, that more young people do not identify with Him as a hero, but turn instead to others for hero worship, is that not enough of us who bear His name let His Person and presence and love and power shine through our daily lives.

John in his Gospel called Jesus the Bread of life, the Good Shepherd, the Light of the world, the Way, the Truth, the Life. Embracing Jesus must not just be a formula recited, a creed stated, a service attended, a church/church leader obeyed. It must first and foremost and, above all else, be a living relationship of love. To be clothed with Christ is a tremendous gift and privilege; to live that life is the challenge given to us all, along with the promise to give us the strength we need to follow through. *"Behold, I stand at the door and knock."* Will we open to Him today, this minute? The choice is ours; and God will always honor our free choices, regardless of the consequences if we knowingly choose wrongly.

SUMMARY FOR REFLECTION AND DISCUSSION:

A real Christian:

1) Seeks above all else to be clothed with Jesus Christ – to be more and more like Him and to follow Him in daily life;
2) Does not let the finery and baubles of the world or the rituals and rites of religion detract from what is truly most important;
3) Hears Jesus knocking at the heart's door daily, and with great eagerness opens up and invites Him in.

SCRIPTURES FOR JOURNALING:

1) Revelation 2-3;
2) Luke 16: 19-23;
3) Mark 14-15;
4) Isaiah 3: 18-24 and 1 Peter 3: 3-4.

REFLECTION 30:

A NEW HEAVEN AND A NEW EARTH

In June of 1992, I attended a Habitat for Humanity meeting at Estes Park, Colorado. Among the many families and groups assembled at the beautiful setting of the YMCA of the Rockies for vacations, retreats and business meetings was a small church group. The name of the group is not significant. Suffice it to say that it was an end-times oriented congregation. Everyone – fathers, mothers, children, grandparents, the pastor and other leaders – wore a tee shirt with the bold phrase "OCTOBER 28, 1992" on it. Many members of the congregation were passing out tracts explaining the significance of that date. They were absolutely convinced that the rapture was upon us and that it would occur on October 28. I remember recalling the Scripture stating that we do not know the day nor the hour – not Jesus, not the angels, only the Father. Frankly, it was saddening to me to see the simple, trusting and misguided faith of the people, especially the children. I wondered how the leaders and the parents would explain the failure of the Lord to return on that day. At the same time, the experience certainly served as a reminder that time is short for each of us; we never know when we will be called home, just as we do not know when the Lord will return. If we are truly walking in the Spirit, the awareness of what is coming will be frequently in our minds and hearts and will give us a sense of urgency to use our time according to God's plan for us. Take a look

Will the Real Christians Please Stand Up!

with me at just a little of what the Word says about this subject – see it as a "preview of coming events":

"Do not let your hearts be troubled. Trust in God; trust also in me. In my Father's house are many rooms; if it were not so, I would have told you. I am going there to prepare a place for you. And if I go and prepare a place for you, I will come back and take you to be with me that you also may be where I am. You know the place where I am going." (John 14: 1-4)…*"Therefore, they are before the throne of God and serve him day and night in his temple; and he who sits on the throne will spread his tent over them. Never again will they hunger; never again will they thirst. The sun will not beat upon them, nor any scorching heat. For the Lamb at the center of the throne will be their Shepherd; he will lead them to springs of living water. And God will wipe away every tear from their eyes."* (Revelation 7: 15-17)

"…He will swallow up death forever. The Sovereign Lord will wipe away the tears from all faces; he will remove the disgrace of his people from all the earth. The Lord has spoken. In that day they will say, 'Surely this is our God; we trusted in him, and he saved us. This is the Lord, we trusted in him; let us rejoice and be glad in his salvation.'" (Isaiah 25: 8-9)

Then I looked and heard the voice of many angels, numbering thousands upon thousands, and ten thousand times ten thousand. They encircled the throne and the living creatures and the elders. In a loud voice they sang: 'Worthy is the Lamb, who was slain, to receive power and wealth and wisdom and strength and honor and glory and praise!'"

"Then I heard what sounded like a great multitude, like the roar of rushing waters and like loud peals of thunder, shouting, 'Hallelujah! For our Lord God Almighty reigns. Let us rejoice and be glad and give him glory! For the wedding of

the Lamb has come, and his bride has made herself ready. Fine linen, bright and clean, was given her to wear.'" (Revelation 19: 6-8)

A good summary of the coming end of time can be taken from the beautiful 21st chapter of Revelation:

"Then I saw a new heaven and a new earth, for the first heaven and the first earth had passed away, and there was no longer any sea. I saw the Holy City, the New Jerusalem, coming down out of heaven from God, prepared as a bride beautifully dressed for her husband. And I heard a loud voice from the throne saying, 'Now the dwelling of God is with men, and he will live with them. They will be his people, and God himself will be with them and be their God. He will wipe away every tear from their eyes. There will be no more death or mourning or crying or pain, for the old order of things has passed away.' He who was seated on the throne said, 'I am making everything new!' Then he said, 'Write this down, for these words are trustworthy and true.' He said to me, 'It is done. I am the Alpha and the Omega, the Beginning and the End. To him who is thirsty I will give to drink without cost from the spring of the water of life. He who overcomes will inherit all this, and I will be his God and he will be my son.'" (Revelation 21: 1-7)

If we are truly Christians, washed in the Blood of the Lamb; if we believe that the Word is God is true; if we believe that the Book of Revelation is a gift of God opening up the portals of heaven and describing life there not as some literary fable, but rather as it is being lived right now; if we have real faith and hope – then these passages have a powerful and lasting impact on us. But what kind of impact?

First, JOY! The Word says that what we look forward to is no more death, mourning, crying or pain, and an eternity of joyous and blissful communion with God. Whatever we are going through now, it is but a snap of the fingers compared to the timelessness of eternity – and it is coming closer with every breath we take.

Second, PEACE! Reflect on the words of that great old hymn, "Blessed Assurance:" "Blessed assurance, Jesus is mine! O what a foretaste of heaven divine! Heir of salvation, purchase of God, born of His Spirit, washed in His Blood. Perfect submission, perfect delight, visions of rapture now burst on my sight. Angels descending bring from above echoes of mercy, whispers of love. Perfect submission, all is at rest, I in my Savior am happy and blest. Watching and waiting, looking above, filled with His goodness, lost in His love. This is my story, this is my song, praising my Savior all the day long." Powerful! And real!

Third, a SENSE OF URGENCY! As a Christian, I believe in eternity; but just as there is a place of union with God, so there is also a place of eternal separation from God. Some so-called "sophisticated" Christians dispute this, but I emphatically state that such denials are a dangerous delusion – it is simply not possible to be a real Christian and deny what is so evident in the Word of God and in the teachings of Jesus. We have seen some beautiful descriptions of glory in Revelation; but reflect as well on some other words in that same Book:

> *"Then I saw a great white throne and him who was seated on it. Earth and sky fled from his presence, and there was no place for them. And I saw the dead, great and small, standing before the throne, and books were opened. Another book was opened, which is the book of life. The dead were judged according to what they had done as recorded in the books. The sea gave up the dead that were in it, and death and Hades gave up the dead that were in them, and each person was judged according to what he had done. Then death and Hades were thrown into the lake of fire. The lake of fire is the second death. If anyone's name was not found written in the book of life, he was thrown into the lake of fire."* (Revelation 20: 11-15)

> *"But the cowardly, the unbelieving, the vile, the murderers, the sexually immoral, those who practice magic arts, the*

idolaters and all liars – their place will be in the fiery lake of burning sulfur. This is the second death...Behold, I am coming soon! My reward is with me, and I will give to everyone according to what he has done. I am the Alpha and the Omega, the First and the Last, the Beginning and the End. Blessed are those who wash their robes, that they may have the right to the tree of life and may go through the gates into the city. Outside are the dogs, those who practice magic arts, the sexually immoral, the murderers, the idolaters and everyone who loves and practices falsehood. I, Jesus, have sent my angel to give you this testimony for the churches. I am the Root and the Offspring of David, and the bright Morning Star...Nothing impure will ever enter it (the New Jerusalem), *nor will anyone who does what is shameful or deceitful, but only those whose names are written in the Lamb's book of life."* (Revelation 21: 8, 12-16, 27)

Daniel writes of these things as well: *"As I looked, thrones were set in place, and the Ancient of Days took his seat. His clothing was white as snow; the hair of his head was white like wool. His throne was flaming with fire, and its wheels were all ablaze. A river of fire was flowing, coming out before him. Thousands upon thousands attended him; ten thousand times ten thousand stood before him. The court was seated and the books were opened. Then I continued to watch because of the boastful words the horn was speaking. I kept looking until the beast was slain and its body destroyed and thrown into the blazing fire...In my vision at night I looked, and there before me was one like a Son of Man, coming with the clouds of heaven. He approached the Ancient of Days and was led into his presence. He was given authority, glory and sovereign power; all peoples, nations and men of every language worshiped him. His dominion is an everlasting dominion that will not pass away, and his kingdom is one that will never be destroyed."* (Daniel 7: 9-14)

As we look toward eternity, it is also a fact that we are the presence of Jesus on earth today, as members of His Body. It is the plan of God to primarily reach people through the Church. We are clearly called to be the instrument of God's saving grace as we journey through this life, sensitive to His leading. We will fail in this mission if we choose not to listen. The Holy Spirit wants to guide us every minute of every day that we have in this fleeting life. Eternity looms – and so many people do not recognize it.

I read in a pamphlet the true story of a Christian who was having a meal in a restaurant. He had a sudden strong urge to witness to the waiter who was serving him. But the restaurant was crowded, and the witnessing seemed out of place. As the customer left the restaurant, the same urge came upon him. He continued to walk down the street; then he stopped and determined at last to listen to that inner voice. He went back to the restaurant and decided to wait outside until it closed; he planned on talking to the waiter as he left to go home. After awhile, the restaurant owner came out, just as a police car and ambulance arrived. The Christian asked the owner what was happening. With a sad shake of his head, he reported that a waiter – the Christian's waiter – had gone into a back room and shot himself.

We never know when we will be called to introduce people to the ever approaching new heaven and new earth, and, above all, to the Lord and Savior Jesus Christ, who wants all to be saved and to come to the knowledge of the truth. If we are not tuned in, if we do not have a spiritual sense of urgency, if we are not acutely aware of the ultimate meaning of life for every human being, people will pass us by and miss the message and light of salvation that the Holy Spirit intended for them – through us as His instruments.

"Blessed assurance, Jesus is mine...Heir of salvation, purchase of God, born of His Spirit, washed in His Blood. This is my story, this is my song, praising my Savior all the day long." Is it just a song? Is it just words? Or am I living the meaning of that song, with the love and joy welling up and overflowing so that others can see, and share?

SUMMARY FOR REFLECTION AND DISCUSSION:

A real Christian:

1) Lives each day with an acute awareness of the existence of the Kingdom of Heaven, and also of hell;
2) With that perspective, keeps the joy of hope in what is to come before his/her spiritual eyes and is constantly reminded that the sorrows and sufferings of this life are transitory;
3) Is filled with a burning desire to see every person saved, is filled with horror at the thought of people missing the joy of heaven and suffering the pain of hell for all eternity;
4) Hears and accepts the call to be a witness to the truth and seeks to share Jesus at every opportunity – recognizing that every Christian is called to be evangelistic and avoiding the trap of thinking that only certain people are so called or of thinking that we have no right to impinge on people's private lives – or all other rationalizations that are so contrary to God's Word and God's plan.

SCRIPTURES FOR JOURNALING:

1) John 14;
2) Revelation 5, 7, 19, 21;
3) Daniel 7 and Revelation 21-22;
4) (Other favorite Scriptures pertaining to eternal life and eternal death)

REFLECTION 31:

YOKE MINISTRY

This reflection is a partial repeat, a reemphasis, and a summary of much that we have focused on as integral to the life of a real Christian. So, what is a "yoke ministry"? We have all heard about ministries to the homeless, to addicts, to gangs, to the sick and disabled, to the imprisoned, to the unsaved throughout our nation and the world – but "yoke ministry"?

It is Scripture exploration time again, as the way to fathom this little mystery. We begin with Psalm 22, the great prophetic Psalm fulfilled on the cross, as Jesus cried out in verse 1: *"My God, My God, why have you forsaken me?"* But let's go on, to better understand the utter horror of Calvary and the physical, emotional and spiritual pain that the Son of God endured. Beginning with verse 2:

"Why are you so far from saving me, so far from the words of my groaning? O my God, I cry out day by day, but you do not answer, by night, am not silent. Yet you are enthroned as the Holy One; you are the praise of Israel. In you our fathers put their trust; they trusted and you delivered them. They cried to you and were saved; in you they trusted and were not disappointed. But I am a worm and not a man, scorned by men and despised by the people." (This is God Himself praying, using the Words that an inspired author

Will the Real Christians Please Stand Up!

wrote centuries before. This is how God Incarnate was treated, and how He felt.) *"All who see me mock me; they hurl insults, shaking their heads. 'He trusts in the Lord; let the Lord rescue him. Let him deliver him, since he delights in him.' Yet you brought me out of the womb, you made me trust in you even at my mother's breast. From birth I was cast upon you; from my mother's womb you have been my God."* (People who consider themselves "pro-choice" should take note; this is another Scripture proclaiming life in the womb. Aren't you glad Joseph did not encourage Mary to have an abortion when he discovered that she was pregnant before marriage?) *"Do not be far from me; for trouble is near and there is no one to help. Many bulls surround me, strong bulls of Bashan encircle me. Roaring lions tearing their prey open their mouths wide against me. I am poured out like water, and all my bones are out of joint. My heart has turned to wax; it has melted away within me. My strength is dried up like a potsherd, and my tongue sticks to the roof of my mouth; you lay me in the dust of death. Dogs have surrounded me; a band of evil men has encircled me, they have pierced my hands and my feet, I can count all my bones; people stare and gloat over me. They divide my garments among them and cast lots for my clothing."* (Now soaring faith and praise take over.) *"But You, O Lord, be not far off; O my Strength, come quickly to help me. Deliver my life from the sword, my precious life from the power of the dogs. Rescue me from the mouth of the lions; save me from the horns of the wild oxen. I will declare your name to my brothers; in the congregation I will praise you. You who fear the Lord, praise him! All you descendents of Jacob, honor him! Revere him, all you descendents of Israel! For he has not despised or disdained the suffering of the afflicted one; he has not hidden his face from him but has listened to his cry for help. From you comes the theme of my praise in the great assembly; before those who fear you will I fulfill my vows. The poor will eat and be satisfied; they who seek the Lord will praise him – may your hearts live forever! All the ends of the earth will remember and turn to the Lord, and all the families of the nations will bow down before him, for dominion belongs to the Lord and he rules over the nations. All the rich of the earth will feast and worship, all who go down to the dust will kneel before him – those who cannot keep themselves alive. Posterity will serve him; future generations will be told about the Lord. They will proclaim his righteousness to a people yet unborn – for he has done it."*

This mighty and accurate description of the death of the Savior of the world gives rich meaning to the words of Jesus in Matthew 16: 24-26:

"If anyone would come after me, he must deny himself and take up his cross and follow me. For whoever wants to save his life will lose it, but whoever loses his life for me will find it. What good will it be for a man if he gains the whole world, yet forfeits his soul? Or what can a man give in exchange for his soul?"

We need be wary of glibly agreeing to take up the cross as Christians, without understanding or accepting the price to be paid. When He asks us to take up the cross and follow Him, He means just that – a willingness to give all for Him and to endure even suffering, rejection, persecution and death.

But Jesus says it differently in Matthew 11: 28-30:

"Come to me, all you who are weary and burdened, and I will give you rest. Take my yoke upon you and learn from me, for I am gentle and humble in heart, and you will find rest for your souls. For my yoke is easy and my burden is light."

When we think of Jesus' yoke, our minds automatically turn to the way of the cross, the way to Golgotha. It was the Roman custom in death by crucifixion to have the condemned prisoner carry the cross beam to the place of execution. Many paintings and movie depictions of the event show Jesus carrying the entire cross. But that is probably inaccurate, though understandable from an imagery and visual message perspective. He carried the heavy beam until He was unable to carry it any longer. His strength was weakened because of the terrible scourging and loss of blood and a sleepless night. We know that a man named Simon, from Cyrene, was forced to carry that cross beam, at least for part of the journey to Calvary. It may well be that Simon took up that beam unwillingly, picked out of the crowd as he was for the unpleasant task. But I believe that at least before the journey was finished Simon carried the beam – the yoke – upon himself with pride and love and even eagerness. It was one of the greatest privileges ever accorded to a human being.

What does "taking the yoke" mean? Quite simply, it means having a servant's heart. It means subjugating our wills to that of our Lord; it means saying and doing what He wants; it means going through life seeking only and always to live as He would have us live, to live as He lived. The good news is that Jesus promises a yoke that ultimately is easy and light; for no matter how difficult the path becomes, no matter how often we fall, no matter who abandons us or what humiliations we endure – if we are walking with the Lord, carrying His yoke, there will be not only the grace to carry on but also a deep inner peace and joy in the midst of the storms of life.

Some other Scriptures beckon to us in this quest to understand the yoke ministry. The following verses may not appear to fit together at the first reading, but they will make a lot of sense as we analyze them with the help of the Holy Spirit:

"For Christ did not enter a man-made sanctuary that was only a copy of the true one; He entered heaven itself, now to appear for us in God's presence. Nor did he enter heaven to offer himself again and again, the way the high priest enters the Most Holy Place every year with blood that is not his own. Then Christ would have had to suffer many times since the creation of the world. But now he has appeared once for all at the end of the age to do away with sin by the sacrifice of himself. Just as man is destined to die once, and after that to face judgment, (sorry, New Agers and other believers in

reincarnation!) *so Christ was sacrificed once to take away the sins of many people, and he will appear a second time, not to bear sin, but to bring salvation to those who are waiting for him."* (Hebrews 9: 24-28)

"Day after day every priest stands and performs his religious duties; again and again he offers the same sacrifices, which can never take away sins. But when this Priest had offered for all time one sacrifice for sins, he sat down at the right hand of God. Since that time he waits for his enemies to be made his footstool, because by one sacrifice he has made perfect forever those who are being made holy." (Hebrews 10: 11-14)

Well, all that about Christ as the great High Priest seems pretty clear. But wait: *"Now I rejoice in what was suffered for you, and I fill up in my flesh what is still lacking in regard to Christ's afflictions, for the sake of his Body, which is the Church."* (Colossians 1: 24)

And further: *"When Christ, who is your life, appears, then you also will appear with him in glory. Put to death, therefore, whatever belongs to your earthly nature."* (Colossians 3: 4-5)... *"And God raised us up with Christ and seated us with him in the heavenly realms in Christ Jesus, in order that in the coming ages he might show the incomparable riches of his grace, expressed in his kindness to us in Christ Jesus."* (Ephesians 2: 6-7)

Now let's put all of this together; it makes for a very rich and exciting message: Christ came to suffer and die. In doing that He became the great High Priest, who offered the perfect and once-for-all-time sacrifice. He is now seated at the right hand of the Father in glory, as the great Mediator and Intercessor. There obviously continues to be a need to apply the benefits of the cross, as He mediates and intercedes with the Father. That is why Paul, under the inspiration of the Holy Spirit, can write those amazingly bold words about making up in his life what is lacking in the sufferings of Jesus. Paul is not on some kind of ego trip. He is rightly saying that the Christian by her/his life is spiritually united with the great Mediator, and that this life is the God-chosen vehicle for Jesus to continue His work of salvation. It is clear that the Christian must continue to put to death the earthly nature, must work at having the mind of Christ, so that the grace of God can touch souls through the Body of Christ, the Church – corporately and individually.

Then Paul writes something equally radical and wondrous. He says that, having Christ as our Savior, we are not only looking for an eternal life after death, we are spiritually and mysteriously right now seated in the heavenly realm, with Jesus Christ. Therefore, our lives of service in obedience to Jesus become living prayers, taken up into the prayer of the High Priest so that they become His prayer. Thus the yoke ministry becomes the essential ministry, the one that infuses and vitalizes all other ministries.

So, every Christian is called to the yoke ministry, no exceptions. Any Christian who does not see that or respond to that call just does not understand what the Christian life is really all about. The yoke ministry: It is about being like Jesus Christ, being a yielded servant doing the Father's will. It means enabling, by our yielded lives, the power of the cross to touch souls – for this is the plan that God has put into motion beginning with the Resurrection and Ascension of Jesus and the birthday of the Church on Pentecost.

But, how do we live the yoke ministry, in a practical way? Though there will be varying nuances for different people in different circumstances, there are some basics that apply to every Christian:

1) A total commitment to service: As we have seen, so many people see yielding one's own will to be weakness rather than strength; but it takes enormous strength – possible only with the help of grace – to subordinate personal desires to the decision to serve others. The yoke ministry means being sensitive to the needs of others, consistently looking for ways to help, never walking past a fellow human being in need no matter what personal feelings about that person may be. It is embracing the AIDS victim, while not condoning actions that

Will the Real Christians Please Stand Up!

may have led to the disease; it is lifting up the alcoholic, recognizing that there but for the grace of God go I; it is putting aside personal ambitions in the corporate scene and putting service to others above ladder-climbing and even personal goal attainment. It is the way Jesus lived – a Servant who was gentle and humble and available, but also a Servant Leader who never compromised the truth and confronted with directness and strength when faced with hypocrisy.

2) Sharing the Gospel, the Good News: The yoke ministry means consistently looking for opportunities to tell people about Jesus and about salvation. It also means being guided by the Holy Spirit with regard to the when and the how. People can be led by misguided zeal and do more harm than good in their sharing. The Holy Spirit knows each heart perfectly and will gently move us to speak when the time is right. And, very often, the best sharing is simply the example of a yielded life. Do not be misled by that last statement. It is not acceptable, based on Jesus' life and His heart, to take the position that I am not called to share the Gospel, not to be "evangelistic." It is part and parcel of every real Christian's life, just expressed in different ways as the Spirit gives direction. As St. Francis of Assisi put it, we should preach Christ always and only if necessary use words. The Holy Spirit will always guide yielded hearts. The yoke ministry includes a desire for the whole world to know and accept the love of Jesus Christ.

3) Being an intercessor: Every Christian is called, as an integral aspect of the yoke ministry, to be a person of prayer. We are united with the great Intercessor, and our prayer becomes His prayer when it is guided by the Holy Spirit for the good of others and the glory of the Father. This means that every day – every single day of our lives – the Holy Spirit will be prompting us to intercede. When someone pops into your mind, pray for that person. When you see someone on TV or read about someone in a magazine or a newspaper, pray for

that person. Pray for the hurting and the suffering and for those who cause it. Pray for those incarcerated and those on death row. Pray for the neighbor next door, the worker in the adjoining cubicle, the town in which you live, your State and your nation. Pray for every nation on every continent. Pray for the lost. Pray for God's Chosen People, the Jews, that they meet and accept the Messiah, Jesus Christ. No matter what our state in life – very busy and active, retired, bedridden, vacationing – we are called to be intercessors. The incredible fact is, God has chosen in His plan to need us, and souls are counting on us! When someone hurts us, pray for that person – it is healing for us and at the same time powerful intercession for the other. It is far better to pray for a child abuser (along with the child abused) than it is to want the abuser to be hung up by the thumbs. Our example, again, is Jesus. He frequently went into solitude to be with His Father; He prayed before beginning His public ministry; He sought the Father's will in all things; He prayed for His murderers while He hung on the cross.

4) Having all my life tuned in to God: That is really the bottom line of the yoke ministry, to be in such union with God that everything I say or do or even consciously think flows from a yielded mind and heart. This is a lifelong journey; but it is, frankly, the only life journey worth taking. Other journeys may bring more passing pleasures and temporary fulfillment; but the journey of the yoke ministry brings lasting happiness, peace, joy and the ultimate perfect fulfillment. It is the greatest and absolutely most important gift we can give our children and those around us – awareness of and accepting the yoke ministry. First, though, we must commit to it ourselves. With the grace of God, it is not only possible, it is an exciting reality and continuous adventure.

This reflection ends with the familiar words of Jesus teaching through the great parable about the end of time:

"When the Son of Man comes in his glory, and all the angels with him, he will sit on his throne in heavenly glory. All the nations will be gathered before him, and he will separate the people from one another as a shepherd separates the sheep from the goats. He will put the sheep on his right and the goats on his left. Then the King will say to those on his right, 'Come, you who are blessed by my Father; take your inheritance, the kingdom prepared for you since the creation of the world. For I was hungry and you gave me something to eat, I was thirsty and you gave me something to drink, I was a stranger and you invited me in. I needed clothes and you clothed me, I was sick and you looked after me. I was in prison and you came to visit me...I tell you the truth, whatever you did for one of the least of these brothers of mine, you did for me...Depart from me, you who are cursed, into the eternal fire prepared for the devil and his angels. For I was hungry and you gave me nothing to eat, I was thirsty and you gave me nothing to drink, I was a stranger and you did not invite me in, I needed clothes and you did not clothe me, I was sick and you did not look after me...I tell you the truth, whatever you did not do for the least of these, you did not do for me.' Then they will go away to eternal punishment, but the righteous to eternal life." (Matthew 25: 31-46)

The yoke ministry is living like Jesus Christ, and that means being guided daily by the Holy Spirit, in whatever we do, think, say. It means being people of prayer, not just of prayers. It means being willing vessels through which the saving power of Jesus Christ can pour into the hearts of others.

In John 7: 37-39*: "On the last and greatest day of the Feast, Jesus stood and said in a loud voice, 'If anyone is thirsty, let him come to me and drink. Whoever believes in me, as the Scripture has said, streams of living water will flow from within him.' By this he meant the Holy Spirit, whom those who believed in him were later to receive. Up to that time* *the Spirit had not been given, since Jesus had not yet been glorified."*

Well, Jesus has been glorified, and the Holy Spirit has indeed been given. Perhaps we do not often think of the role of the Holy Spirit in our living out the yoke ministry. But the Spirit seeks to tell us about Jesus and to give us the grace us to live like Him. Without the Holy Spirit it is impossible for us to live with servants' hearts. Do I really thirst? The real Christian does – thirsting daily for more and more of God's grace and guidance, thirsting to have ever more completely the mind and heart of Christ, so that streams of living water may flow to a parched and dying world. "Take My yoke upon you."

SUMMARY FOR REFLECTION AND DISCUSSION:

A real Christian:

1) Seeks to be yoked with Christ, knowing that two are always yoked together and in this case the partner is Christ – explaining why *"the yoke is easy and the burden is light;"*
2) Walks to a different drummer than the world, rejoicing in being a servant to others;
3) Thirsts for the salvation of souls and yearns to be an instrument for evangelism.

SCRIPTURES FOR JOURNALING:

1) Matthew 11: 28-30;
2) Psalm 22;
3) Hebrews 9; Colossians 1.

REFLECTION 32:

WHAT A CHRISTIAN IS NOT – AND IS

We begin this final reflection with the first verses of the Book of Acts:

"In my former book, Theophilus, I wrote about all that Jesus began to do and teach until the day he was taken up to heaven, after giving instructions through the Holy Spirit to the apostles he had chosen. After his suffering, he showed himself to these men and gave many convincing proofs that he was alive. He appeared to them over a period of forty days and spoke about the kingdom of God. On one occasion, while he was eating with them, he gave them this command: 'Do not leave Jerusalem, but wait for the gift my Father promised, which you have heard me speak about. For John baptized with water, but in a few days you will be baptized with the Holy Spirit.' So when they met together, they asked him, 'Lord, are you at this time going to restore the Kingdom to Israel?' He said to them: 'It is not for you to know the times or dates the Father has set by his own authority. But you will receive power when the Holy Spirit comes on you; and you will be my witnesses in Jerusalem, and in all Judea and Samaria, and to the ends of the earth.'"

Will the Real Christians Please Stand Up!

There they were – the apostles and disciples, their minds reeling because of the events of the past months: Their Master preaching and teaching, performing mighty miracles culminating in the raising of Lazarus from the dead; His going to Jerusalem where His enemies were waiting; His betrayal by one of their own who subsequently committed suicide; their leader denying Him and then repenting; ashamed because only His mother and one of the twelve had the courage to approach the cross while He was dying. Dying! The Messiah they believed in executed as a common criminal! Their fear and horror turning to bewildered joy when they saw Him risen and glorified (and even then one of them doubting until he touched the Lord's wounds). Their memories of meeting and eating with Him periodically from the day of Resurrection until the day of Ascension, and even then still not understanding as they asked Him if He was going to restore Israel and therefore triumph as a political and military Messiah. They were dull of heart and mind, weak in faith, grasping for hope, fearful and intimidated, gazing into the heavens as He departed from them – and at last going to Jerusalem in obedience to His command and waiting, praying, not sure what to expect next, recognizing that Jesus' enemies were gloating and calling His promises the empty words of a madman or a charlatan.

The followers of Jesus did not understand why they were asked to wait and pray, for ten days, while Jews from all over began gathering in Jerusalem for their Feast called Pentecost, or Feast of Weeks, celebrated fifty days after the Passover. This was also called the Feast of the Harvest and the Day of the First Fruits. So it was that the harvest of the New Covenant began on that day, and the first fruits of the sacrifice of Jesus the Christ were brought into the storeroom.

The apostles and disciples needed strength and power to be transformed into witnesses – and into true Christians, the first Christians. They needed the promised Comforter, the Holy Spirit; and He, the living Love of God, swept into that upper room in Jerusalem, cleared the cobwebs from their minds and filled their hearts with a bursting love for their Lord and Master. The Spirit gave them that flash of recognition that Jesus was truly God, that

Will the Real Christians Please Stand Up!

He had come to fulfill the prophecies of old, and that the Kingdom that was to be ushered in, starting that day, was one far greater than any political revolution they had mistakenly been hoping for.

On the Day of Pentecost the Church of Jesus Christ began its life when a band of followers became servant leaders – and 3,000 people became Christians. The Church was, and always will be, a band of believing people in union with Jesus Christ – indeed, a band that is a remnant among many others who believe they are Christians but do not get what the Christian life is all about. The Christian life is servanthood, seeking to have the mind and heart of Jesus, guided by the Holy Spirit, for the salvation of souls and the glory of the Father. Peter's first sermon, the one that resulted in those conversions of thousands of Jews to Christianity, was very simple:

> *"'Jesus of Nazareth was a man accredited by God to you by miracles, wonders and signs, which God did among you through him, as you yourselves know. This man was handed over to you by God's set purpose and foreknowledge; and you, with the help of wicked men, put him to death by nailing him to the cross. But God raised him from the dead, freeing him from the agony of death, because it was impossible for death to keep its hold on him...Therefore let all Israel be assured of this: God has made this Jesus, whom you crucified, both Lord and Christ.' And when the people, moved deeply, asked what they should do, Peter replied: 'Repent and be baptized, every one of you, in the name of Jesus Christ for the forgiveness of your sins. And you will receive the gift of the Holy Spirit.'"* (Acts 2: 22-24, 38)

The message was Jesus! It was Jesus who was the Promised One. It was Jesus who fulfilled the prophecies of old. It was Jesus who was sent by the Father. It was Jesus who brought freedom from sin's deadly clutches. It was Jesus who brought salvation. Only in His Name was there to be found release from Satan's bondage, and only in accepting Him as Savior could there be opened the door to the transforming love and power of the Holy Spirit. The early Church flourished, grew and blossomed because of a belief in and a

Will the Real Christians Please Stand Up!

following of a living Jesus Christ. The people prayed together, broke bread together, listened to those who had walked with the Lord, witnessed to anyone who would listen and drew strength from one another as the early favor bestowed upon them quickly turned to hatred and persecution. The blood of the martyrs further nourished this amazing phenomenon known as the "Way," made up of people eventually called "Christians," people who refused to bow before Jewish leaders and Roman emperors, people who faced suffering and death with peace and even joy, proclaiming that their death was only an event ushering them into the eternal presence of their beloved Jesus.

Stephen, the first martyr, at the moment of truth, when he would either capitulate to the demands of the Jewish leaders or face death, cried out:

> *"You stiff-necked people, with uncircumcised hearts and ears! You are just like your fathers. You always resist the Holy Spirit! Was there ever a prophet your fathers did not persecute? They even killed those who predicted the coming of the Righteous One. And now you have betrayed and murdered him – you who have received the law that was put into effect through angels but have not obeyed it...Look, I see heaven open and the Son of Man standing at the right hand of God...Lord Jesus, receive my spirit...Lord, do not hold this sin against them."* (Acts 7: 51-63, 56, 59)

And later Paul, who was holding the robes of those who stoned Stephen, long after he met Jesus on the road to Damascus and had his entire life changed, would write in his letter to the Romans that he would be willing to be separated from Jesus if it meant that his brethren, the Jews, would find Jesus. (Romans 9: 3)

Folks, these are expressions of deep and abiding love. That is being Christ-centered to the max. That is walking as the Master walked, willing to give one's life for the sake of others. Only a committed love for someone can possibly lead to such willing sacrifice; and in this case that Someone is Jesus Christ. Jesus was truly the center of the life of the early Church.

Will the Real Christians Please Stand Up!

But, something happened. As time went on, even though on the one hand God raised up holy and learned leaders through whom He solidified the truths He had revealed, the initial fervor of the Church waned. To be sure, it was necessary to develop doctrine, in order to combat the heresies that began cropping up on every side. But in that battle a side effect was the development in too many people of a gradual transfer from heart knowledge, with focus on relationship, to head knowledge, with focus on correctness. The soul began to rule over the spirit. Truth took precedence over relationship with the Way, the Truth and the Life. Religion began to take precedence over spirituality for far too many Christians. To be sure, there was always a remnant of people who remained true to the message of the Gospel – the focus on relationship with Jesus Christ as the cornerstone of Christian faith. God promised that He would be with us always; the Church can never be destroyed. Nonetheless, as more time passed, the words of Jesus in Revelation 2:4 echoed strongly through the Church: *"You have forsaken your first love."*

As a deep, personal – yes, even fanatical – love for the living Person Jesus Christ became for many secondary to creed and doctrine, the Holy Spirit, the living Love of God, became thwarted in His desire to mold the hearts of all Christians. The fields were still ripe for the harvest, the need for laborers was still there, the guidance and power of the Holy Spirit were still vitally important – but the ugly head of religion raised itself and began impeding the free flow of God's grace.

As the centuries passed, the clergy became a powerful group within the Church. Rules began to become more and more important. Worship began to become more of a spectator sport than a living expression of the true Church, the people of God. And, then, a catastrophe: In the fourth century the Roman emperor, Constantine, became a Christian. No, that was not the catastrophe; praise God for his conversion. What happened as a result of that was something that caused joy in the hearts of many at the time – save undoubtedly for the prophets in their midst. The Christian Church was proclaimed to be the state religion of the Roman Empire. The seeds of religion, already planted and watered, now took full bloom. Remember, it was "religion" that killed Jesus Christ. It was now religion that was to

Will the Real Christians Please Stand Up!

bludgeon Christianity and turn it into something far too formal and impersonal for far too many Christians. Keep in mind the concept of the remnant; there were always committed Christians, both clergy and laity. Keep in mind, too, that it was Christendom that both proclaimed the truth of and preserved the Bible. God used monasteries, Councils of Church leaders, dedicated and holy members of the laity to preserve His truth, even in the midst of strife and sin.

Because of some doctrinal differences but primarily because of disputes about Church authority Eastern and Western Christianity separated. And then the Church in the western world was split asunder by the Protestant Reformation. There is no doubt in my mind that God permitted the Reformation to keep western Christianity from imploding. But the Reformation also created problems, which continue to the present day. Jesus and the New Testament writers and the early Church were focused on the themes of love and unity; what happened as a result of the Reformation was the proliferation of denominations into the incredible number we have today – thousands upon thousands, and growing annually. Martin Luther started out correctly, seeking passionately to reform the Church; but he ended by moving from spiritual reform to doctrinal change, and that opened the floodgates. Church leaders of that time are just as accountable as Luther and other reformers; many leaders were so hidebound in their sinful lives and scandalous practices that the Holy Spirit could not reach them. Just as Satan attacked the Church through encouraging layers of religiosity in the 4th century and after, so he attacked the Church through inciting division and disunity in the 16th century and beyond, even to the present day. But the Church in its essence is still the Church, the Bride of Christ. God is wonderful in turning what Satan plans for bad into something good. The 4th century laid a foundation of stability for the Christian Church, especially in the western world. The 16th century provided a way for the Holy Spirit to ensure both preservation and growth of the Church's essential beauty. The Eastern Church, Roman Catholicism and Protestantism are all expressions of the Body of Christ; all proclaim the Lordship of Jesus Christ. And visionary leaders within all of these expressions of Christianity are praying and working toward Christian unity, that, as Jesus prayed, "all may be one."

Will the Real Christians Please Stand Up!

So, as we look around today at the many varied churches and congregations, just what is a Christian? These reflections have attempted to answer that. As a summary, though, let's first look at what a Christian is not, then at what a Christian is:

First, a Christian is not a "compartmentalizer." I realize that this sounds like an egg-headish kind of word; but the meaning is simple. A compartmentalist is a person who neatly and conveniently places his or her spiritual life in one room of the house of life. There are also rooms for work, for play, for family, for community service, and so on. This type of person focuses on being "religiously correct." But God did not tell us to love Him just on Sunday, or during evening devotions. He said, *"Love the Lord your God with all your heart, with all your soul, with all your strength, and with all your mind."* (Luke 10: 27 and Deuteronomy 6: 5) If we take God at His word, then the call is to be totally committed to Him and His ways. It is our relationship with Him that gives meaning to everything else and makes every thought, word and action an expression of that relationship of love. Family, work, social and community activities all become consecrated and meaningful in light of – and only in light of – our walk with Father, Son and Holy Spirit. If we are compartmentalizers, we are not real Christians. Jesus told us to take up our cross and follow Him. He also told us that no one who has put hand to the plow and looks back is fit for the Kingdom of God. He really means it to be all or nothing for His followers.

Second, a real Christian is not a "compromiser." Jesus Christ was anything but a wimp. He absolutely refused to water down the truth. He stood His ground, so unlike many of the so-called ecumenists of today who water down essential Christian truth in the name of holding hands and displaying a superficial and false unity. They proclaim we are all going to the same place, just by different paths. Jesus, on the other hand, stated firmly that the path to eternal life is narrow and the one to destruction is broad. Jesus did not hesitate to tell it like it is, even while He loved His detractors. He refused to conform to what was popular in order to gain a following and, at the end, to even save Himself. Remember, it was the loving Jesus who entered the Temple area and threw out the moneychang-

329

ers, bringing down on Himself the wrath of the religious leaders. He did not mince words: *"It is written, 'My House will be called a house of prayer, but you are making it a den of robbers.'"* (Matthew 21: 13, and all the other Gospels). At His trial, Jesus could have tried to avoid execution; instead, He spoke the truth, stating that He was truly the Son of God and that they would see Him coming on the clouds of heaven. (Matthew 26: 64) By those words, He ensured His death – which was His plan all along. Earlier in His ministry, Jesus gave the great teaching of Himself as the Bread of heaven and said that people must eat this Bread to have eternal life. When many of His disciples and friends were scandalized and walked away, Jesus did not call for them to come back. Rather, He looked at the Twelve and asked if they were going to walk away also. It is so much easier to compromise – and it is one of the great temptations of our modern society. It is becoming harder and harder to walk the narrow path – in fact, it is impossible without the guidance of the Holy Spirit. But, in the final analysis, a real Christian simply does not compromise the truth.

Third, a true Christian is not a "legalist." Why? Because Jesus was not one. To be sure, He held great respect for the Law of Moses. In fact, He said that He came to fulfill it. He, in effect, told the people to do what the religious leaders said, but not to do what they did. For those leaders, He had tough words. For example, read Chapter 23 of Matthew. Here are a few examples:

"Everything they (the teachers of the law and the Pharisees) *do is done for men to see...They love the place of honor at banquets and the most important seats in the synagogues; they love to be greeted in the marketplaces and to have men call them 'Rabbi.' But you are not to be called 'Rabbi,' for you have only one Master and you are all brothers...The greatest among you will be your servant. For whoever exalts himself will be humbled, and whoever humbles himself will be exalted. Woe to you, teachers of the law and Pharisees, you hypocrites! You travel over land and sea to win a single convert, and when he becomes one, you make him twice as much a son of hell as you are. Woe to you,*

blind guides!...Woe to you, teachers of the law and Pharisees, you hypocrites. You are like whitewashed tombs, which look beautiful on the outside but on the inside are full of dead men's bones and everything unclean...You snakes! You brood of vipers! How will you escape being condemned to hell?"

And while He was saying these things, He was deeply loving them, yearning for them to see the truth about His Father and Himself.

Jesus became angry at the religious leaders when they watched to see if He would cure a man on the Sabbath. Jesus said that the Sabbath was made for man, and not man for the Sabbath. Jesus told the woman at the well that the time was coming when people would worship in spirit and in truth. No, Jesus was no legalist – and He was put to death for his audacity to challenge the established religious and political leadership of the time.

Fourth, a real Christian is not a "materialist." I believe that the period of the 70's, 80's, 90's, and even today, will be known in future times as the era of the TV evangelists. Now, I will be the first to state that TV evangelism has done much good, including in my life and that of my family. God touched us, for example, through the PTL Club, especially in the 70's. That is why I refuse to join in the mocking and tongue-wagging of people about Jim Bakker's fall; that is also why I pray for him and his family and his new ministry in the Branson, MO area, right in my own backyard. But at the same time, if we step back and look at the TV evangelists in their heyday, some focused far too heavily on the things of the world – including Jim, by his own admission. Sadly, for many the emphasis on God's promises of prosperity was a ploy to obtain funds for the continuance of expensive airtime – and for many the purchase of expensive homes and other material benefits. The Biblical principle of unselfish giving was perverted into a gimmick, with an unhealthy emphasis on physical health and material gain. One evangelist who boldly claimed years ago that we are deceived if we do not think Jesus was a wealthy man in Galilee and is therefore a role model for the obtaining of material riches (!!) is still on the air today. Just recently I heard (briefly, before I quickly changed the channel) a well-known pastor and evangelist say as a guest on a Christian interview show, "Those 'name-it-and-claimers'? Put me right at the head of the line!" Now, in fairness, perhaps he was making a deeply spiritual point that I just did not wait long enough to hear. What makes the majority of the TV evangelists stand out, especially in years past, was a contrasting thread running through them that was pure gold: Billy Graham. Focus on the man, his message, his lifestyle, and one realizes just how God really intends the airwaves to be used for His glory and the spreading of the Kingdom. Unfortunately, compare Billy Graham to some others, and one can begin to understand why the world snickers at the very poor presentation by these other people, some of whom are just plain hucksters, of what real Christianity is all about. Sadly, people have been suckered by the millions. Good, Godly people have been moved by subtle misinterpretations of Scripture, beautiful choirs and soloists, and Christianized subliminal advertising. To use an analogy: I used to order from a magazine subscription service that offered the opportunity to win prizes; frankly, I enjoyed it. I knew, deep down, that ordering or not ordering did not impact the chances of winning something. But the subliminal message was there that maybe, just maybe, my not ordering something would impair my chances of winning. So it has been with too many of the TV ministries. Give or do not give, order a tape or book and send a contribution or not – but if you really want to be blessed by God (the unspoken message), if you do not want to be overlooked in His outpouring of material blessings, then you had really better give. There is no doubt that we are called to give to God; there is no doubt that God is faithful. But we live in a society in which materialism not only runs rampant in the world around us, it has also influenced the Church. It is not unlike Jesus' time. Many of the religious leaders gained wealth at the expense of the people (Matthew 23 again). But it is more subtle today. Today the message spewed by some is that wealth, luxury and possessions are our birthright as Christians. If we do not have them, there is obviously something wrong with our faith and with our lives. This is what I call "Christian materialism." It is entirely contrary to the life, teaching and example of Jesus Christ. Do not let anyone convince you otherwise, I urge you. Just read the Gospels with an open mind and heart. Learn there what a real Christian is with regard to the attitude toward wealth. Then read Paul's letters and the rest of the New Testament. Wealth is not wrong; the attitude toward it can be terribly wrong, however. *"Blessed are the poor in spirit, for theirs is the kingdom of heaven."* (Matthew 5: 3)

Finally, a true Christian is not "lukewarm." Some say that the Book of Revelation is the most difficult in the Bible to understand. Well, not really. When a person seeks the guidance of the Holy Spirit in reading the Word, this Book, like the others, comes alive. Oh, there are to be sure theological debates and nuances of interpretations, but if we read with faith, take the Word of God as it is given to us, and recognize that every passage has a meaning today and a meaning tomorrow as well as, frequently, an historical meaning in the mind of the writer, then God speaks clearly and meanings leap off the page. Some of the most powerful words spoken by Jesus were actually spoken to the author of the Book of Revelation. The glorified Christ instructed John to write to the seven churches, certainly actual groups of Christians at the time but also clearly representing the Church of today. Listen to Jesus speaking to each of us right now (the Word is living and true):

"...I hold this against you. You have forsaken your first Love. Remember the height from which you have fallen! Repent and do the things you did at first. If you do not repent, I will come to you and remove your lampstand from its place...You have a reputation of being alive, but you are dead. Wake up! Strengthen what remains and is about to die, for I have not found your deeds complete in the sight of my God. Remember, therefore, what you have received and heard; obey it, and repent. But if you do not wake up, I will come like a thief, and you will not know at what time I will come to you...I know your deeds, that you are neither cold nor hot. I wish you were either one or the other! So, because you are lukewarm – neither hot nor cold – I am about to spit you out of my mouth." (Revelation 2: 4-5; 3: 1-3; 3: 15-16)

Forsaken first love...wake up...neither hot nor cold: These are very pointed words, spoken from heaven, directed to the Church (which means to each of us in the Church). The message is clear: Integral to the definition of a Christian is a state of being on fire for God, absolutely and totally dedicated to the things of God, and above all to the Persons of God, seeking to know, love and follow the Lord Jesus Christ before and above all else. Christianity is not intended to include fence-sitting, going through the motions, doing just what is necessary to get by. A lukewarm Christian is not a real Christian.

So, then, just what is a "real Christian?" The key is Jesus. He also says in Revelation that He stands at the door and knocks; that He is waiting patiently for us; that He wants to come into our hearts and our lives. Perhaps a Scripture from another Book of the Bible best summarizes what a true Christian is: *"This is how we know we are in him. Whoever claims to live in him must walk as Jesus did"*. (1 John 2: 6) Must walk as Jesus did: In other words, must seek above all else to be like Him in everything we say, everything we do, and even in everything we consciously think. This requires a passionate desire and commitment to get to know Him better; to spend time with Him in prayer; to study His Word; to listen to the Holy Spirit who seeks to tell us about Him. It is more important than focus on family, work, recreation, service, than on life itself. For without that kind of passion, we are really only serving ourselves. Prayerfully study His life, and you will find a person who was totally yielded to the Father's will, totally led by the Holy Spirit, engaged in spiritual warfare against the forces of darkness and against the sterile ways of empty and hypocritical religious practices that were not based on true worship of God and service in His Name.

Jesus calls Himself the Light of the world (John 8: 12), the Way, Truth and Life for each of us (John 14: 6). Paul tells us that only those who are led by the Spirit of God are truly the sons of God (Romans 8: 14). Paul also tells us to come out from the world and be separate (2 Corinthians 6: 17). There is a warning here to the Christians of today. This issue is not whether a church has few or many rites and rituals, whether a church follows a particular order of service or relies on the guidance of the Holy Spirit in each service. No, all of this can become very religious, devoid of true fervor and love. It is what is in our hearts that counts.

Does our light shine? It simply cannot if we are not daily, living reflections of the love and presence of Jesus Christ. It is time for an inner "altar call," as we bow before God and ask in all sincerity, humility and openness if we are real Christians, if we are truly living the Christian life. Are we involved in a passionate love relationship with Jesus Christ, or are we Christians in name only, going through the religious motions of life and kidding ourselves?

I can think of no better way to end this reflection than to refer to the words of Paul, while an old man in prison, pouring out his heart to the people of God. Let his prayer be our prayer:

"And this is my prayer, that your love may abound more and more in knowledge and depth of insight, so that you may be able to discern what is best and may be pure and blameless until the day of Christ, filled with the fruit of righteousness that comes through Jesus Christ – to the glory and praise of God...Your attitude should be the same as that of Christ Jesus: Who, being in very nature God, did not consider equality with God something to be grasped, but made himself nothing, taking the very nature of a servant, being made in human likeness. And being found in appearance as a man, he humbled himself and became obedient to death – even death on a cross...But whatever was to my profit I now consider loss for the sake of Christ. What is more, I consider everything a loss compared to the surpassing greatness of knowing Christ Jesus my Lord, for whose sake I have lost all things. I consider them rubbish, that I may gain Christ and be found in him, not having a righteousness of my own that comes from the law, but that which is through faith in Christ – the righteousness that comes from God and is by faith. I want to know Christ and the power of his Resurrection and the fellowship of sharing in his sufferings, becoming like him in His death, and so, somehow, to attain to the resurrection from the dead." (Philippians 1: 9-11; 2:

5-8; 3: 7-11)

SUMMARY FOR REFLECTION AND DISCUSSION:

A real Christian:

1) Does not compartmentalize life, but lets faith and love permeate all of life;
2) Does not compromise the truth, but stands up for the truth in all situations;
3) Does not become a legalist, does not focus on superficial aspects of faith and ignore what is most important – love and relationship with Jesus and with others;
4) Does not live as a materialist who is more interested in the things of the world than in the things of God;
5) Is not lukewarm, but lives a passion to grow ever closer to God and for the salvation of all souls;
6) Lets the light and love of Jesus shine through daily life, illuminating the way for others who cross the path of life.

SCRIPTURES FOR JOURNALING:

1) Acts 1-3;
2) Acts 7;
3) Matthew 7: 13-14; 21; 26;
4) Revelation 1-3

CONCLUSION

So, in final analysis now, just what is a "real Christian?" A Christian is someone who has repented of his/her sins, confessed them to God, has accepted the invitation to proclaim Jesus as personal Savior – and has made the firm commitment to truly make Him the Lord of one's entire life. It is this last statement that becomes a critical element in the definition of a true Christian. To be sure, a Christian is someone who has been cleansed by the shed blood of Jesus Christ, who is a living temple wherein dwell the Father, the Son and the Holy Spirit, who believes that Jesus Christ is both God and Man and is now at the right hand of the Father in glory and will come again. So, you see, I am not challenging the essence of true Christianity which the Church teaches and holds fast to. Regardless of the vast number of Christian denominations and non-denominations (which are really denominations because they have a body of belief), we Christians, as I have previously stated in this book, believe almost everything in common and tend to fuss over the relatively small amount of differences. There are certainly some non-negotiables: Show me a church that does not believe in the Trinity, or that Jesus is God, or that there is a heaven and a hell, or a church that believes that we can become gods – just to name some essentials – and I will state firmly that such a church may call itself "Christian" but in reality is not Christian at all.

I stated in the Introduction that we must differentiate between the beliefs of a real Christian and the lifestyle of a real Christian.

The beliefs are black and white (for the most part), readily understood from Scripture and the teaching authority of the Body of Christ. The lifestyle, however, is a process, moving hopefully to ever greater holiness, greater yieldedness as a servant, ever increasing in the degree to which one has the mind and heart of Jesus Christ.

What I strongly suggest for your prayerful consideration is an underlying and critical question of this entire book: Is it possible, really possible, to be a "real Christian" and to have a lifestyle that is not consonant with or is in opposition to what Christianity is all about? I wrote earlier and I reemphasize now that I am not the judge of anyone's spiritual state. That is God's job and right, not mine. But I can look at my own life and can state with sorrow, and with gratitude to God for His patient love, that for many years I considered myself a "real Christian:" I believed the right things, I studied about and talked about, and even to, Jesus; I even wore my Christianity on my sleeve, ensuring that people knew where I stood on the issue of Christian beliefs (though with some significant lack of consistency and courage) – but it was academic and intellectual. I talked the talk, but I did not walk the walk. Finally, God's grace got through, and I made a genuine commitment. Oh, believe me, I falter and fall and stumble and stutter, but at least now I am aware of what Jesus means when He asks me to follow Him. The entire purpose of this book is to assist or at least encourage you, the reader, to move your faith from your head to your heart – for Jesus' love is all about the heart while not minimizing the importance of knowledge.

So, permit me to provide a brief, summary look at both beliefs and lifestyle:

BELIEFS: Some years ago I wrote a letter of protest to a local pastor who was sponsoring an ecumenical Good Friday prayer service. Among the clergy participating, and publicized as a participant, was the pastor of a church which proclaimed to be Christian but in reality was not because of an essential belief in contradiction to Christian truth. When I wrote a letter to the coordinating pastor, suggesting that the ministerial alliance publish a statement of essen-

Will the Real Christians Please Stand Up!

tial Christian beliefs, I received in return a scathing letter accusing me of bigotry. It was an eye-opening experience for me to see how Christians are falling into the trap of turning the solid food of Christian doctrine into some bland, blended mush. I know that this pastor truly loved the Lord and served Him; but he failed to recognize the importance of identifying what marks a Christian and what does not. Years later, when I had the privilege of beginning and administering a regional prayer team seeking to have 24 hour a day and 7 day a week prayer for spiritual transformation in our area, the Steering Committee approved a card that on one side explained the mission and vision of the team and on the other side listed a simple statement of beliefs, the essential beliefs of every true Christian. That way we could state clearly that this is a Christian prayer team and that volunteers simply have to read the card to see if their beliefs are consonant with the ones printed there. Following is what is printed on the card. I can say with absolute certainty that a Christian must believe at least these things in order to be a true Christian in terms of doctrine:

STATEMENT OF BELIEFS

WE BELIEVE: That God is a Trinity of Three Persons, one God...

WE BELIEVE: That God is the Creator of heaven and earth and that we are all Created in the image and likeness of God...

WE BELIEVE: That the Second Person of the Trinity became a Man, Jesus of Nazareth, that He is the Christ, the promised Messiah who was conceived by the Holy Spirit (the Third Person of the Trinity) and was born of a virgin...

WE BELIEVE: That mankind sinned and became cut off from an intimate union with God, and that Jesus Christ, through His death and Resurrection paid the ultimate price for the forgiveness of our sins and made possible again an intimate and eternal union with God, in His Most Holy Trinity, in Heaven *("In him we have redemption through his blood, the forgive-*

ness of sins, in accordance with the riches of God's grace that he lavished on us with all wisdom and understanding.")...

WE BELIEVE: That Jesus Christ ascended into heaven and will come again...

WE BELIEVE: That the Holy Spirit is the living Love of God and is with us as Comforter and Counselor and to bring to our minds and hearts all that Jesus has taught and teaches us...

WE BELIEVE: That the Bible is the only written Word of God and is both inspired by the Holy Spirit and is true...

WE BELIEVE: That there is a fallen angel (Lucifer), who is Satan, and that there exists an eternal Hell...

WE BELIEVE: That God calls His people to prayer, and that prayer is communion with God...

WE BELIEVE: That we are invited to fellowship with God and are called to love, serve and obey God and to serve one another with yielded hearts.

LIFESTYLE: A real Christian is on a journey to an ever deeper union with God the Father, God the Son and God the Holy Spirit; is a follower of Jesus Christ and seeks above all else in life to love and serve God and be an instrument for God's love and grace to reach others. Following, in summary form, are some characteristics of the true Christian, the one who takes the relationship with God seriously and the one who is not just "trying to get by and somehow sneak into heaven" (or the one who believes that she/he "has it made" and so can just take it easy).

Lives and walks with the awareness of the presence of God within...

Prays without ceasing, by making all of life a prayer...

Recognizes the daily call to service as a member of the Body of Christ...

Lives in daily awareness of an eternal life to come and that this life is passing...

Will the Real Christians Please Stand Up!

Lives in hope and trust in the love and promises of God...

Fervently seeks that all be saved and is a living witness to others as led by the Holy Spirit...

Puts Jesus Christ first in everything, considers Him not only Lord and Savior but also best Friend...

Is a yielded servant, seeking only to follow Jesus and do God's will...

Sees and uses the Bible as God's revelation, as a living Word, and as one form of direct communication with God...

Is goal-minded, with regard to the Christian life and eternal life...

Has personally and intimately experienced the risen Christ and has a relationship with Him deeper than any human one...

Rejoices in wonder at the gift of salvation and at the immense and personal love of God...

Gives thanks consistently for all of the gifts of God, natural and supernatural...

Sees God's guiding hand in all circumstances of life and believes that He has a plan and is in control...

Recognizes and seeks the daily guidance of the Holy Spirit...

Thirsts to know and love and be like Jesus...

Sees the taking up of the cross as the calling of every Christian...

Daily places himself/herself on the altar of sacrifice, dedicating life to God, and sees life as the privilege of being a yielded sacrifice of love and service...

Believes in angels, both good and fallen, and recognizes spiritual warfare at work in all of life and all of history until the end of the world...

Never ignores the presence and workings of Satan, but also knows that she/he has no power in the presence of Jesus Christ...

Loves every person, regardless of race, creed, size or shape, whether friend or enemy, and shows that love by actively serving and loving...

Forgives readily, regardless of how deep the hurt...

Does not condone or participate in bigotry, gossip or backbiting...

Will the Real Christians Please Stand Up!

Is acutely aware of the horror of sin and tries consistently to flee from it...

Has the trusting heart of a child in the providence of God...

Uses gifts given by God as fully and wisely as possible, and knows that every Christian has gifts to use for the spreading of the Kingdom and the building up of the Body of Christ...

Has a sense of urgency that all be saved and has a passion to be used toward that end...

Never equates religion with spirituality...

Knows the value of and seeks quiet time with God, and listens as well as speaks...

Has a "burning heart" when reading the Word, knowing that the Holy Spirit is speaking...

Yearns and works for revival in the Church and transformation in communities, nations, the world...

Has her/his treasure in heaven, not on this earth...

Knows that the Jesus of the Gospels is the same Jesus alive today...

Daily puts on spiritual armor to do battle with the enemy...

Sees the Old Testament as having its ultimate meaning and fulfillment in the New...

Consciously believes that he/she is a living temple...

Sees every day as an opportunity to live the reality of the Resurrection...

Prays and seeks that every person with whom she/he has contact during life whether directly or indirectly, consciously or unconsciously, receives the grace of salvation...

Seeks to let the living and glorified Jesus shine through daily life...

Seeks to have the mind of Christ...

Does not let the allure, the problems, the tasks of the life in the world distract from what is most important...

Hears Jesus knocking daily and opens the door to communication, love and service...

Seeks the guidance of the Holy Spirit in all decisions...

Leans not on his/her own understanding...

Will the Real Christians Please Stand Up!

Does not ignore people in need, regardless of the circumstances, but reaches out to help and becomes actively involved in the lives of these people...

Has her/his heart totally fixed on Jesus...

Does not compartmentalize faith, but lets it permeate every aspect of life...

Finds life's greatest happiness in bringing light, vision, hope and help to others through, with and in Jesus Christ...

Knows that the Jews continue to be God's Chosen People, loves them as brothers and sisters, prays for Israel and that the Jewish people find Jesus as the Messiah...

Does not compromise the truth in relationships with people of other faiths, but also loves every human being without reservation...

Keeps giving and serving no matter what happens...

Even during times when God's felt joy and peace are absent, keeps on serving, loving, and walking with faith toward the prize to come.

Please add to this list from your own prayer, reflection and discussion with others. Keep journaling – reading Scripture, making notes and prayers and sharing thoughts with others. The many Scriptures provided in this book can never be exhausted of their richness, and they are but a sample of the amazing Word of God. My prayer is that you see the conclusion of these reflections not as an end but as a new beginning in your Christian journey. Please pray for my family, my associates and for me. Please pray for Herschend Family Entertainment Corporation. Please pray that God's perfect will be done in Southwest Missouri, in the State of Missouri, in Northwest Arkansas, in the United States of America and in the world. Please pray that the Body of Christ grow in love and unity.

Peace to you and yours!

Printed in the United States
46381LVS00001B/157-255